Kaplan Publishing are constantly finding new ways to support students looking for exam success and our online resources really do add an extra dimension to your studies.

This book comes with free MyKaplan online resources so that you can study anytime, anywhere. **This free online resource is not sold separately and is included in the price of the book.**

Having purchased this book, you have access to the following online study materials:

CONTENT	AAT	
	Text	Kit
Electronic version of the book	✓	✓
Knowledge Check tests with instant answers	✓	
Mock assessments online	✓	✓
Material updates	✓	✓

AF874496

How to access your online resources

Received this book as part of your Kaplan course?
If you have a MyKaplan account, your full online resources will be added automatically, in line with the information in your course confirmation email. If you've not used MyKaplan before, you'll be sent an activation email once your resources are ready.

Bought your book from Kaplan?
We'll automatically add your online resources to your MyKaplan account. If you've not used MyKaplan before, you'll be sent an activation email.

Bought your book from elsewhere?
Go to **www.mykaplan.co.uk/add-online-resources**
Enter the ISBN number found on the title page and back cover of this book.
Add the unique pass key number contained in the scratch panel below.
You may be required to enter additional information during this process to set up or confirm your account details.

This code can only be used once for the registration of this book online. This registration and your online content will expire when the examinations covered by this book have taken place. Please allow one hour from the time you submit your book details for us to process your request.

Please scratch the film to access your unique code.

Please be aware that this code is case-sensitive and you will need to include the dashes within the passcode, but not when entering the ISBN.

KAPLAN PUBLISHING

ACCA

Applied Skills

Corporate and Business Law
(LW GLO)

Study Text

British library cataloguing-in-publication data

A catalogue record for this book is available from the British Library.

Published by:

Kaplan Publishing UK
179 - 191 Borough High Street,
London,
SE1 1HR

ISBN 978-1-83735-251-7

Printed and bound in Great Britain

Acknowledgements

We are grateful to the Association of Chartered Certified Accountants and the Chartered Institute of Management Accountants for permission to reproduce past examination questions. The answers have been prepared by Kaplan Publishing.

Contents

Introduction

How to use the Materials

These Kaplan Publishing learning materials have been carefully designed to make your learning experience as easy as possible and to give you the best chances of success in your examinations.

The product range contains a number of features to help you in the study process. They include:

(1) Detailed study guide and syllabus objectives

(2) Description of the examination

(3) Study skills and revision guidance

(4) Study text

(5) Question practice

The sections on the study guide, the syllabus objectives, the examination and study skills should all be read before you commence your studies. They are designed to familiarise you with the nature and content of the examination and give you tips on how to best to approach your learning.

The **study text** comprises the main learning materials and gives guidance as to the importance of topics and where other related resources can be found. Each chapter includes:

- The **learning objectives** contained in each chapter, which have been carefully mapped to the examining body's own syllabus learning objectives or outcomes. You should use these to check you have a clear understanding of all the topics on which you might be assessed in the examination.
- The **chapter diagram** provides a visual reference for the content in the chapter, giving an overview of the topics and how they link together.
- The **content** for each topic area commences with a brief explanation or definition to put the topic into context before covering the topic in detail. You should follow your studying of the content with a review of the illustration/s. These are worked examples which will help you to understand better how to apply the content for the topic.
- **Test your understanding** sections provide an opportunity to assess your understanding of the key topics by applying what you have learned to short questions. Answers can be found at the back of each chapter.
- **Summary diagrams** complete each chapter to show the important links between topics and the overall content of the paper. These diagrams should be used to check that you have covered and understood the core topics before moving on.
- **Question practice** is provided at the back of each text.

Quality and accuracy are of the utmost importance to us so if you spot an error in any of our products, please send an email to mykaplanreporting@kaplan.com with full details, or follow the link to the feedback form in MyKaplan.

Our Quality Coordinator will work with our technical team to verify the error and take action to ensure it is corrected in future editions.

Icon Explanations

Definition – Key definitions that you will need to learn from the core content.

Key point – Identifies topics that are key to success and are often examined.

Illustration – Worked examples help you understand the core content better.

Test your understanding – Exercises for you to complete to ensure that you have understood the topics just learned.

Supplementary reading – These sections will help to provide a deeper understanding of core areas. The supplementary reading is **NOT** optional reading. It is vital to provide you with the breadth of knowledge you will need to address the wide range of topics within your syllabus that could feature in an exam question. **Reference to this text is vital when self studying.**

Links to other syllabus areas – This symbol refers to areas of interaction with other parts of your syllabus, either in terms of other ACCA papers that you have studied, or may go on to study, or even further professional qualifications that you may decide to pursue on completion of ACCA.

On-line subscribers

Our on-line resources are designed to increase the flexibility of your learning materials and provide you with immediate feedback on how your studies are progressing.

If you are subscribed to our on-line resources you will find:

(1) On-line referenceware: reproduces your Study Text on-line, giving you anytime, anywhere access.

(2) On-line testing: provides you with additional on-line objective testing so you can practice what you have learned further.

(3) On-line performance management: immediate access to your on-line testing results. Review your performance by key topics and chart your achievement through the course relative to your peer group.

Ask your local customer services staff if you are not already a subscriber and wish to join.

ACCA Support

For additional support with your studies please also refer to the ACCA Global website.

Study skills and revision guidance

This section aims to give guidance on how to study for your ACCA exams and to give ideas on how to improve your existing study techniques.

Preparing to study

Set your objectives

Before starting to study decide what you want to achieve – the type of pass you wish to obtain. This will decide the level of commitment and time you need to dedicate to your studies.

Devise a study plan

Determine which times of the week you will study.

Split these times into sessions of at least one hour for study of new material. Any shorter periods could be used for revision or practice.

Put the times you plan to study onto a study plan for the weeks from now until the exam and set yourself targets for each period of study – in your sessions make sure you cover the course, course assignments and revision.

If you are studying for more than one paper at a time, try to vary your subjects as this can help you to keep interested and see subjects as part of wider knowledge.

When working through your course, compare your progress with your plan and, if necessary, re-plan your work (perhaps including extra sessions) or, if you are ahead, do some extra revision/practice questions.

Effective studying

Active reading

You are not expected to learn the text by rote, rather, you must understand what you are reading and be able to use it to pass the exam and develop good practice. A good technique to use is SQ3Rs – Survey, Question, Read, Recall, Review:

(1) **Survey the chapter** – look at the headings and read the introduction, summary and objectives, so as to get an overview of what the chapter deals with.

(2) **Question** – whilst undertaking the survey, ask yourself the questions that you hope the chapter will answer for you.

(3) **Read** through the chapter thoroughly, answering the questions and making sure you can meet the objectives. Attempt the exercises and activities in the text, and work through all the examples.

(4) **Recall** – at the end of each section and at the end of the chapter, try to recall the main ideas of the section/chapter without referring to the text. This is best done after a short break of a couple of minutes after the reading stage.

(5) **Review** – check that your recall notes are correct.

You may also find it helpful to re-read the chapter to try to see the topic(s) it deals with as a whole.

Note-taking

Taking notes is a useful way of learning, but do not simply copy out the text. The notes must:

- be in your own words
- be concise
- cover the key points
- be well-organised
- be modified as you study further chapters in this text or in related ones.

Trying to summarise a chapter without referring to the text can be a useful way of determining which areas you know and which you don't.

Three ways of taking notes:

Summarise the key points of a chapter.

Make linear notes – a list of headings, divided up with subheadings listing the key points. If you use linear notes, you can use different colours to highlight key points and keep topic areas together. Use plenty of space to make your notes easy to use.

Try a diagrammatic form – the most common of which is a mind-map. To make a mind-map, put the main heading in the centre of the paper and put a circle around it. Then draw short lines radiating from this to the main sub-headings, which again have circles around them. Then continue the process from the sub-headings to sub-sub-headings, advantages, disadvantages, etc.

Highlighting and underlining

You may find it useful to underline or highlight key points in your study text – but do be selective. You may also wish to make notes in the margins.

Revision

The best approach to revision is to revise the course as you work through it. Also try to leave four to six weeks before the exam for final revision. Make sure you cover the whole syllabus and pay special attention to those areas where your knowledge is weak. Here are some recommendations:

Read through the text and your notes again and condense your notes into key phrases. It may help to put key revision points onto index cards to look at when you have a few minutes to spare.

Review any assignments you have completed and look at where you lost marks – put more work into those areas where you were weak.

Practise exam standard questions under timed conditions. If you are short of time, list the points that you would cover in your answer and then read the model answer, but do try to complete at least a few questions under exam conditions.

Also practise producing answer plans and comparing them to the model answer.

If you are stuck on a topic find somebody (a tutor) to explain it to you.

Read good newspapers and professional journals, especially ACCA's Student Accountant – this can give you an advantage in the exam.

Ensure you know the structure of the exam – how many questions and of what type you will be expected to answer. During your revision attempt all the different styles of questions you may be asked.

Further reading

You can find further reading and technical articles under the student section of ACCA's website.

Paper introduction

Paper background

The aim of ACCA **Corporate and Business Law**, is to develop knowledge and skills in the understanding of the general legal framework, and of specific legal areas relating to business, recognising the need to seek further specialist legal advice where necessary.

Objectives of the syllabus

- Identify the essential elements of different legal systems including the main sources of law, the relationship between the different branches of a state's constitution, and the need for international legal regulation, and explain the roles of international organisations in the promotion and regulation of international trade, and the role of international arbitration as an alternative to court adjudication.
- Recognise and apply the appropriate legal rules applicable under the United Nations Convention on Contracts for the International Sale of Goods, and explain the various ways in which international business transactions can be funded.
- Recognise different types of international business forms.
- Distinguish between alternative forms and constitutions of business organisations.
- Recognise and compare types of capital and the financing of companies.
- Describe and explain how companies are managed, administered and regulated.
- Recognise the legal implications relating to insolvency law.
- Demonstrate an understanding of corporate fraudulent and criminal behaviour.

Core areas of the syllabus

- Essential elements of the legal system.
- International business transactions.
- Transportation and payment of international business transactions.
- The formation and constitution of business organisations.
- Capital and the financing of companies.
- Management, administration and regulation of companies.
- Insolvency law.
- Corporate fraudulent and criminal behaviour.

ACCA Performance Objectives

In order to become a member of the ACCA, as a trainee accountant you will need to demonstrate that you have achieved nine performance objectives. Performance objectives are indicators of effective performance and set the minimum standard of work that trainees are expected to achieve and demonstrate in the workplace. They are divided into key areas of knowledge which are closely linked to the exam syllabus.

There are five Essential performance objectives and a choice of fifteen Technical performance objectives which are divided into five areas.

The performance objectives which link to this exam are:

1 Ethics and professionalism (Essential)

2 Governance risk and control (Essential)

The following link provides an in depth insight into all of the performance objectives:

https://www.accaglobal.com/content/dam/ACCA_Global/Students/per/PER-Performance-objectives-achieve.pdf

Progression

There are two elements of progression that we can measure: first how quickly students move through individual topics within a subject; and second how quickly they move from one course to the next. We know that there is an optimum for both, but it can vary from subject to subject and from student to student. However, using data and our experience of student performance over many years, we can make some generalisations.

A fixed period of study set out at the start of a course with key milestones is important. This can be within a subject, for example 'I will finish this topic by 30 June', or for overall achievement, such as 'I want to be qualified by the end of next year'.

Your qualification is cumulative, as earlier papers provide a foundation for your subsequent studies, so do not allow there to be too big a gap between one subject and another. We know that exams encourage techniques that lead to some degree of short term retention, the result being that you will simply forget much of what you have already learned unless it is refreshed (look up Ebbinghaus Forgetting Curve for more details on this). This makes it more difficult as you move from one subject to another: not only will you have to learn the new subject, you will also have to relearn all the underpinning knowledge as well. This is very inefficient and slows down your overall progression which makes it more likely you may not succeed at all.

In addition, delaying your studies slows your path to qualification which can have negative impacts on your career, postponing the opportunity to apply for higher level positions and therefore higher pay.

You can use the following diagram showing the whole structure of your qualification to help you keep track of your progress.

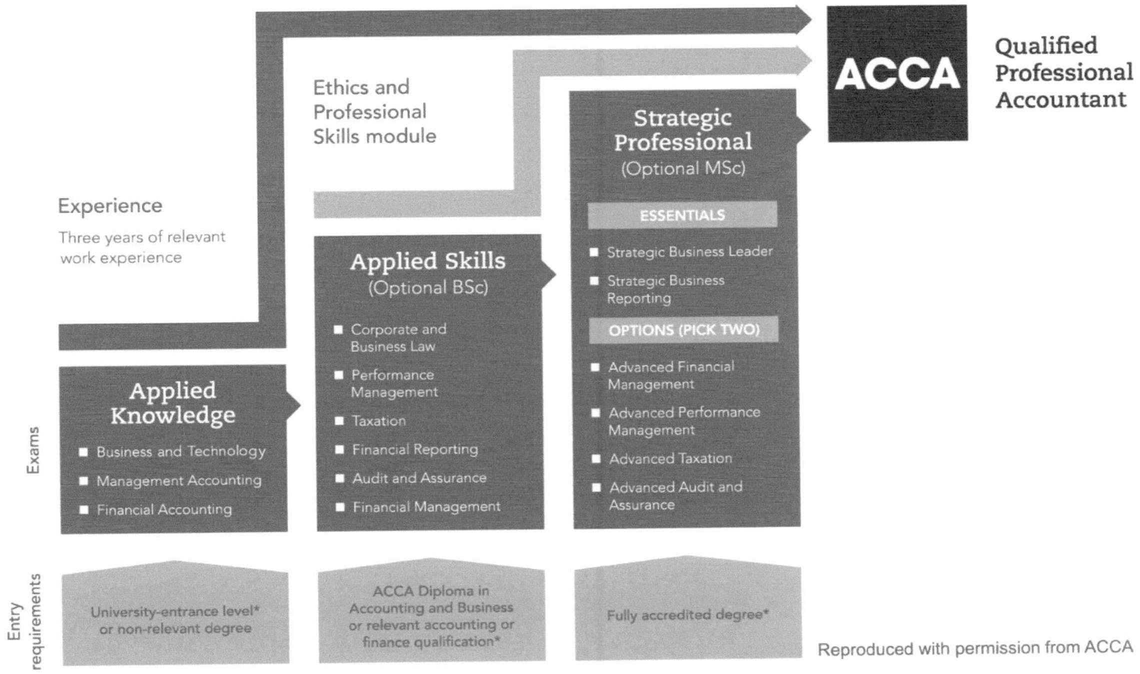

Reproduced with permission from ACCA

Syllabus objectives

We have reproduced the ACCA's syllabus below, showing where the objectives are explored within this book. Within the chapters, we have broken down the extensive information found in the syllabus into easily digestible and relevant sections, called **Content Objectives**. These correspond to the objectives at the beginning of each chapter.

Syllabus learning objective	Chapter reference
A ESSENTIAL ELEMENTS OF LEGAL SYSTEMS	
1 Business, political and legal systems	
(a) Explain the inter-relationship of economic and political and legal systems.[2]	1
(b) Explain the doctrine of the separation of powers and its impact on the legal system.[2]	1
(c) Explain the distinction between criminal and civil law.[1]	1
(d) Outline the operation of the following legal systems:[1]	1
(i) Common law	
(ii) Civil Law	
(iii) Sharia law	
2 International trade, international legal regulation and conflict of laws	
(a) Explain the need for international legal regulation in the context of conflict of laws.[2]	1
(b) Explain the function of international treaties, conventions and model codes.[2]	1
(c) Explain the roles of international organisations, such as the UN, ICC, WTO, the OECD, UNIDROIT, UNCITRAL and courts in the promotion and regulation of international trade.[1]	1
3 Alternative Dispute Resolution mechanisms	
(a) Explain the operation, and evaluate the distinct merits, of court-based adjudication and alternative dispute resolution mechanisms.[2]	1
(b) Explain the role of the international courts of trade including the International Court of Arbitration.[1]	
(c) Explain and apply in detail the provisions of the UNCITRAL Model Law on International Commercial Arbitration.[2]	2
(d) Describe the arbitral tribunal.[2]	2
(e) Explain arbitral awards.[2]	2

Syllabus learning objective	Chapter reference
B INTERNATIONAL BUSINESS TRANSACTIONS	
1 Introduction to the United Nations Convention on Contract for the International Sale of Goods and ICC Incoterms	
(a) Explain the sphere of application and general provisions of the Convention.[1]	3
(b) Explain and be able to apply the rules for creating contractual relations under the Convention.[1]	3
(c) Explain the meaning and effect of the ICC Incoterms.[1]	3
2 Obligations of the seller, and buyer and provisions common to both	
(a) Explain and be able to apply the rules relating to the obligations of the seller under the Convention:[2]	4
(i) delivery of goods and handing over documents	
(ii) conformity of the goods and third party claims	
(iii) remedies for breach of contract by the seller.	
(b) Explain and be able to apply the rules relating to the obligations of the buyer under the Convention:[2]	4
(i) payment of the price	
(ii) taking delivery	
(iii) remedies for breach of contract by the buyer.	
(c) Explain and be able to apply the rules relating to the provisions common to both the seller and the buyer under the Convention:[2]	4
(i) breach of contract and in particular anticipatory breach and instalment contracts	
(ii) damages	
(iii) interest	
(iv) exemptions	
(v) effects of avoidance	
(vi) preservation of the goods.	
(d) Explain and be able to apply the rules relating to the passing of risk under the Convention.[2]	4

Syllabus learning objective			Chapter reference
C	**TRANSPORTATION AND PAYMENT OF INTERNATIONAL BUSINESS TRANSACTIONS**		
1	**Transportation documents and means of payment**		
	(a)	Define and explain the operation of bills of lading.[1]	5
	(b)	Explain the operation of bank transfers.[1]	5
	(c)	Explain and be able to apply the rules of UNCITRAL Model Law on International Credit Transfer.[2]	5
	(d)	Explain and be able to apply the rules of the UN Convention on International Bills Of Exchange and International Promissory Notes.[2]	5
	(e)	Explain the operation of letters of credit and letters of comfort.[2]	5
D	**FORMATION AND CONSTITUTION OF BUSINESS ORGANISATIONS**		
1	**Agency law**		
	(a)	Define the role of the agent and give examples of such relationships paying particular regard to partners and company directors.[2]	6
	(b)	Explain how the formation of the agency relationship.[2]	6
	(c)	Define the authority of the agent.[2]	6
	(d)	Explain the potential liability of both principal and agent.[2]	6
2	**Partnerships**		
	(a)	Demonstrate a knowledge of the legislation governing the partnership, both unlimited and limited.[1]	7
	(b)	Discuss the formation of a partnership.[2]	7
	(c)	Explain the authority of partners in relation to partnership activity.[2]	7
	(d)	Analyse the liability of various partners for partnership debts.[2]	7
	(e)	Explain the termination of a partnership and partners' subsequent rights and liabilities.[2]	7

Syllabus learning objective			Chapter reference
3	**Corporations and legal personality**		
	(a)	Distinguish between sole traders, partnerships and companies.[1]	7
	(b)	Explain the meaning and effect of limited liability.[2]	8
	(c)	Analyse different types of companies, especially private and public companies.[1]	8
	(d)	Illustrate the effect of separate personality and the veil of incorporation.[2]	8
	(e)	Recognise instances where separate personality will be ignored (lifting the veil of incorporation).[2]	8
4	**The formation and constitution of a company**		
	(a)	Explain the role and duties of company promoters, and the breach of those duties and remedies available to the company.[2]	8
	(b)	Explain the meaning of, and the rules relating to, pre-incorporation contracts.[2]	8
	(c)	Describe the procedure for registering companies, both public and private, including the system of streamlined company registration.[1]	8
	(d)	Describe the statutory books, records and returns, including the confirmation statement and the register of people with significant control, that companies must keep or make.[1]	8
	(e)	Analyse the effect of a company's constitutional documents.[2]	8
	(f)	Describe the contents of model articles of association.[1]	8
	(g)	Explain how articles of association can be changed.[2]	8
	(h)	Explain the controls over the names that companies may or may not use.[2]	8

Syllabus learning objective		Chapter reference
E	**CAPITAL AND FINANCING OF COMPANIES**	
1	**Share capital**	
	(a) Examine the different types of capital.[2]	9
	(b) Illustrate the difference between various classes of shares, including treasury shares, and the procedure for altering class rights.[2]	9
	(c) Explain allotment of shares, and distinguish between rights issue and bonus issue of shares.[2]	9
	(d) Examine the effect of issuing shares at either a discount, or at a premium.[2]	9
2	**Loan capital**	
	(a) Define companies' borrowing powers.[1]	9
	(b) Explain the meaning of loan capital and debenture.[2]	9
	(c) Distinguish loan capital from share capital and explain the different rights held by shareholders and debenture holders.[2]	9
	(d) Explain the concept of a company charge and distinguish between fixed and floating charges.[2]	9
	(e) Describe the need and the procedure for registering company charges.[2]	9
3	**Capital maintenance and dividend law**	
	(a) Explain the doctrine of capital maintenance and capital reduction.[2]	9
	(b) Explain the rules governing the distribution of dividends in both private and public companies.[2]	9

Syllabus learning objective			Chapter reference
F	**MANAGEMENT, ADMINISTRATION AND REGULATION OF COMPANIES**		
1	**Company directors**		
	(a)	Explain the role of directors in the operation of a company, and the different types of directors, such as executive/non-executive directors or de jure and de facto directors, and shadow directors.[2]	10
	(b)	Discuss the ways in which directors are appointed, can lose their office and the disqualification of directors.[2]	10
	(c)	Distinguish between the powers of the board of directors, the managing director/chief executive and individual directors to bind their company.[2]	10
	(d)	Explain the duties that directors owe to their companies, and the controls imposed by statute over dealings between directors and their companies, including loans.[2]	10
2	**Other company officers**		
	(a)	Discuss the appointment procedure relating to, and the duties and powers of, a company secretary.[2]	11
	(b)	Discuss the appointment procedure relating to, and the duties and rights of, a company auditor and their subsequent removal or resignation.[2]	11
3	**Company meetings and resolutions**		
	(a)	Distinguish between types of meetings: general meetings and annual general meetings.[1]	11
	(b)	Distinguish between types of resolutions: ordinary, special and written.[2]	11
	(c)	Explain the procedure for calling and conducting company meetings.[2]	11

Syllabus learning objective	Chapter reference
G LEGAL IMPLICATIONS RELATING TO COMPANIES IN DIFFICULTY OR IN CRISIS	
1 Insolvency	
(a) Explain the meaning of and procedure involved in voluntary liquidation, including members' and creditors' voluntary liquidation.[2]	12
(b) Explain the meaning of, the grounds for and the procedure involved, in compulsory liquidation.[2]	12
(c) Explain the order in which company debts will be paid off on liquidation.[2]	12
(d) Explain administration as an alternative to liquidation.[2]	12
(e) Explain the way in which an administrator may be appointed, the effects of such appointment and the powers and duties of an administrator.[2]	12
H CORPORATE FRAUDULENT AND CRIMINAL BEHAVIOUR	
1 Fraudulent and criminal behaviour	
(a) Recognise the nature and legal control over insider dealing.[2]	13
(b) Recognise the nature and legal control over market abuse.[2]	13
(c) Recognise the nature and legal control over money laundering including the following policies, procedures and controls: (i) risk management practices (ii) internal controls (iii) customer due diligence (iv) reliance and record keeping (v) the monitoring and management of compliance with, and the internal communication of, such policies, controls and procedures.[2]	13
(d) Recognise the nature and legal control over bribery.[2]	13
(e) Discuss potential criminal activity in the operation, management and liquidation of companies.[2]	13
(f) Recognise the nature and legal control over fraudulent and wrongful trading, including the failure to prevent the facilitation of tax evasion and the meaning of relevant body.[2]	13

The superscript numbers in square brackets indicate the intellectual depth at which the subject area could be assessed within the examination. Level 1 (knowledge and comprehension) broadly equates with the Knowledge module, Level 2 (application and analysis) with the Skills module and Level 3 (synthesis and evaluation) to the Professional level. However, lower level skills can continue to be assessed as you progress through each module and level.

The examination

Examination format

	Number of marks
Section A:	
– 25 × 2 mark objective test questions	50
– 20 × 1 mark objective test questions	20
Section B:	
– 5 × 6 mark multi-task questions	30
	100

Total time allowed: 2 hours

Chapter

1

Essential elements of legal systems

Chapter learning objectives

Upon completion of this chapter you will be able to:

- explain the interrelationship of economic, political and legal systems
- explain the separation of powers and its impact on the legal system
- explain the different types and systems of law
- explain the distinction between civil and criminal law
- explain the operation of common, civil and Sharia law
- explain the distinction between public and private international law
- explain the need for international regulation in the context of conflict of laws
- explain the function of international treaties, conventions and model codes
- explain the roles of international organisations, UN, ICC, WTO, COE, OECD, UNIDROIT, etc. and the courts in the regulation of international trade
- explain the operation, and evaluate the distinct merits, of court-based adjudication and arbitration as a means of settling civil disputes.

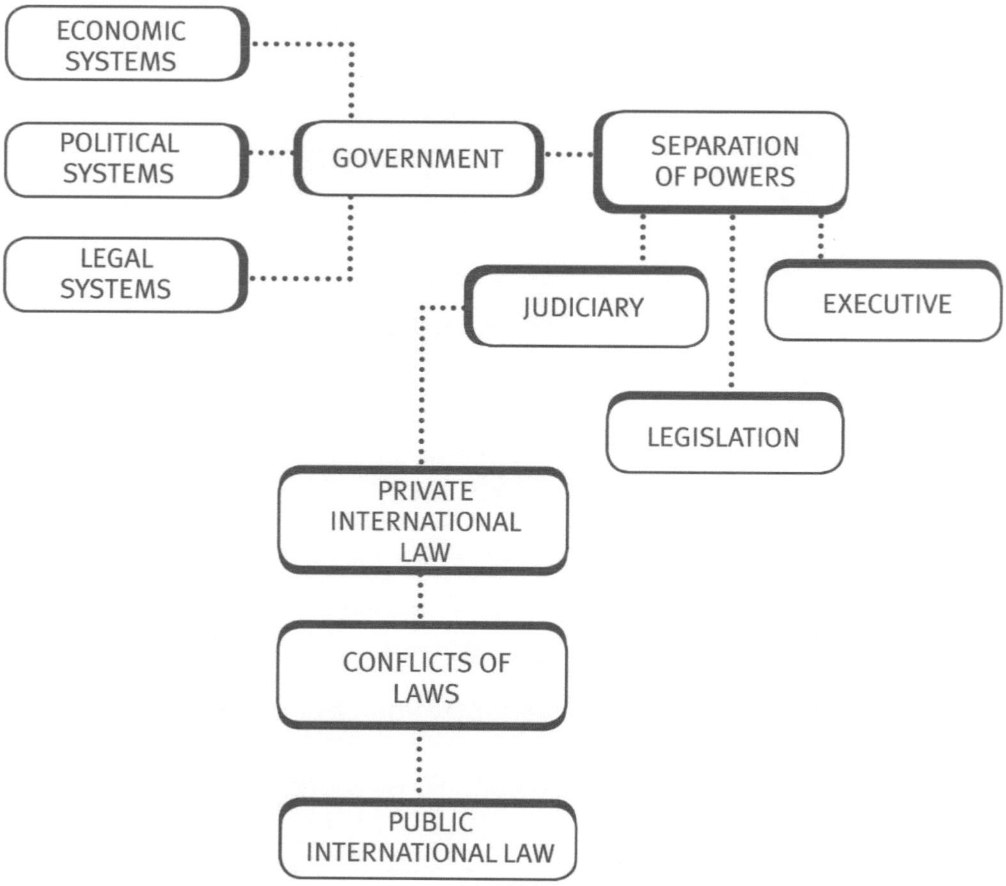

1 Economic, political and legal systems

The inter-relationship between economic, political and legal systems

A country's political economy refers to its political, economic and legal systems.

These systems are interdependent, and interact and influence each other. The political and economic system of a country will be influenced by its legal system and will have implications for the practice of international business.

Economic systems

A country's economic policy decides how that society finances itself, that is, what it produces, how it produces it and for whom.

There are three main types of economic system:

- Planned – where decisions and choices are made by the government, e.g. how natural resources in the country are to be used and what prices should be paid for them.

- Market – where decisions and choices are left to market forces of supply and demand, e.g. the price is set by how much will be paid for the resources and how much of it is needed. If a particular resource is easily obtainable, the price will usually be lower. The reverse is also true – if a particular resource is rare, the price will usually be high.
- Mixed – which is a mixture of the two types above (in practice, most countries have a mixed economy, and what makes the difference is the proportion between market forces and planned economy in that country).

Test your understanding 1
Define a planned economy.

Political systems

Politics refers to how countries are managed.

A country might be run by a dictator (political system: a dictatorship) and individual freedom might be heavily regulated.

In contrast, a country might be run by an elected body (political system: democracy) and individuals may be more free to regulate their own lives, still being subject to an overall body of law made by the elected government.

The nature of the political system:

- affects the way that laws are made
- affects the way that economies are run.

Test your understanding 2
What is democracy?

Legal systems

Law is the body of rules that exists in a society, under which its members operate.

Law is therefore:

- usually understood in 'local' rather than 'global' terms
- historically in writing as societies changed from tribal/family government to nation states
- often outlined in basic terms in a country's constitution
- made by the people governing the country.

There are three broad 'types' of legal system which operate in the world:

- common law (e.g. in the UK and the US)
- civil law (e.g. in France and Germany)
- Sharia law (for example, in Pakistan and Iran).

These will be looked at in more detail later in this chapter.

Many countries in the world have a constitution setting out its citizens' basic legal rights. For example, the US has a written constitution.

Increasingly, countries are trading internationally.

- This can cause problems where legal, economic and political systems are so different as to make agreeing terms between the parties difficult.
- This has led to an increasing interest in creating 'international' law, particularly with regard to international commercial transactions, which is what this syllabus focuses on.

Test your understanding 3
Define law.

Separation of powers

Separation of powers is the ancient constitutional principle that different 'powers' involved in the government of a state should be separate from one another. The fear was that if two or more 'powers' in the same state get into the same hands, then they are likely to rule as tyrants. Many modern dictators bear out this observation. The concept is understood in various ways. Modern thinking analyses the 'powers' of government as being three: a legislature to make the law, and executive to implement it, and a judiciary to interpret it in cases of dispute. What varies is how (if at all) the principle is applied – are the organisations involved to be separate, the personnel different in each 'power', no organisation to be able to control another – or some combination of those.

The US constitution was designed with separation of powers in mind. Thus, the President (in charge of the executive limb of the constitution) may not be a member of Congress (the legislature). However, the US also has an intricate system of 'checks and balances' to link the 'powers' together and keep them accountable to each other – so that one tyrant will not merely be replaced by three. For example, although the US Supreme Court (the most senior judicial body) may declare laws made by the US Congress to be invalid, the members of that Court are chosen by the President, subject to the approval of the senior (upper) chamber of Congress, which is called the Senate.

The UK has what is often called an unwritten constitution: its key rules have never been formally collected together into one enactment. The UK constitution has evolved over centuries, rather than ever been 'designed,' and so it does not reflect this criterion. On the one hand, it is a basic principle that – contrary to the theory of separation of powers – the most senior members of the executive are chosen from the legislature. This is known as the 'Westminster Model' and has been copied extensively worldwide: it is seen as promoting the executive's responsibility to the legislature and so the people that they represent. On the other hand, His Majesty the King as Monarch has potentially significant powers of a legislative (calling elections), executive (appointing ministers) and judicial (pardoning criminals) nature.

These powers are now considered, briefly, in turn as they relate to the law.

The legislature:

- is the primary law maker in a state
- will usually indicate if a state is to be considered democratic or not by whether its membership is wholly or substantially elected
- may either have unlimited law-making power (in which case it is called 'sovereign' or 'supreme') or be subject to legal limits on its power ('subordinate') – limits that are often imposed by that state's written constitution. Those limits (if any) are often enforced by that state's judiciary, who may be given power to declare invalid laws made by the legislature that are inconsistent with those limits.

One of the key rules of UK unwritten constitution is that the UK Parliament is sovereign. The courts (that is, the judiciary) have no power to declare its law to be invalid: if a law made by Parliament is flawed, then it is for Parliament to put the matter right. It would be seen as unconstitutional (an abuse of separation of powers) for a UK court to criticise the soundness of an Act of Parliament. Whether the law in question is to be changed remains a matter for Parliament.

The executive:

- implements the law (that is, brings it into effect)
- is usually the numerically largest of the 'powers', consisting of central and local government, the civil service, government ministers, the police, the armed forces, the tax authorities, etc.
- in states that seek fully to practise separation of powers (such as France or the US, in different ways), will be largely independent of the legislature and the judiciary. In states that follow the Westminster Model (see above) it will by contrast be a constitutional requirement that the leading members of the executive be chosen from and accountable to the legislature.

The separation of powers allows for the legislature and the executive, which may be expected to function semi-independently of each other, to be elected individually. That will be especially likely to happen if they are controlled by different political parties. Under the Westminster Model, there is more likely to be only one set of elections, which chooses the legislature and the executive at the same time, and so gives the new government both the power and the duty (called the doctrine of mandate) to enact as laws the promises and policies that they made in their successful election manifesto.

The judiciary:

- decides authoritatively questions that arise about what is the law of that state, and about its application to particular cases. Judicial activity may be classified as criminal – matters between state and citizen concerned with punishing those guilty of crime – or civil – matters between citizens usually about compensation for loss of some kind.
- is usually wholly or largely outside the legislative process. Where the legislature is not sovereign, the judiciary may well have power to declare unconstitutional (or otherwise legally unsound) laws made by it to be invalid. This may be the role of all the courts or just one or more specialist courts.
- in a common law legal system like that of the UK of the USA, i.e. one where the law is found in many, many case decisions of the courts – there will be a further important function of the judiciary: it will be their function to interpret the law, and (usually) to lay down authoritative rulings (called precedent) about what is the law. In a civil law legal system like that of France, the law is instead to be found in a comprehensive code (a very long enactment), and it will be said that the judiciary do not need to interpret the code, they just apply it.
- in both common law and civil law systems courts exercise limited control over the actions of public bodies by way of a judicial review. The review usually takes place at the instance of an individual whose rights have been infringed by the public body and who claims that that public body acted either illegally or ultra vires – outside their powers. Judicial review applications are heard by the King's Bench Division of the High Court. On application, the court will not determine whether any individual decision of the public body was correct on its merits. It will only determine whether that public body had the authority to make such a decision and whether the decision was taken according to proper procedures. If the courts determine that the decision was taken by a body that did not have the appropriate authority or proper procedures were not followed, it will quash the decision and will ask the relevant public body to reconsider the decision on its merits.

Test your understanding 4

Define the function of the legislature.

Test your understanding 5

Explain the concept of separation of powers.

2 Different legal systems

Types of law

Each country has its own set of national laws which regulate how entities relate to each other and to the state. International law on the other hand reflects the interrelationship of states and will seek to resolve problems where there is a conflict of national laws.

Each country will also distinguish between civil and criminal law.

Criminal law versus civil law (the UK)

Criminal law	Civil law
Criminal law relates to conduct of which the State disapproves and which it seeks to control. It is a form of public law.	Civil law is a form of private law and involves the relationships between individual citizens.
Purpose – the enforcement of particular forms of behaviour by the State, which acts to ensure compliance.	**Purpose** – to settle disputes between individuals and to provide remedies.
In criminal law the case is brought by the **State** in the name of the Crown. A criminal case will be reported as R v ..., where R stands for Regina or Rex. Regina means the Latin for 'queen' and Rex for 'king'.	In civil law the case is brought by the **claimant**, who is seeking a remedy. The case will be referred to by the names of the parties involved in the dispute, such as Brown v Smith.
Burden of proof – on the prosecution.	**Burden of proof** – on the claimant.
Standard of proof – guilt must be shown **beyond reasonable doubt** (high standard of proof).	**Standard of proof** – liability must be shown on the **balance of probabilities** (lower standard of proof).
Object – to regulate society by the threat of punishment.	**Object** – usually financial compensation to put the claimant in the position he or she would have been in had the wrong not occurred.
If found guilty the criminal court will sentence the accused and it may fine him or her or impose a period of imprisonment. If innocent the accused will be acquitted.	The civil court will order the defendant to pay damages or it may order some other remedy, e.g. specific performance or injunction.

Conflicts of laws

A conflict of laws occurs when parties from different legal jurisdictions interact and trade with each other and their respective legal rules conflict.

This is where international law steps in and will regulate the relationship between the parties and their rights and duties towards one another.

Sources of international law

International law is derived from various sources:

- International treaties and conventions
- International custom
- The general principles of law.

Common law

Common law derives from the body of law built up in England between 1066AD and 1400AD. It has been exported to various countries, notably the USA.

Key principles of common law:

- Principles of law do not become inoperative through lapse of time (therefore a principle applied in a court case of 1066AD may be relevant to a case today).
- New laws developed by the legislature are presumed not to alter the existing law (unless they state that they do so).
- Judges apply the law and must apply decisions reached in previous cases subject to certain conditions, e.g. that there is no material difference between the cases in question. This is the doctrine of judicial precedent, which is an important concept in common law.

Sources of law in common law systems:

- Common law: the body of law referred to above, which has evolved through the application of the doctrine of judicial precedent.
- Equity: the system of rules developed by Chancery to overcome the perceived rigidity of common law.
- Statute: law made by the legislature.
- Delegated legislation.
- Custom (historic law): customs still plays a part in commercial transactions.
- The constitution: in common law countries that have a constitution.
- European Union (EU) law: in all countries that are also part of the European Union. Many European Union countries have a civil system.

BREXIT

On Thursday 23rd June 2016 a referendum was held and the UK voted to leave the EU.

The UK left the EU on 31st January 2020, meaning that European Union law no longer applies in the UK. Prior to leaving, European Union law took precedence over all other sources of law in the UK.

All of the EU law that directly applied to the UK at 31st January 2020 was brought within the UK's domestic legal framework as a new category of law known as retained EU law.

Legislation and delegated legislation

Legislation is the law created by the Parliament as the highest sovereign law making body in the UK. UK Parliament consists of the House of Commons and the House of Lords. For any Act to be enacted the Bill (proposed Act) must be approved by the House of Commons, House of Lords and a Royal Assent by the Monarch must be given.

Acts may be passed to:

1 Create a new law

2 Authorise taxation

3 Codify existing law

4 Consolidate existing statute

5 Overrule an existing precedent.

The process of enacting Acts of Parliament is very time consuming and burdensome. It would not be possible to regulate every legal aspect by an Act of Parliament or considered every minute detail of each relevant section. To facilitate law making process and to save Parliamentary time, the Parliament is able to authorise another body to enact secondary legislation. This type is usually called delegated or secondary legislation. This means that the legislation is done on behalf of the Parliament.

There are many types of delegated legislation:

1 Orders in Council – it permits the government, through the Privy Council to enact new law. The Privy Council is nominally a non party-political body of eminent parliamentarians. Orders in Council are usually used in times of national emergency, for example to mobilise the Armed Forces on the outbreak of hostilities.

2 Statutory Instruments – they are usually made by government ministers in which particular regulations are enacted.

3 By-laws – they are made by local authorities or other local bodies. The application of by-laws is limited to a specific geographic territory.

4 Court Rule – made by Court Rule Committees to govern the procedures in the particular courts under the Supreme Court Act 1981, the County Court Act 1984, and the Magistrates' Courts Act 1980.

5 Professional regulations – made by e.g. the Law Society under the Solicitors' Act 1974 to regulate and control the conduct of practising solicitors.

The role of judges

The role of judges in common law systems is to:

- apply the law consistently with previous decisions of judges unless there are valid reasons for overruling previous decisions
- interpret the statutes made by the legislative
- review the law to determine whether it conflicts with the overriding principles of law (for example the US Constitution). This is not a feature of a UK judicial role.

UK Courts and their hierarchy

The UK Court structure is divided into civil law courts and criminal law courts.

The Supreme Court – is the highest appellate court in UK for both civil and criminal cases.

Court of Appeal – the second highest court in UK. It has two divisions: criminal and civil. Appeals are normally considered in the Court of Appeal before they can be heard in the Supreme Court. Civil division hears appeals from the County Courts and the High Court of Justice. Criminal division hears appeals from the Crown Court.

Civil cases	Criminal cases
High Court – for jurisdiction purposes the High Court is divided into three divisions: the King's Bench Division, the Chancery Division and the Family Division. The King's Bench Division deals mainly with contract and tort disputes. The Chancery Division deals with land law, trusts, probate, copyright, company law, partnership law, revenue law and insolvency cases. The Family Division deals with matrimonial matters. **County Courts** – court of first instance for civil claims in contract, tort, land and tenant, probate, and insolvency.	**Crown Courts** – deal with serious criminal offences where the defendant is tried by the judge and the jury. **Magistrates' Courts** – deal with other criminal offences and some limited family matters.

Doctrine of judicial precedent

The system adopted by the judges, of following the decisions in previous cases is called the doctrine of judicial precedent.

- Some precedents are **binding** (meaning they **must** be followed in later cases).
- Others are merely **persuasive** (meaning that a judge in a later case **may** choose to follow it but he or she is not bound to do so).

The application of consistency is the basis of judicial precedent, which has the following rules.

- A precedent must be based on a proposition of law not of fact.
- The facts of the case being considered must be materially the same as the case in which the precedent was laid down.
- The previous court must have had the power to bind the court making the current decision (it must be a superior court).
- In order for a precedent to be binding on a judge in a later case, the material facts of the two cases must be the same. If they are significantly different, the precedent will be persuasive rather than binding.
- A precedent can be overruled by a higher court. Please note that the Supreme Court can overrule itself.

Rules of statutory interpretation

Statutory interpretation is the process by which judges assign meanings to ambiguous words or phrases in statutes.

Literal rule

Words must be given their ordinary dictionary meaning, even if this produces an undesirable outcome.

Fisher v Bell (1961)

Facts: The court had to consider the meaning of the wording 'offer for sale'. It was an offence to 'offer for sale' offensive weapons. A shopkeeper had flick-knives with price tags attached on display in his shop window.

Held: The court applied the fundamental principles of contract law in a literal fashion, accepting that the display of flick-knives was an invitation to treat. It was the customer who made an offer to buy. In consequence, the shopkeeper was found not to be acting illegally. The aim of Parliament, however, had been to prevent sales of offensive weapons.

Golden rule

Where the literal rule gives more than one meaning or provides an absurd result, the golden rule is used to ensure that preference is given to the meaning that does not result in the provision being an absurdity.

Adler v George (1964)

Facts: A conviction was challenged on the basis of what appeared to be a miswording in the Official Secrets Act (1920). This Act made it an offence to obstruct a member of the armed forces `in the vicinity of' particular locations, but not actually `in' those locations. The defendant was actually inside an Air Force base at the time of the incident, which he claimed was beyond the literal scope of the Act.

Held: The words 'in the vicinity of' a prohibited place in the Official Secrets Act were held to cover the acts of the defendant which took place 'within' a prohibited place.

Mischief rule

Used to interpret a statute in a way which provides a remedy for the mischief the statute was enacted to prevent.

Gorris v Scott (1874)

Facts: The Contagious Diseases (Animals) Act 1869 provided that any ship carrying animals should contain them in pens. The defendant neglected his duty, and some of the claimant's sheep were washed overboard and lost.

Held: Since the purpose of the statute was to prevent the spread of contagious disease, and not to guard against the danger of the property being washed overboard, the claim failed.

Purposive Rule

This is a more modern approach. Here the court is not just looking to see what the gap was in the old law, it is making a decision as to what they felt Parliament meant to achieve.

Gardiner v Sevenoaks RDC (1950)

Facts: The purpose of an Act was to provide for the safe storage of film wherever it might be stored on 'premises'. The claimant argued that 'premises' did not include a cave and so the Act had no application to this case.

Held: The purpose of the Act was to protect the safety of persons working in all places where film was stored. If film was stored in a cave, the word 'premises' included the cave.

Eiusdem generis

General words mean the same kind of thing as the specific words they follow.

Powell v Kempton Park Racecourse Co (1899)

Facts: Section 1 of the Betting Act 1853 prohibited betting in a 'house, office, room or other place'. The issue was whether a ring at a racecourse was an 'other place' for the purposes of this statute.

Held: The Lords decided that if the eiusdem generis rule was applied, the specific words such as 'room' and 'office' that preceded the general phrase 'or other place' created a class of indoor places. As a ring on a racecourse was outside it would not fall within this category. Therefore the Act did not apply to restrict gambling here.

Expressio unius exclusio alterius

Where a statute seeks to establish a list of what is covered by its provisions, then anything not expressly included in that list is specifically excluded.

Presumptions

There are presumptions which will generally apply unless the legislation specifically states otherwise, for example:

- A statute will not bind the Crown.
- A statute cannot conflict with international law. An Act should therefore be interpreted as giving effect to international obligations.
- A statute does not have any retrospective effect.
- A statute does not alter the common law.
- A statute does not exclude the jurisdiction of the court.
- Legislation does not extend beyond the territorial jurisdiction of the UK.

Civil law systems

Civil law is the law historically developed from Roman law, based on codes of written law.

Principles of civil law:

- Comprehensibility: law is contained in codes, which are drafted as general principles, which should answer any situation.
- Certainty: derived from the above, questions of law should be decided predictably, in the context of the codes. Judges only have limited powers of interpretation.

Sources of law:

- countries' constitutions
- (in EU members) EU law
- statute (much of which is codified, as noted above)
- administrative regulations
- custom.

Role of judges:

- The distinction between those who draft the law and those who apply it tends to be greater in civil law systems than can be the case in common law systems.
- Judges apply the law.
- Judges create precedents (in effect law) which must be followed by other judges.

Principles of judicial interpretation:

- In general terms, judges are not supposed to interpret the law but apply it.
- However, when some interpretation is required, judges are required to identify the social purpose of the law and apply it in a manner that ensures that purpose is enacted.
- Also judges may look at the historic intention of the law and seek to apply it in the way that it would have been drafted to cover modern situations.

e.g

Illustration 1 – Different legal systems

There are a number of specific interpretational rules in France, such as that judges must follow the clear meaning of the law and not seek a different meaning. In addition, the law must be interpreted in accordance with its spirit, not to its letter, when the meaning is ambiguous.

e.g

Illustration 2 – Different legal systems

Certain common law countries have developed a system whereby the judiciary may decide whether any given statute is constitutional.

Germany has constitutional courts which exist for this purpose.

Test your understanding 6

Give two examples of countries which have a civil law system.

Test your understanding 7

Judges in a civil law system are required to interpret the law.

True or false.

Common law and civil law distinguished

The differences between common law and civil law can be seen in the descriptions above.

- Sources of law: In civil law, codes and statutes are supposed to be comprehensive. In common law, they are supplementary to the body of historic law created by judges.
- Role of judges: In civil law, judges are required to apply the law, whereas in common law, they have a much more interpretative and creative role.

Illustration 3 – Different legal systems

Auguste is a judge in France. Alison is a judge in the UK. They are presiding over cases which have similar facts. Auguste will refer to the relevant code and apply the law as stated within that code. Alison will have to consider the relevance of statutory law to the case. She will also have to consider if there has been a similar case previously decided by a superior court and apply any decision of law made in that case to the present facts.

Test your understanding 8

Compare and contrast statutory interpretation in common law and civil law systems.

Sharia law

Sharia law is law based in the religion of Islam.

Principles of Sharia law:

- Sharia is law given by Allah and is the divine way ordained for mankind.

Sources of Sharia law:

- Quran: Allah's divine revelation to his prophet Mohammed.
- Sunnah: record of what has come to be the acceptable course of conduct, derived from sayings of the prophet, known as Ahadith.

- Madhab: schools of thought based on writings and thoughts of major historical jurists. There are broadly speaking two schools, the Sunni and the Shiite. The Sunnis form the majority, and the schools under the Sunnis can be further subdivided into the Hanafi School, the Maliki School, the Shafii School and the Hanbali School.'
- Constitution of the country.

Role of judges:

- Judges in Sharia law are generally clerics, given the religious nature of the law although some countries also have secular judges.
- Judges are required to apply the law.
- There are limited powers of interpretation, given that the law was ordained by Allah.

Interpretation of the law:

- If clear guidance is not available in the Quran, a cleric may refer to the Sunnah to confirm, explain, or clarify the law.
- If the Quran does not give guidance on a specific matter, the Sunnah may do so.
- Within the Sunnah, Ahadith are classified according to their reliability: Mutawatir are virtually guaranteed, Mashhur are less certain and Ahads have little certainty about their reliability.
- There is controversy in the Muslim world whether further interpretation of law may be required.
- Taqlid is the theory that the law has been interpreted sufficiently and does not require further interpretation.
- Ijtihad are the historic processes used for interpreting the law (the specific types of Ijtihad are: Ijma', Qiyas, Istihan, Maslahah mursalah, 'Urf, and Istishab).

Ijtihad:

- Must not be carried out on certain matters (such as whether Allah exists).
- Must be carried out by a suitably qualified person, known as a Mujtahid, who has studied the Quran and the traditions of the prophet, understands the principle of Ijma', understands the conditions for Qiyas and is a just, reliable, trustworthy and good practising Muslim.

Ijma' is a consensus of opinion of jurists.

Qiyas is comparison of two things with a view to evaluating one in the light of the other.

Illustration 4 – Different legal systems

Because taking alcohol is forbidden by the Quran, the principle of Qiyas applies the same rule to matters which have a similar effect to alcohol, such as taking illegal drugs.

Istihan is the concept of equity or fairness, exercised within the bounds of what the Quran says.

Riba is an unjustified increment in borrowing or lending money, paid in kind or in money above the amount of loan.

Judicial review:

- May exist in some Muslim countries to ensure that issued statutes are based on Sharia law principles.

Test your understanding 9

Define Sharia law.

Test your understanding 10

Judges have the power to interpret Sharia law.

True or false.

Test your understanding 11

Define Qiyas.

3 International trade, international legal regulation and conflict of laws

Public and private international law

Private international law is a set of national, domestic rules to determine jurisdiction and applicable law in international contracts. Private international law, despite its name, is not an international law – it is purely domestic law. It also deals with the enforcement and recognition of foreign judgments.

Public international law is law which is recognised by a group of nations, such as Conventions and Treaties, international custom and general principles of law recognised by civilised nations.

Illustration 5 – Public international law

In this syllabus, we shall look at various examples of public international law, such as the UN Model Law on Arbitration or the UN Convention on Contracts for the International Sale of Goods (UNCCISG).

Test your understanding 12

Define public international law.

Test your understanding 13

Define private international law.

Conflict of laws and international legal regulation

Conflict of laws will arise where the law of two different countries produces different outcomes, making it difficult for parties in those countries to trade with one another.

Illustration 6 – Conflict of laws

This issue can be illustrated by thinking about the HSBC advertisements run on television or when you arrive at London's Heathrow Airport. The point of these advertisements is that the same thing (e.g. the colour red) can mean very different things in two different nations: e.g. in the UK red implies danger, in China it implies good luck. A similar situation may exist with the law. In Country A, negotiations to a contract may form part of the contract, in Country B, only agreed and signed terms may be included.

Suppose Constance, in Country A, wants to buy some goods from Dimitri, in Country B.

If Constance were dealing with someone in Country A, she would enter into negotiations with him. When they had agreed the terms of their sale she would engage a solicitor to write up those terms, and those terms would not become binding on either party until both had signed.

In Country B however, Dimitri is accustomed to less formality in relation to contracts. He understands that once the parties have agreed the terms, the terms are binding. So once negotiations with Constance have been finalised, he makes and sends her the goods.

Constance finds an alternative supplier prepared to give her a better deal than Dimitri before she has signed her contract with Dimitri and decides to contract with the alternative supplier instead. Then she receives goods from Dimitri. She is surprised, because she does not believe she has a contract with Dimitri. He, however, expects her to accept and pay for the goods.

Ultimately, if this situation were to be taken up in the courts of each nation, Country A (where Constance is) would say there was no contract, so Constance does not have to accept or pay for the goods. Country B would say that there was a contract, and Constance has to accept and pay for the goods. But Constance is not in Country B, so the judgement against her cannot be enforced, and Dimitri loses out.

This is the problem of conflict of laws. Parties will not want to trade with one another when their laws and customs are different, and could leave them exposed to loss.

Test your understanding 14

Define conflict of laws.

International treaties, conventions and model codes

Public international law arises out of the problem of conflict of laws.

- Nations negotiate treaties and model codes so that parties can refer to that agreed code of conduct when carrying out international trade rather than their own domestic laws.
- International bodies (which we will look at below) exist to help create, manage and amend those agreed international laws.

Illustration 7 – Public international law

Examples of public international law were given above. They include the UN Model Law on Arbitration, the UNCCISG, the UN Model Law on International Credit Transfers, the UN Convention on International Bills of Exchange and International Promissory Notes.

Illustration 8 – Public international law

Various organisations are associated with international law, as we shall see below. However, as you can tell from the names of the model laws listed above, a key organisation is the United Nations (UN).

Illustration 9 – Public international law

There are also various bodies involved in adjudicating international law. For example, the International Chamber of Commerce set up the International Court of Arbitration.

Conventions

UN Conventions are binding under international law on member states. The Rome Convention 1980 sets out policy on what law should govern the validity of international contracts. It sets down the principle that if the parties have a written contract and have expressed preference for a particular law in that contract, that law should govern the contract.

The New York Convention 1958 sets out the agreement of countries relating to referring cases to arbitration.

4 International organisations

United Nations (UN)

The UN is a global body which has almost every country in the world as a member, which exists to maintain peace and security, develop friendly relations between nations, co-operate in solving economic, social, cultural and humanitarian problems and to promote respect for human rights and international freedoms.

As you can see, the UN's remit is wider than international law. It has various legal departments, such as:

- UN Commission on International Trade Law (UNCITRAL) (www.uncitral.org).
- The International Court of Justice (ICJ) (www.icj-cij.org).

UNCITRAL is the legal body of the UN which has largely harmonised and unified public international law. It is formed of 61 states elected by the UN general assembly and it has issued various model laws and conventions, including those mentioned above which are covered in this syllabus.

UNCITRAL:

- was established in 1966 by the general assembly of the UN
- has a general mandate to harmonise and unify the international law on trade
- is composed of 60 member states elected by the general council
- carries out work at annual session, which may be observed by any party

- has six working groups that conduct preparatory research work on topics in its programme
- issues model laws and conventions relating to international trade as we have seen and will look at in more detail.

Test your understanding 15
What is UNCITRAL?

International Chamber of Commerce (ICC)

The ICC is an organisation created by business leaders from various countries which aims to 'serve world business community by promoting trade and investment, open markets for goods and services, and the free flow of capital'.

The ICC:

- has thousands of member companies and associations from 130 countries
- co-operates with and advises the UN in formulating international law
- provides practical services to businesses
- seeks to combat commercial crime (such as money laundering)
- has a website, which is www.iccwbo.org
- has a World Council, national committees and groups, International Secretariat.

The World Council is the supreme authority of the ICC.

The World Council:

- consists of delegates of business executives from members of ICC nominated by national committees
- elects the executive board, which is responsible for implementing ICC policy. It has between 15 and 30 members who serve for three years, with one third retiring at the end of each year
- elects the chairman and the vice-chairman of the board who make recommendations for the board to implement.

The national committees:

- represent the ICC in their nation states
- ensure that ICC takes account of their national business concerns in determining policy
- elect a member to the World Council.

The Secretariat:

- works closely with the national committees to carry out the ICC's work programme
- is headed by a general secretary (currently Guy Sebban, from France).

Test your understanding 16
What is the ICC?

World Trade Organisation (WTO)

The WTO is an organisation which provides rules for the system of international trade. It was formed in 1995 from the old General Agreement on Tariffs and Trade (GATT) which had existed since 1948. The WTO provides guidance on trade in goods, services, inventions, creations and intellectual properties. It has 149 members, accounting for over 97% of the world's trade.

The purposes of the WTO are to:

- assist the free flow of trade by removing obstacles
- publicise world trade rules
- give individuals, companies and governments confidence that there will be no sudden changes of policy.

The WTO:

- administers trade agreements
- acts as a forum for trade negotiations
- settles trade disputes
- reviews national trade policies
- assists developing countries in trade policy issues
- cooperates with other international organisations
- has a website (www.wto.org).

The WTO's agreements:

- include individual countries' commitments to lower customs tariffs and other trade barriers
- set procedures for settling disputes (through the Dispute Settlement Body)
- prescribe special treatments for developing countries
- require governments to make trade policies transparent by frequent reporting to, and periodic scrutiny by, the WTO.

The structure of the WTO is:

- a Secretariat based in Geneva, which supplies technical support for councils and committees
- the Ministerial Conference, which is the top decision-making body and meets at least once every two years
- the General Council, comprising ambassadors based in Geneva, but sometimes officials are sent from member countries which meets several times a year in Geneva
- sub-councils, such as the Goods Council or the Services Council, which report to the general council
- specialised committees and working groups.

Decisions of the WTO are taken:

- by consensus generally (although a majority vote is permitted)
- by the entire membership.

The General Council is also known as the Dispute Settlement Body when relevant. It has the authority to:

- establish a panel of three or up to five experts from different countries to hear a case (chosen in consultation with the countries in dispute)
- accept or reject the panel's findings
- accept or reject (by consensus) an appeal on a point of law within 30 days
- monitor the implementation of rulings and recommendations.

Appeals are heard by three members of the Appellate Body which:

- is a permanent body
- is made up of seven members who have to be individuals with recognised standing in the field of law and international trade and not affiliated with any government
- can uphold, modify or reverse the original panel's findings.

e.g

Illustration 10 – International organisations

The country of Aredia has a dispute with the country of Banovia. It has been referred to a panel of three experts. The two countries in dispute have agreed to the following members of the panel:

- Carl, an expert from Dunvin.
- Egor, an expert from Francia.
- Gertrude, an expert from Hanu.

The panel delivers a verdict. However, Aredia is not happy with the verdict and so appeals. The appeal will be heard by three members of the Appellate Body. The Appellate Body modifies the verdict. The Dispute Settlement Body then confirms that Appellate Body's verdict. Aredia and Banovia are required to comply with the terms of the verdict, and the Dispute Settlement Body monitors the implementation of the ruling.

Test your understanding 17

Idria and Jamelistan have a dispute which has been referred to a panel of WTO experts. The panel delivers a ruling, but Jamelistan is not happy with the verdict.

1 **Jamelistan may appeal this verdict.**

Tue or false

2 **An appeal would be heard before:**

A the original panel of experts

B the Appellate Body

C the Dispute Settlement Body

D the Secretariat

3 **The Dispute Settlement Body has the power to:**

A accept the appeal ruling

B modify the appeal ruling

C reject the appeal ruling

D monitor the implementation of the appeal ruling

Organisation for Economic Co-operation and Development (OECD)

The OECD is a group of member countries whose modern aim is to be a forum for discussing, developing and refining economic and social policies.

The OECD:

- has 38 member countries from most continents
- has relationships with a further 70 countries
- was historically an organisation set up to administer US and Canadian aid to Europe after World War II
- creates legally-binding agreements and non-binding guidelines for countries (members and otherwise) to subscribe to
- provides guidance, e.g. on corporate governance (how companies are managed) – the OECD Principles of Corporate Governance
- has a website (www.oecd.org).

Test your understanding 18

What is the OECD?

International Institute for the Unification of Private Law (UNIDROIT)

UNIDROIT is an independent, inter-governmental organisation.

UNIDROIT:

- studies needs and methods of harmonising private commercial law
- has 61 member states from five continents
- is financed by contributions from member states
- has a website (www.unidroit.org)
- draws up international conventions which are designed to have the force of law in priority to existing domestic law where adopted
- draws up model laws for states to take into consideration when drafting their own private law
- draws up general principles addressed to judges or arbitrators who are free to decide whether to implement them or not
- its work has served as a basis for conventions issued by other bodies, such as the UN CCISG
- has a three-tiered structure, with a Secretariat, a Governing Council and a General Assembly.

The Secretariat:

- is responsible for carrying out the day-to-day work programme of UNIDROIT
- is run by the Secretary-General nominated by the Governing Council
- consists of civil servants and ancillary staff.

The Governing Council:

- is made up of one ex officio member, who is the President, and 25 elected officials (judges, practitioners, civil servants)
- supervises the work of the secretariat.

The General Assembly:

- is the decision-making body of UNIDROIT
- elects the governing council every five years
- approves the work programme every three years
- is made up of one official from every member state.

Test your understanding 19
What is UNIDROIT?

5 International courts

International Court of Justice (ICJ)

The ICJ is one of the components of the UN, as discussed above.

The ICJ:

- settles disputes put before it by states
- provides legal advice on issues put before it by international organisations
- is not a court for individuals
- has 15 judges elected by the General Assembly of the UN for a term of nine years. No two judges must have the same nationality. Elections are held every three years for one third of the seats and retiring judges may be re-elected.

States may submit a dispute to the court:

- by specific agreement
- by virtue of a jurisdictional clause in a treaty to which they are a party
- by virtue of the Statute (if the dispute is with other signatories to the UN Statute).

Procedures of the court:

- are governed by the rules of Court under the Statute
- there are written procedures and then a public oral phase
- there is no appeal.

The International Court of Arbitration (ICA)

The ICA is a body set up by the International Chamber of Commerce to oversee all aspects of the arbitration process when members refer disputes between them to arbitration.

The ICA:

- has a list of arbitrators that can be appointed to conduct the arbitration proceedings
- decides on challenges to arbitrator
- approves arbitral awards
- fixes arbitrators' fees.

Test your understanding 20

1 **The ICJ can try cases relating to individuals.**

True or False.

2 **The ICA can try cases relating to individuals.**

True or False.

Test your understanding 21

What is the ICA?

6 Courts versus arbitration

Operation of the courts

Courts are where legal disputes have historically been settled.

In a court case:

- parties present their claim before a judge (and sometimes a jury of 'ordinary citizens') who decides the merits of the case
- parties are often represented by legal personnel such as solicitors or barristers
- parties have a right of appeal to a superior court if they disagree with the outcome.

Advantages and disadvantages of court-based adjudication

The main advantage of going to court is that it can provide a helpful legal solution.

The disadvantages are that choosing to go to court can be expensive and time consuming. The cost of legal representation coupled with court fees can act as a deterrent of going down this route especially where the case may proceed through the appeal courts.

Illustration 11 – Courts versus arbitration

In the UK, there are two systems of courts. The criminal system deals with offences against the state and the civil system deals with legal disputes between citizens. Both systems have a structure of courts so that the case will be heard in a court of 'first instance' but, if a party does not agree with the outcome, the case can then be referred to an 'appellate' court.

The UK civil court structure contains five levels of courts. The main court of first instance is the county court. From the County Court, an appeal can be made to the High Court or the Court of Appeal (depending on the nature of the appeal). If the case is still disputed, an appeal can be made from the High Court to the Court of Appeal and from the Court of Appeal to the Supreme Court (previously House of Lords).

The Supreme Court is the UK's superior court (that is, it is the final court in the UK to which an appeal can be taken).

Test your understanding 22

What is a court of first instance?

Arbitration

Arbitration is one example of what is collectively called alternative dispute resolution (ADR). It is a way of settling disputes without going through the courts, by referring the issue to a third party for resolution.

Arbitration is:

- a popular way of settling commercial disputes
- the subject of the UN Model law on International Commercial Arbitration (covered in **Chapter 2**)
- governed in the UK by the Arbitration Act 1996, which states that its principles are to allow resolution of disputes without unnecessary delay and expense, with the free agreement of the parties as to how the dispute will be settled subject only to such safeguards as are necessary in the public interest. The 1996 Act increases the role of the arbitrator and reduces the role of the court to a residual level of intervention where legal assistance is required.

Test your understanding 23

Define arbitration.

Advantages and disadvantages of arbitration

- **Privacy.** Arbitration tends to be held in private, in contrast to proceedings in a court which are public. This means that sensitive information can be kept private and damaging publicity can be kept to a minimum.
- **Informality.** Proceedings can be less formal than a court case and can be scheduled flexibly for the parties involved. However, arbitration now tends to be very formal with full use of legal representation so this advantage is diminishing in importance.
- **Speed.** Generally a court case takes much longer than an arbitration.
- **Cost.** Partly due to speed, arbitration can be cheaper than a court case. However, the cost of the experts involved in arbitration can still be significant.
- **Expertise.** When a case is arbitrated, it is heard before a third party who may be an expert in the specific area under dispute and therefore the expert forms the judgement in line with accepted practice in that area. Parties are free to choose the arbitrator and decide on what expertise he or she must possess. He or she may be a legal expert or he or she may have expertise in the required field.
- **Finality.** There is more limitation on appeals from an arbitration award than from the decision of the court. Recourse after a decision has been made is therefore limited. The award can be enforced through court action under the UN Convention on Recognition and Enforcement of Foreign Arbitral Awards.
- **Neutral forum.** Parties in international dispute will usually wish to avoid litigation in a foreign country. Arbitration may take place in a neutral forum which offers no advantage to either party to a dispute. (This is often perceived to be the biggest advantage of arbitration.)
- Note that the advantages of arbitration are in many cases the disadvantages of court action (particularly privacy, informality, speed and expertise).

Advantages of court action

- Judges are legal experts and may have greater expertise in evaluating evidence.
- Court decisions are taken within a framework of precedent, so in theory the outcome is more predictable than in arbitration where decisions are made on a case-by-case basis.
- There is much more scope for appeal in the court system.
- Note that the advantages of the court system in general are disadvantages of the arbitration system. Parties will have to determine what the most important factors are for them in each case.

Illustration 12 – Courts versus arbitration

Sanjay and Thomas have a dispute as a result of a contract for the international sale of goods. There is no clause in their contract referring to how disputes should be settled. The case involves a dispute with regard to the quality of goods supplied by Thomas. Thomas would prefer that this alleged lack of quality is not made public, as this might harm his relationships with other customers. Thomas and Sanjay are keen to resolve this matter quickly and amicably, as Thomas has always been Sanjay's preferred supplier and he has a number of outstanding orders with him at the moment.

In this case, it would be to both Thomas' and Sanjay's advantage to refer the case to arbitration rather than to take it to court. Arbitration would give Thomas the privacy he would prefer, and it would result in a quicker effective resolution.

Test your understanding 24

Indicate which of the following are advantages of arbitration or court proceedings. Place A (arbitration) or C (court proceedings) after the relevant sentence.

- Proceedings are likely to be swifter.
- Proceedings will be private.
- The person presiding over the dispute will be chosen by the parties.
- The person presiding over the dispute will be a judge.
- There will be significant scope for appeal.

Test your understanding 25

Valerie and Wong have a dispute as a result of a contract for the international sale of goods. There is no provision for the settlement of disputes in the contract. They both want a speedy resolution to the issue which relates to a fairly obscure part of trade law. Wong feels that some recent disputes have been settled unfairly against him however, and wants to be able to appeal the decision if he does not agree with it.

Advise Wong.

7 Chapter summary

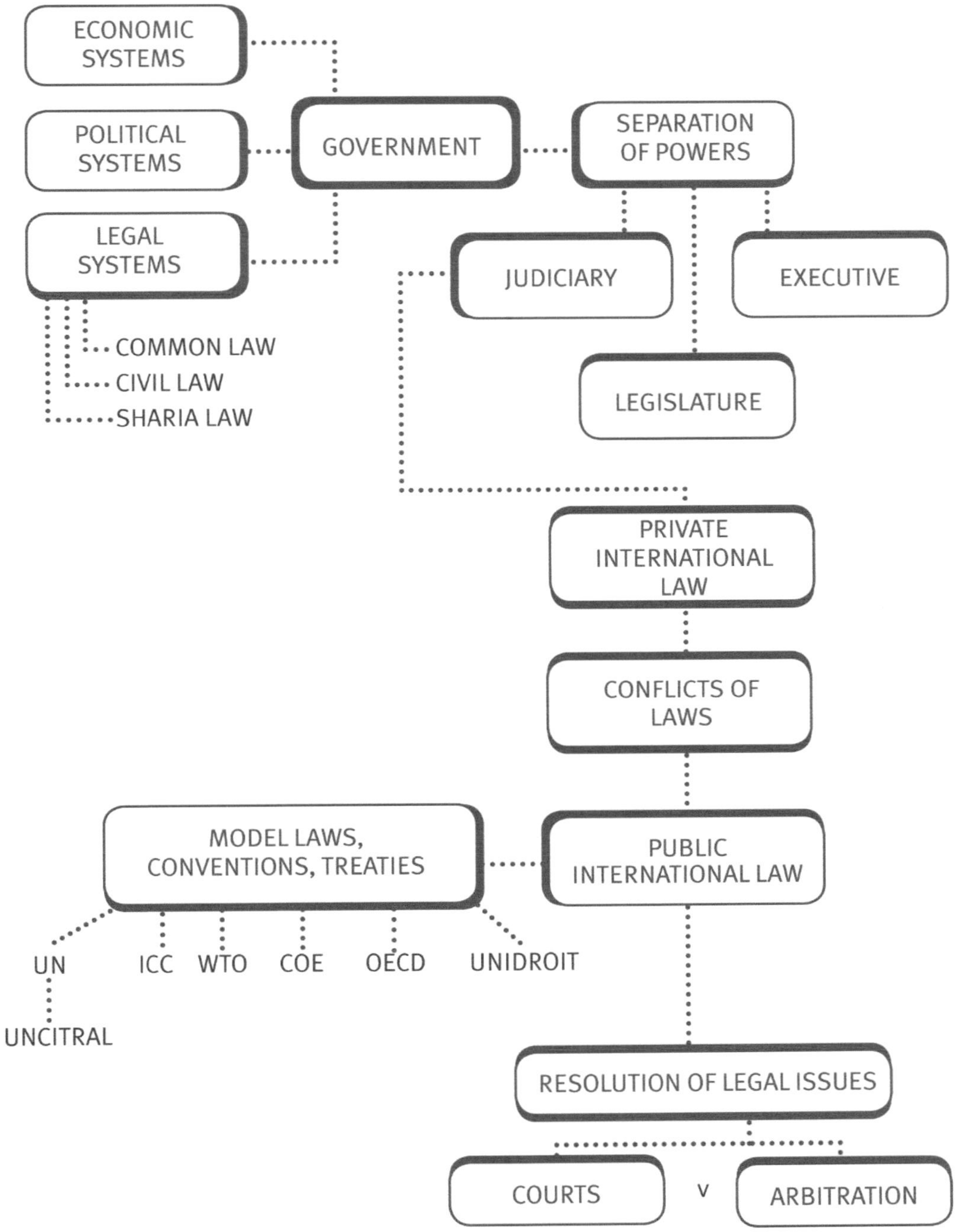

Test your understanding answers

Test your understanding 1

A planned economy is one where the government makes the decisions and choices that direct the economy, e.g. what prices shall be paid for things and where resources will be used.

Test your understanding 2

Democracy is a political system whereby the citizens of a country elect the government which rules them.

Test your understanding 3

Law is the body of rules under which society operates.

Test your understanding 4

The legislature is the primary law maker of a state.

Test your understanding 5

The concept of separation of powers involves the division between different persons or organisations (or both) of the three 'powers' of government in a state. These powers are the legislature, who make the law, the executive, who implement it, and the judiciary, who resolve disputes concerning it. The idea behind this division is that it will make tyranny less likely.

Test your understanding 6

France and Germany. Note that France and Germany are only two examples. Nearly all European jurisdictions (except England and Wales, Ireland and Northern Ireland) are based on civil law.

Test your understanding 7

False It is a general principle of civil law that they are not supposed to interpret the law but apply it.

Test your understanding 8

In a common law system, judges have a number of rules and principles to apply in interpreting statutes, which will have been drafted in great details. These include the fact that statutes do not override existing law, and do not concern matters not covered by the law.

In a civil law system, judges are required not to interpret the law but merely apply it. If interpretation is required, judges should try and implement the social purpose behind the law and seek to apply the intention to the present day.

Test your understanding 9

Sharia law is law ordained by Allah, as set out in the Quran. It is based on hadith, precedents and interpretation.

Test your understanding 10

In general terms, this is false. Much of the interpretation of Sharia law has been carried out already by the Prophet and in historic Ijtihad. A strong school of thought exists that further interpretation is unnecessary.

Test your understanding 11

Qiyas is a method of interpreting how to apply law to a matter by comparing that matter with one on which the Quran is clear. For example, a comparison between the effects of taking alcohol and taking illegal drugs leads to the conclusion that taking illegal drugs is forbidden by the Quran, because taking alcohol is forbidden. (Please note that taking medications is not affected.)

Test your understanding 12

Public international law is law which is recognised by a group of nations. Examples are conventions and treaties, international custom and general principles of law recognised by civilised nations.

Test your understanding 13

Private international law is a set of national, domestic rules to determine jurisdiction and applicable law in international contracts.

Test your understanding 14

Conflict of laws will arise where the law of two different countries produces different outcomes, making it difficult for parties in those countries to trade with one another.

Test your understanding 15

UNCITRAL is the legal body of the UN which has largely harmonised and unified public international law. It is formed of 61 states elected by the UN General Assembly and it has issued various model laws and conventions.

Test your understanding 16

The International Chamber of Commerce is an organisation created by business leaders from various countries which aims to 'serve the world business community by promoting trade and investment, open markets for goods and services, and the free flow of capital'.

Test your understanding 17

1 True

2 **B** – The Appellate Body

3 The Dispute Settlement Body does not have the power to modify the appeal ruling (B); it can simply accept (A) or reject it (C). It would also monitor the implementation of the ruling (D).

Test your understanding 18

The OECD is a group of member countries whose modern aim is to be a forum for discussing, developing and refining economic and social policies.

Test your understanding 19

UNIDROIT is the International Institute for the Unification of Private Law. It is an independent, intergovernmental organisation.

Test your understanding 20

1 **False:** the ICJ only has jurisdiction over cases involving states, not individuals.

2 **False:** the ICA does not 'try' cases as such, it facilitates the arbitration process in disputes which can be between individuals or individual companies. We shall look at the difference between courts and arbitration in the next section.

Test your understanding 21

The ICA is the International Court of Arbitration, which is an arm of the International Chamber of Commerce. It exists to facilitate the arbitration process, by maintaining approved lists of arbitrators, overseeing cases and awards and approving arbitrators' fees.

Test your understanding 22

A court of first instance is the court where a legal dispute or case is heard primarily. If there is any dispute with the judgement in the case when it has been heard in a court of first instance, it is then referred to an appellate court.

Test your understanding 23

Arbitration is a procedure whereby the parties in dispute refer the issue to a third party for resolution rather than taking the issue to the courts.

Test your understanding 24

- Proceedings are likely to be swifter. (A)
- Proceedings will be private. (A)
- The person presiding over the dispute will be chosen by the parties. (A)
- The person presiding over the dispute will be a judge. (C)
- There will be significant scope for appeal. (C)

Test your understanding 25

Wong's desire to appeal if he is unhappy with the decision suggests that court proceedings might be his best option. However, this has to be balanced against the advantages of arbitration, which would give a swifter decision, and would be heard in front of an expert in the 'fairly obscure' area of trade law to which it relates. Arbitration awards can be challenged only in very limited circumstances, and although he may be smarting from the results of previous arbitrations, arbitration might still be the better option in this case. It is likely to be the best option for Valerie, and if Wong wants to keep a good future relationship with Valerie, this would be another reason for preferring arbitration.

Chapter

2

International Commercial Arbitration

Chapter learning objectives

Upon completion of this chapter you will be able to:

- explain and apply the provisions of the UNCITRAL Model Law on International Commercial Arbitration
- describe the arbitral award
- explain arbitral awards.

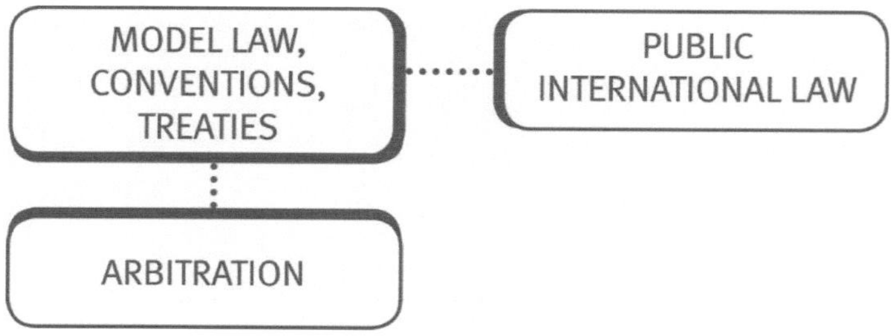

1 Model Law on International Commercial Arbitration

Model Law on International Commercial Arbitration

Under Article 1(3) arbitration is international if:

- the parties to the arbitration have their places of business in different states at the time of conclusion of the arbitration agreement
- or one of the following places is situated outside the State in which the parties have their place of business:
  - the place of arbitration if determined, in or pursuant to, the arbitration agreement
  - or the place where a substantial part of the obligations of the commercial relationship from which the dispute arises is in a different state from where the parties have their business
  - or the parties have expressly agreed that the subject matter of the arbitration agreement relates to more than one country.

Under Article 3:

- Unless the parties have agreed otherwise, any written communication (excluding those relating to court proceedings) is deemed to have been received if it is delivered to the addressee personally or it is delivered at his or her place of business, habitual residence or mailing address.
- If the place of business, habitual residence or mailing address cannot be determined after reasonable enquiry, a written communication is deemed to have been received if it is sent by registered letter (or other method which provides a record of the attempt to deliver it) to the addressee's last known place of business, habitual residence or mailing address.
- The communication is deemed to have been received on the day it is delivered.
- The provisions of this article to do not apply to communication in court proceedings.

Under Article 4:

- A party waives his or her right to object to non-compliance with this Model law or an aspect of the arbitral agreement if he or she does not make his or her objection without undue delay or if a time-limit is provided within such period of time.

Under Article 5:

- No court shall intervene in matters covered by this law unless the law so provides.

2 Arbitration agreement

An arbitration agreement is an agreement by the parties to submit to arbitration all or certain disputes which have arisen or which may arise between them in respect of a defined legal relationship, whether contractual or not. An arbitration agreement may be in the form of an arbitration clause in a contract or in a form of a separate agreement.

Under Article 7 an arbitration agreement:

- shall be in writing (in a document signed by the parties, or in an exchange of letters, telex, telegrams or other means of telecommunication which provide a record of the agreement in which the existence of an agreement is alleged by one party and not denied by the other)
- results in any court action being referred to arbitration by the court to which a matter is brought unless the agreement is found to be null and void, inoperative or incapable of being performed (arbitral proceedings may be carried out while the court is determining this).

Under Article 9 it is declared that it is not incompatible with an arbitration agreement for a party to request, before or during the arbitral proceedings, from a court an interim measure of protection and for court to grant such a measure.

e.g

Illustration 1 – Model Law

Albert and Brigitte have exchanged a series of letters in which Albert asserted that their agreement contained an arbitration agreement. Brigitte did not refute this claim. Therefore, in the event of dispute, under the Model law their dispute will be settled by arbitration. Under the agreement between them, Albert is due to deliver a number of machines made to Brigitte's specifications in instalments over a period of six months. She disputes the quality of the first instalment and refuses to pay for it. Albert has delivered the second instalment. Brigitte refers the dispute to arbitration, but also seeks an injunction through the courts to prevent Albert manufacturing the rest of the machines as there appears to be an error in how he is interpreting her instructions.

Test your understanding 1

Define an arbitration agreement.

Test your understanding 2

An arbitration agreement shall be in writing under the Model Law.

True or false.

3 Arbitral tribunal

In respect of arbitrators:

- the number shall be determined by the parties (Article 10(1))
- if the parties do not determine the number, there shall be three arbitrators (Article 10(2))
- no one shall be precluded from being an arbitrator due to nationality, unless the parties agree otherwise (Article 11(1))
- the parties are free to agree on a procedure of appointing the arbitrator or arbitrators (Article 11(2))
- if the parties do not agree the procedure, each party shall appoint one arbitrator and the two arbitrators thus appointed shall appoint the third one. If a party fails to appoint an arbitrator within 30 days of a request by the other party to do so, or the two appointed arbitrators fail to appoint a third, the appointment shall be made by the relevant court or authority, on request of one of the parties (Article 11(3)(a))
- the relevant court or authority is the one specified by each particular state when enacting the Model Law Article 6.

e.g

Illustration 2 – Model Law

Clare, from the Canade, and Derek, from Danmark, have a dispute which has been referred to arbitration. Clare has failed to appoint her arbitrator, and Derek requested that she do so 40 days ago. Derek has therefore asked High Court of Danmark to appoint the arbitrator, as Danmark law states that the High Court is the relevant court in relation to this Model Law.

The appointment of an arbitrator may be challenged:

- if circumstances exist which give rise to justifiable doubts as to his or her impartiality or independence or if he or she does not possess qualifications agreed by the parties (Article 12(2))
- by the party that appointed him or her, or was involved in his or her appointment, only if that party becomes aware of facts relating to impartiality or qualifications after the appointment has been made (Article 12(2))
- through a procedure agreed by the parties (Article 13(1))
- if the parties have not agreed to a procedure, by a party sending a written statement of the reasons for his or her challenge to the arbitral tribunal within 15 days of becoming aware of who was on the tribunal (Article 13(2)).

The challenge is determined by (Article 13(2)):

- the challenged arbitrator, if he or she resigns from the tribunal as a result of the challenge
- the parties to the dispute if they both agree on the challenge
- the arbitral tribunal if the arbitrator does not withdraw and the parties do not agree.

Under Article 13(3) – If a challenge is not successful:

- the challenging party may request a decision on the challenge from the relevant court
- the challenging party must make such a request within 30 days of hearing the decision
- the decision of the relevant court will not be subject to appeal
- the arbitral tribunal including the challenged arbitrator may continue with proceedings while such a request is being made/decided by the court.

An arbitrator:

- may withdraw if he or she becomes unable to act for any reason whether de facto or de jure (Article 14(1))
- if an arbitrator withdraws, a substitute arbitrator shall be appointed in the same way as the original arbitrator had been (Article 14(2)).

Test your understanding 3

A party may challenge the appointment of an arbitrator if there is justifiable doubt about his or her impartiality or his or her qualifications.

True or False.

4 Arbitral proceedings

Under Article 16 a plea that the arbitral tribunal does not have proper jurisdiction to decide the case:

- must be made before the submission of the statement of defence
- can be made despite the pleader having participated in appointing an arbitrator
- can be decided by the arbitral tribunal, after which the pleader may appeal to the specified court.

A plea that the arbitral tribunal has overstepped its jurisdiction during proceedings:

- shall be raised as soon as the alleged incident has taken place
- however, a tribunal may consider a later plea if it considers the delay justified.

Subject to any different agreement between the parties to the contrary:

- the arbitral tribunal may order either party to take interim measures in respect of the subject matter of the dispute only (this is a very important restriction on the tribunal's powers) (Article 17).

During the proceedings:

- the parties shall be treated with equality and shall be given full opportunity to present their cases (Article 18)
- the parties are given freedom to agree on the procedures (Article 19(1))
- if the parties do not agree on procedure, the arbitral tribunal may carry out proceedings in any way it sees fit (Article 19(2))
- the parties are free to agree on the pace of arbitration (Article 20(1))
- regardless of the parties' agreement, the tribunal may meet wherever it sees fit to consult, hear witnesses, inspect goods or other property or documents (Article 20(2))
- unless otherwise agreed by the parties, proceedings commence on the date on which a request for that dispute to be referred to arbitration is received by the respondent (Article 21)
- the parties shall agree the language in which the proceedings will be carried out. If the parties do not agree on language, the tribunal will determine which language to use (Article 22(1))
- the tribunal may order that documentary evidence be translated into the language in which the tribunal is being conducted (Article 22(2))
- the tribunal will decide whether the hearings will be oral or documentary (unless the parties have agreed otherwise). The tribunal may decide whether the proceedings shall be conducted on the basis of documents and other materials. However, unless the parties have agreed that no such hearings shall be held, the arbitral tribunal shall hold such hearings at an appropriate stage of the proceedings if so requested by the parties (Article 24(1))
- all documents, statements and other information submitted shall be communicated to the other party (Article 24(3))
- all documents or expert report used by the tribunal in making a decision shall be communicated to the parties (Article 24(3))
- if any party fails to appear at a hearing or produce documentary evidence, the tribunal will continue proceedings and make the award on the basis of the evidence before it (Article 25(c)).

Under Article 25 statements of claim and defence:

- must be made within the time agreed by the parties or determined by the tribunal
- the statement of claim must state the facts supporting the claim, the points at issue and the relief or remedy sought
- the defence shall state the defence in respect of the same particulars
- all relevant documents to the claims may be submitted with these statements
- the claim or defence may be supplemented during the proceedings, unless the parties agree otherwise
- unless otherwise agreed by the parties, if a party fails to make a statement of claim without reasonable excuse, the tribunal shall terminate proceedings
- under Article 25(b), if the respondent fails to communicate his or her statement of defence in accordance with Article 23(1), the arbitral tribunal shall continue the proceedings without treating such failure in itself as an admission of the claimant's allegations.

Experts and evidence (Article 26):

- the tribunal may appoint one or more expert witnesses to report on specific issues determined by the tribunal
- the tribunal may require a party to give the expert witness information or documents
- unless agreed by the parties, the expert may participate in a hearing after the presentation of his or her expert report so that he or she may take questions
- the tribunal (or a party with the tribunal's approval) may request the assistance of a competent court in taking evidence.

Test your understanding 4
In which language shall tribunal proceedings be conducted?

5 Awards

The arbitral tribunal shall make the arbitral decision:

- by a majority decision (Article 29)
- in accordance with whichever rules of law are chosen by the parties (Article 28(1))
- if the parties have not agreed on the applicable rules of law, the arbitral tribunal shall apply the law determined by the conflicts of laws rules which it considers applicable (Article 28(2))

- unless the parties have settled the dispute during proceedings, whereupon proceedings end (and, if the parties request it and the tribunal does not disagree, the tribunal records the agreed terms as the arbitral award) (Article 30)
- in writing and signed by all the arbitrators (or a majority of them, if reasons are given for omitted signatures) (Article 31(1))
- shall state the reasons on which it is based unless the parties have agreed otherwise (Article 31(2))
- shall state the date and place of arbitration (Article 31(3))
- shall be delivered to each party (Article 31(4)).

Arbitral proceedings are terminated:

- by the final award (Article 32(1))
- by order of the tribunal, if a party withdraws his or her claim (unless the respondent objects and the tribunal recognises a legitimate interest on his or her part in obtaining a final settlement of the dispute) (Article 32(2)a)
- if the parties agree to end the proceedings (Article 32(b))
- by order of the tribunal if the tribunal finds that the proceedings have become unnecessary or impossible (Article 32(c)).

Article 33 specified when correction of the award may be possible:

- either party may request within 30 days that errors in computation or clerical errors or any other errors of similar nature in the award by corrected
- if previously agreed by the parties, either party may request an interpretation of a specific point, with notice to the other party
- if the arbitral tribunal considers either request to be justified, it shall make the correction or give the interpretation within 30 days of receipt. This interpretation will form part of the award
- the tribunal may correct such errors by its own initiative within 30 days of the date of the award
- additional awards in respect of claims made during the tribunal may be requested by a party within 30 days of receipt of the award
- the tribunal shall make such award, if it considers it to be justified, within 60 days
- arbitral awards shall be recognised as binding and enforceable in a competent court subject to the provisions of the Model Law.

> **Illustration 3 – Model Law**
>
> Gio and Hafeez have received the notification of the award in respect of their arbitration on 30 May. Hafeez has noticed a computational error meaning that he is due to pay compensation of $25,000 rather than $15,000. Gio has noticed that one of the issues he covered in his claim document does not appear to be mentioned in the award, although Hafeez did not present a defence to that part of the claim and it appeared to be uncontested through the course of the arbitration.
>
> Both parties have 30 days (i.e. until 29 June) to raise these issues with the arbitral tribunal. If the arbitral tribunal finds that the requests are justified, it should address the error by 29 July and the question of the additional award by 28 August.
>
> It is 1 September. The arbitral tribunal corrected the original award to $15,000, but issued an additional award in respect of Gio's query of $7,500. Hafeez has paid the $15,000 but refuses to pay the additional $7,500. Gio may enforce the payment of this award in court.

6 Recourse

Under Article 34 an arbitral award may only be set aside by the court designated in the agreement if:

- the party making the application for it to be set aside proves:
  - that the arbitration agreement was not valid
  - they were not given proper notice of the appointment of an arbitrator and were unable to present their case
  - the award deals with a dispute falling outside of the scope of the arbitration agreement
  - the tribunal or its procedure was not in accordance with the model law, or
- the court finds that the subject matter of the dispute was not capable of settlement by arbitration under the law of the land, or that the award is contrary to public policy.

7 Recognition and enforcement

Under Article 35:

- regardless of which country the arbitral award was made in, it will be recognised as binding; and
- upon application in writing to the court, shall be enforced subject to the provisions of Article 36.

Under Article 36 recognition or enforcement of an arbitral award, irrespective of the country in which it was made, may be refused only:

(a) at the request of the party against whom it is invoked, if that party furnishes to the competent court where recognition or enforcement is sought proof that:

  (i) a party to the arbitration agreement referred to in article 7 was under some incapacity; or the said agreement is not valid under the law to which the parties have subjected it or, failing any indication thereon, under the law of the country where the award was made; or

  (ii) the party against whom the award is invoked was not given proper notice of the appointment of an arbitrator or of the arbitral proceedings or was otherwise unable to present his or her case; or

  (iii) the award deals with a dispute not contemplated by or not falling within the terms of the submission to arbitration, or it contains decisions on matters beyond the scope of the submission to arbitration, provided that, if the decisions on matters submitted to arbitration can be separated from those not so submitted, that part of the award which contains decisions on matters submitted to arbitration may be recognised and enforced; or

  (iv) the composition of the arbitral tribunal or the arbitral proceedings was not in accordance with the agreement of the parties, or failing such agreement, was not in accordance with the law of the country where the arbitration took place; or

  (v) the award has not yet become binding on the parties or has been set aside or suspended by a court of the country in which, or under the law of which, that award was made; or

(b) if the court finds that:

  (i) the subject matter of the dispute is not capable of settlement by arbitration under the law of this State; or

  (ii) the recognition or enforcement of the award would be contrary to the public policy of this State.

8 Chapter summary

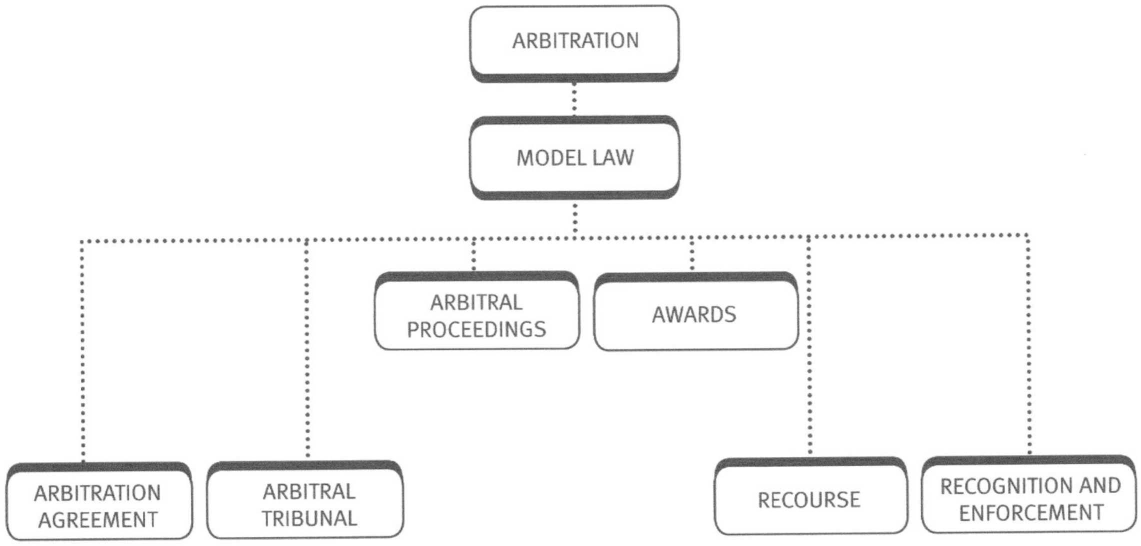

Test your understanding answers

Test your understanding 1

An arbitration agreement is an agreement by the parties to submit to arbitration all or certain disputes which have arisen or which may arise between them in respect of a defined legal relationship, whether contractual or not. An arbitration agreement may be in the form of an arbitration clause in a contract or in the form of a separate agreement.

Test your understanding 2

True

Test your understanding 3

True

Test your understanding 4

Whatever language is determined by the parties, or, if they cannot agree, the tribunal decides.

Chapter

3

International business transactions: formation of the contract

Chapter learning objectives

Upon completion of this chapter you will be able to:

- explain the sphere of application and general provisions of the United Nations Convention on Contracts for the International Sale of Goods 1980 (UNCCISG)
- explain the meaning and effect of the International Chamber of Commerce (ICC) Incoterms
- explain and be able to apply the rules for creating contractual relations under UNCCISG.

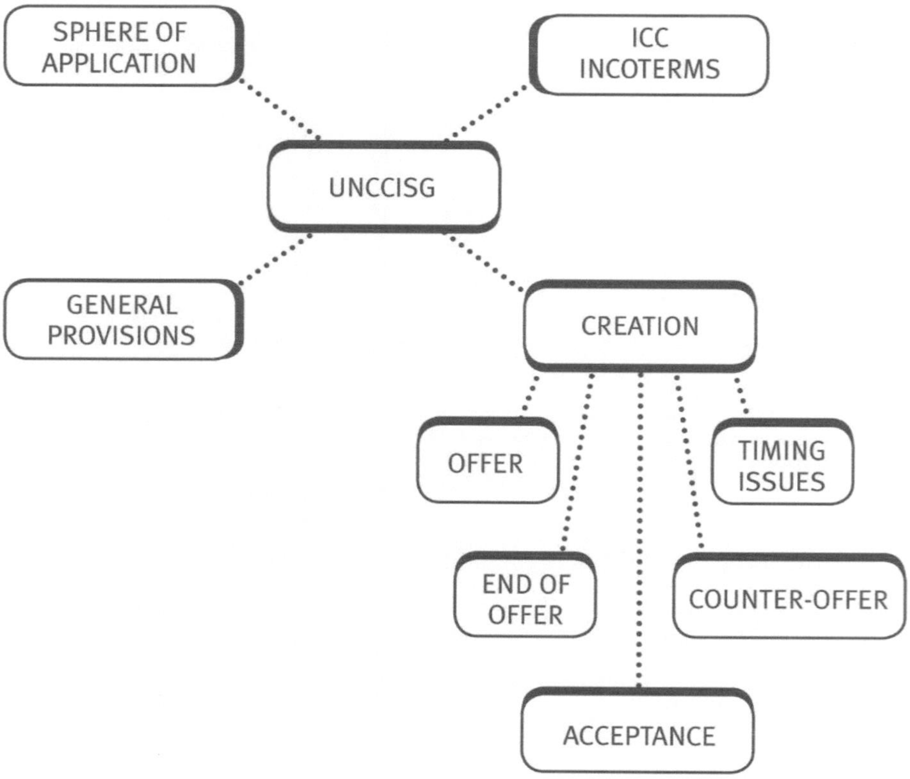

United Nations Convention on Contracts for the International Sale of Goods 1980 (UNCCISG)

UNCCISG is a Convention adopted by parties to the Convention to govern the way contracts for the sale of goods are carried out between those states.

1 Sphere of application

The Convention applies to:

- sales of goods (Article 1(1))
- made between parties whose places of business are in different states and
- when the states are contracting states (Article 1(1)(a)) or
- where the private international law rules appoint the law of a CISG state in a case of international sales (Article 1(1)(b)).

Sale of goods

Sale of goods means the sale of goods, that is, the supplier provides the materials and produces goods or obtains goods to be sold to the buyer.

Sale of goods

The following are not sales of goods:

- the supply of goods to be manufactured when the buyer undertakes to supply a substantial part of the materials necessary for the manufacture (this is in essence a contract for labour and manufacture only) (Article 3(1))
- contracts where the preponderant part of the obligations of the seller is the supply of labour or other services, even though he or she provides the raw materials (Article 3(2)).

The following types of sales are specifically excluded from the scope of the Convention:

- goods bought for personal, family or household use unless the seller didn't know they were for such use and had no way of so knowing (Article 2(a))
- auction sales (Article 2(b))
- sales made on execution or otherwise by authority of law (Article 2 (c))
- sales of stocks, shares, investment securities, negotiable instruments or money (Article 2(d))
- sales of ships, vessels, hovercraft or aircraft (Article 2(e))
- sales of electricity (Article 2(f)).

Place of business

- If a party has more than one place of business, the relevant place of business is the one which is most closely connected with the contract (Article 10(a)).
- If a party has no place of business, reference will be made to his or her habitual residence (Article 10(b)).

Place of business

The 'place of business' rules are important to determine whether the Convention applies or not. This is because a company may have places of business in many countries, some of which are contracting parties to the UN Convention, some of which may determine by their national law that the UN Convention applies even though they are not a party to it, some of which may not apply the UN Convention.

In such a situation, the other party needs to be clear whether the Convention applies or not. This is determined by looking at which part of the business (in which country) the contract applies.

Illustration 1 – Sphere of application

Company A, a company in Country Y (a contracting state to the Convention) is entering into a contract for the sale of goods with Company B, a company in Country Z (which is not a contracting state, but whose national law states that the provisions of the Convention should be applied in such contracts). In this case, the place of business rules for the purposes of qualifying as CISG under the Convention are met.

In a different scenario, you might have Company C, a multinational company which has operations in Countries X, W, V and U. While X, W and V are contracting states to the Convention, U is not, and its national law does not apply the Convention. Company D, from Country T, a contracting state, wants to enter into a contract (CISG) with Company C. In order to determine whether the Convention will apply to the contract, Company C will have to tell Company D which branch of Company C it is contracting with, and which country that branch is in.

Please note that:

- The examiner may use real countries or made up ones in the examination.
- You do not need to know which real countries are actually contracting states to the UNCCISG for the purposes of the examination.
- If place of business rules are relevant in a multi-task question, it will be clear whether countries mentioned are contracting states or whether their national law makes the Convention relevant.
- You therefore need only learn the rules concerning place of business and apply them in the examination.

Summary

- 'CISG will apply where the private international law rules appoint the law of a CISG state in a case of international sales.'

Sales of goods	+	Parties in contracting states	=	CISG per Convention
Sales of goods	+	Parties in states whose private law applies the Convention	=	CISG per Convention
Sales of goods	+	Parties who have chosen the convention to apply on the basis of party autonomy	=	CISG per Convention
Sales of goods	+	Parties in non-contracting states	=	Not CISG per Convention
Sale of labour or manufacture	+	Parties in contracting states	=	Not CISG per Convention

Extent of application of the Convention

The Convention only governs:

- the formation of the contract of sale and the rights and obligations of the seller and the buyer arising from the contract (Article 4).

The Convention is therefore not concerned with:

- the validity of the contract, its provisions or any usage (Article 4(a))
- the effect which the contract may have on the property in the goods sold (that is, who owns the property) (Article 4(b))
- liability of the seller for death or personal injury caused by the goods to any person (Article 5).

The parties to the contract may:

- state that the Convention does not apply to the contract between them (Article 6)
- amend the effects of any specific clauses of the Convention subject to Article 12 – Article 6
- if they are in states that apply Article 96 of the Convention, any contractual agreement must be in writing.

Test your understanding 1

Alison carries out a business manufacturing and selling kitchen equipment in Burchania, which is a contracting state to the UNCCISG. Chet carries out a similar business in Dimistan, a contracting state.

Edwin, from Francia, a contracting state, wants to enter into contracts with both Alison and Chet.

Alison is to manufacture 1,000 saucepans for Edwin to his design. As the quality of metal Alison can obtain in Burchania is not up to the standard that Edwin requires, he is to provide the metal for casting the body of the saucepans. Chet is to manufacture 1,000 colanders for Edwin. Chet will source the materials from his usual supplier.

Subsequent to the contracts being completed, it is discovered that the colanders have a flaw. The handles are prone to coming loose. A number of claims have been made to Edwin from members of the public sustaining personal injury through burns.

1 **The contract between Alison and Edwin potentially comes within the scope of the Convention because:**

- A Burchania is a contracting state
- B Francia is a contracting state
- C The countries of both parties to the contract are contracting states
- D All contracts for the sale of international goods are subject to the Convention

2 **The contract between Chet and Edwin comes within the scope of the Convention because Edwin's country is a contracting state.**

True or false

3 **The contract between Alison and Edwin is:**

- A for the sale of goods
- B for the supply of services only
- C predominantly for the sale of goods
- D predominantly for the supply of services

4 **Therefore, the contract comes within the scope of the Convention.**

True or false

2 General provisions

Interpretation

According to Article 7, when interpreting the Convention, parties should bear in mind:

- its international character
- the need to promote uniformity in its application
- the observance of good faith in international trade
- questions not expressly settled within the Convention should be settled in conformity with the general principles on which it is based.

Intent

Rules for interpreting the meaning of intent have been provided in Article 8.

- The statements of a party should be interpreted according to their intent.
- The conduct of a party should be interpreted according to their intent.

This can only be the case where:

- the other party was aware of that intent, or
- the other party could not have been unaware what that intent was.

If one party could not have been aware of the other party's intent:

- statements and conduct should be interpreted according to the understanding that a reasonable person of the same kind as the other party would have had in the same circumstances
- all relevant circumstances (including negotiations, established practice between the parties, usages and subsequent conduct of the parties) of the case should be considered.

Established practice

- The parties are bound by established conduct between themselves if they have made similar contracts before (Article 9(1)).
- The parties are bound by a usage which they both knew of (or ought to have done) and which is widely known and used in international trade contracts of the same type (Article 9(2)).

Established practice

If the parties had contracted between themselves many times for the same items and it was always the case that the items were delivered by sea, then it would be an implied term of future contracts between them that the goods were to be delivered by sea, unless they clearly stated to the contrary in their agreement.

If two parties had never contracted before, but they had had similar contracts with other parties and the contract involved goods that are habitually delivered by sea in international contracts, it would be implied in the contract that the goods should be delivered by sea unless they clearly stated to the contrary in their agreement.

Example

Ali, whose place of business is Baru, a contracting state, and Celia, whose place of business is Damico, a contracting state, are negotiating a contract for the international sale of goods.

Ali has many times contracted for Celia to source and supply metal parts which are a key component in his manufacturing process. In this instance, he requires 300 units of Part TIX345, which he has bought from her on a number of occasions. The price of a Part TIX345 is $40 and Celia usually ships them to Ali within 30 days.

If they make no further reference to the price, or the method and timing of delivery for this order for 300 parts of TIX345, then due to the established practice between the parties, the price under the contract for each unit of TIX345 will be $40 and Celia will be required to ship the goods within 30 days of the contract being agreed.

Form

Under Article 11 a contract under the Convention:

- does not have to be concluded in writing
- does not have to be evidenced in writing
- is not subject to any other requirement as to form
- may be proved by any means, including witnesses.

Unless:

- the relevant contracting state has made a declaration under Article 96 of the Convention stating that contracts or variations from the Convention must be made in writing.

Under Article 13, the word 'writing' includes:

- telegram
- telex.

Test your understanding 2

Adele has her place in business in Binaria, a contracting state. Celeste has her place of business in Doman, a contracting state. Estelle has her place of business in Finisterre, which is not a contracting state. Gracia has places of business in Hinland, a contracting state, and Idistan, which is not a contracting state. The business in Hinland is a manufacturing operation, while Gracia sources most of the raw materials required in production from her operation in Idistan. Adele needs to make contracts to buy goods from Celeste, Estelle and Gracia.

Adele has contracted with Celeste on a number of occasions for similar goods, and so negotiations with Celeste are limited. Celeste and Adele agree on the telephone that Celeste will deliver 200 units. They make no further provisions in the contract.

Adele has never contracted with Estelle or Gracia before, so meticulous negotiations take place and the contract between them is detailed with regard to price and delivery. The contracts are in writing and signed by both parties.

Adele intends to use the goods delivered by Celeste for her private use. She has not done this before, and has not made Celeste aware of this fact.

1 **Explain whether the contracts with Celeste, Estelle and Gracia fall within the scope of the Convention.**

2 **Explain what terms will exist in the contract between Adele and Celeste and why.**

3 **Explain the rules in the Convention regarding form of the contract and discuss the impact these rules have on the contracts with Celeste, Estelle and Gracia.**

3 International Chamber of Commerce (ICC) Incoterms

Incoterms is an abbreviation of International Contract Terms. They are a collection of standard contract terms published by the International Chamber of Commerce. Most contracts for the international sale of goods will include these standard terms.

There are 11 standard terms, divided into 4 categories:

- Departure (E terms)
- Main Carriage Unpaid (F terms)
- Main Carriage Paid (C terms)
- Arrival (D).

The terms all start with the first letter of the category they fall in.

Departure (E terms)

- EXW. This stands for Ex works. The seller has carried out his or her requirements with regard to delivery when he makes the goods available to the buyer at his or her own place of work. The buyer is responsible for collecting the goods and loading them on his or her collection vehicle himself. This means that the buyer bears all the costs and risks of delivery, unless otherwise agreed between the parties.

Main carriage unpaid (F terms)

- FOB. This stands for Free on Board. This Incoterm is specific to delivery by ship. The seller has delivered the goods when they pass the ship's rail at the named port of shipment. The seller bears the responsibility for clearing the goods for export, but the buyer is responsible for the goods from when they are placed on the ship and bears the costs from then on.
- FAS. This stands for Free Alongside Ship. This term is also specific to delivery by ship. In this case the seller also has to bear export charges, but has delivered the goods once they are standing alongside the ship at the port. The buyer is responsible for getting them on the ship and from them on.
- FCA. This stands for Free Carrier. This means that the seller has discharged his or her obligations when he or she delivers the goods, cleared for export, to a carrier named by the buyer. In practice, the person named does not have to be a carrier, but can be another agent. In this case, the seller has discharged his or her obligations when the goods are with the agent.

Main carriage paid (C terms)

- CFR. This stands for Cost and Freight. This means that the seller must pay the cost and freight involved in getting the goods to a named destination, but the risk passes to the buyer when the goods are placed with on the ship.
- CIF. This stands for Cost, Insurance and Freight. This means the same as CFR, except that, in addition, the seller must pay for insurance to cover the goods when they are in transit. The seller need only pay for the minimum insurance, so if the buyer wants more comprehensive insurance, the buyer must make arrangements for that.
- CPT. This stands for Carriage Paid to. This means that the seller pays for the freight of the carriage of the goods to the named destination. The seller is required to clear the goods for export. The risk passes from the seller when the goods are at the named destination.
- CIP. This stands for Carriage and Insurance Paid to. This means the same as CPT, except that, in addition, the seller must pay for insurance for the goods during carriage. CPT and CIP may be used irrespective of the mode of transport of the goods.

Illustration 2 – ICC incoterms

Ali and Brenda have negotiated a contract for the international sale of goods. The clause on delivery contains the following abbreviation, 'CPT'. This means that Brenda, the seller, will be responsible for paying for the carriage of the goods to a named destination, and clearing them for export.

Arrival (D terms)

- DPU. This stands for Delivered at Place Unloaded. This means that the seller delivers when the goods, once unloaded from the arriving means of transport, are placed at the disposal of the buyer at a named terminal at the named port or place of destination. "Terminal" includes a place, whether covered or not, such as a quay, warehouse, container yard or road, rail or air cargo terminal. The seller bears all risks involved in bringing the goods to and unloading them at the terminal at the named port or place of destination.
- DAP. This stands for Delivered At Place. This means that the seller delivers when the goods are placed at the disposal of the buyer on the arriving means of transport ready for unloading at the named place of destination. The seller bears all risks involved in bringing the goods to the named place.
- DDP. This stands for Delivered Duty Paid. This is in effect the opposite of EXW, the first Incoterm outlined above, and imposes the minimum requirements on the buyer. It means that the seller delivers the goods when the goods are placed at the disposal of the buyer, cleared for import on the arriving means of transport ready for unloading at the named place of destination. The seller bears all the costs and risks involved in bringing the goods to the place of destination and has an obligation to clear the goods not only for export but also for import, to pay any duty for both export and import and to carry out all customs formalities.

Illustration 3 – ICC incoterms

Caroline and Daudi have negotiated a contract for the international sale of goods. The clause on delivery terms includes the abbreviation, 'DAP'. This means that the seller, Daudi, is responsible for delivering the goods to the named port of destination. Caroline will have access to the goods on the ship there, and will be responsible for the goods from then on, including paying import costs on those goods.

Test your understanding 3

Define the following incoterm: FCA.

Test your understanding 4

State the most appropriate Incoterm for a buyer who wants to avoid as many of the costs and burdens of delivery as possible.

4 Formation of contract

A contract is concluded at the moment when an acceptance of an offer becomes effective in accordance with the provisions of this Convention.

5 Offer

An **offer** is a proposal for concluding a contract addressed to one or more specific persons which is sufficiently definite and indicates the intention of the offeror (person making the offer) to be bound in case of acceptance (Article 14).

It must be sufficiently definite: in the context of an offer it means that the proposal indicates the goods in question and expressly or implicitly fixes or makes provision for determining the quantity of the goods and the price.

Illustration 4 – Offer

Compare the following proposals:

1 'To: Seller, MainCo

From: Buyer, BuyCo

Please provide 100 units of item XC34GH at price indicated in 2006 catalogue.'

2 'Ben, I have 200 units of 2AW2594 available at the moment, do you want some at the usual price?'

3 (Posted on a website) 'I am interested in buying some plastic parts. Can anyone do business with me?'

	Proposal 1	Proposal 2	Proposal 3
Addressed to specific person	Yes	Yes	No
Indicates the intention of the person to be bound in case of acceptance	Yes	Almost certainly	No
Indicates the goods	Yes	Yes	Not specific goods
Fixes or makes provision for the quantity of the goods	Yes	Yes	No
Fixes or makes provision for the price of the goods	Yes	Yes	No
Conclusion	Yes	Almost certainly offer	Mere proposal

There are a number of points illustrated in the illustration above that you might want to look at again more closely.

Intention of the parties

This matter is judgemental, as people will rarely end their proposal to another party with a statement such as 'I am prepared to enter into a contract with you'. In other words, their intention is implied in the level of detail in their proposal. For example, Proposal 1 clearly shows that the Buyer at BuyCo wants to place an order with MainCo and is prepared to enter a contract with them by the detail and tone in his or her message. By contrast, in proposal three, the request is very general – it is not addressed to one person. It more represents 'window-shopping', that is, an attempt to find out what is out there, than a firm intention to contract with anyone who might reply. The fact that the matter is judgemental is why Proposal 2 is marked 'almost certainly yes'. Although the proposal is specific, it could be a proposal made to several people, hoping that one person will take it up. In this case, the seller would not be prepared to enter into contract with all interested parties. However, as the proposal is addressed to Ben, it is most likely that it is specific to Ben and the seller wants to make a contract with Ben.

Specific goods

In order to constitute an offer, a proposal has to 'indicate the goods'. All three proposals above refer to 'goods' but there is a contrast between the specific, named parts indicated in Proposals 1 and 2, and the more general 'plastic parts' indicated in Proposal 3. There is likely to be a large range of plastic parts available in the world, and therefore use of the phrase 'plastic parts' is insufficiently specific to constitute an indication of the goods required for the proposal to be an offer.

An invitation to treat is the name given to a mere proposal that does not constitute an offer.

Test your understanding 5
Define 'offer' according to the rules laid out in the Convention.

Test your understanding 6
Define 'invitation to treat' according to the rules laid out in the Convention.

Offer becoming effective

An offer becomes effective when it reaches the offeree (person being made the offer). Under Article 15 an offer reaches the offeree when:

- it is made orally to the offeree (Article 24)
- it is delivered to the offeree personally at their business or mailing address (Article 24)
- (if they have no business address) it is delivered to them personally at their habitual residence (Article 24).

6 End of offer

An offer may be terminated in three different ways:

- withdrawal (Article 22)
- revocation (Article 16)
- rejection (Article 17)
- by replying to the offer as a purported acceptance but contains addition, limitations or other modifications.

Withdrawal is where the person making the offer changes his or her mind (withdraws the offer). An offer can only be withdrawn before, or at the same time as, the offer reaches the offeree.

Revocation is where the person making the offer changes his or her mind (revokes the offer). An offer can only be revoked before the offeree has despatched an acceptance.

An offer cannot be revoked if:

- It indicates that it is irrevocable. It might state that it is irrevocable, or it might have a fixed time for acceptance, indicating that the person being made the offer may use that time to decide and the offer will not be revoked during that time. It is worth noting at this stage that this is different under English law.
- It was reasonable for the offeree to assume the offer was irrevocable and they have relied on that fact (that is, they have not accepted immediately because they believed the offer to be irrevocable). This might be the case if, e.g. the parties have contracted before and all previous offers have been irrevocable.

Rejection is where the person receiving the offer does not accept the offer. Rejection may be express (the offeree tells the offeror they are not accepting the offer) or implied (the offeree's conduct indicates the offer is not being accepted). Acceptance will be detailed in the next section. Something that is not acceptance is rejection.

Conduct of the offeree implying rejection of the offer might be accepting the offer of another party in respect of the same goods, for example. Silence does not generally constitute acceptance.

End of offer

The difference between withdrawal and revocation is timing. The intention on the part of the person making the offer is the same – the person no longer wants to be bound in contract.

If this notice of no longer wanting to be bound in contract arrives before the original offer, it is withdrawal. If it arrives after the original offer but before the acceptance has been despatched, it is revocation.

If it arrives after acceptance has been despatched, it is pointless. Once acceptance has been despatched, the offeror is bound in contract with the offeree.

Test your understanding 7

Explain the 'reaching' rule in the context of an offer.

7 Acceptance

Acceptance is a statement made by, or other conduct of, the offeree indicating assent to an offer. Silence and inactivity do not amount to acceptance (Article 18(1)).

Counter-offer is a reply to an offer which appears to be acceptance but which contains additions, limitations or other modifications regarding the price, payment, quality of the goods, quantity of the goods, delivery, extent of liability or dispute settlement. Counter-offer is a rejection of the offer. However, minor amendments to the terms of the offer are permitted and will not constitute a rejection of the offer (Article 19).

e.g

Illustration 5 – Acceptance

Compare the following statements

'I accept your offer of 12.12.06.'

'I accept your offer of 12.12.06, but I only want 10 items, not 20.'

In the first instance, the statement is unequivocal acceptance of the offer. In the second, the offeree wants to change the terms of the offer relating to the quantity of the goods under the contract. This is therefore a counteroffer, not acceptance. However, note that a counter-offer is a valid offer capable of being accepted, so if the original offeror wants to accept the counter-offer, he or she may do so, and thereby create a contract.

Effectiveness of acceptance (Articles 18 to 21)

Acceptance of an offer becomes effective when indication of assent reaches the offeror (Article 18). Note that the 'reaching rule' is the same as that outlined in respect of offer:

- acceptance is made orally to the offeror
- it is delivered to him or her personally at his or her business or mailing address
- (if he or she has no business address) it is delivered to him or her personally at his or her habitual residence.

Acceptance is not effective if:

- it does not reach the offeror within the time fixed by him or her with the original offer
- if no time was fixed, it does not reach the offeror within a reasonable time
- the offer was oral, and is not accepted immediately (unless circumstances indicate later acceptance is reasonable, for example, the offeror says 'I'll leave you to think about it', or 'let me know by close of business tomorrow').

Late acceptance can be effective, if:

- the offeror orally tells the offeree so
- the offeror despatches a notice to the offeree stating late acceptance was effective
- lateness was due to circumstances which were not normal (e.g. a postal strike).

Late acceptance due to circumstances which were not normal will be ineffective if:

- the offeror orally tells the offeree that he or she believes that the offer had lapsed
- the offeror despatches a notice to the offeree stating that the offer has lapsed.

'Reasonable time' in the context of acceptance of offer will be judged according to the circumstances of the transaction. This includes the rapidity of the means of communication used by the offeror.

e.g

Illustration 6 – Acceptance

Imagine, for instance, that Violet has sent Winnie an offer. Winnie accepts by post. However, Violet has used airmail and Winnie has used surface mail. Winnie's acceptance has taken four times as long to get to Violet than her offer took to get to Winnie. In the meantime, Violet has assumed that Winnie does not want to contract and has entered negotiations with someone else. In this case, it could be argued that Winnie has not answered in a reasonable time, as it reasonable to suppose she would reply by the same method that Violet originally offered. If Winnie had used a different but faster method of responding, such as fax, telephone or email, her acceptance would have been valid.

Consider also the following situation:

Yazmin is negotiating with ZinZan to purchase a specific batch of perishable goods. Yazmin sends ZinZan an email, offering to buy the goods, but ZinZan does not accept her offer for a week. In the meantime the goods have perished and Yazmin has bought similar goods from someone else. ZinZan's acceptance is not in a reasonable time due to the nature of the goods, and Yazmin is not bound in contract with him.

Acceptance by an act

A party may accept an offer by an act if:

- the parties have established practices between themselves setting precedent for acceptance of an offer being made by an act
- the act is performed within a given timetable or a reasonable timetable if none is given, according to the rules set out above.

If acceptance is indicated by an act, it is effective once the act has been carried out.

Illustration 7 – Acceptance

Hudson is Imogen's sole supplier of Part AB135. He has supplied her with the same part for a number of years. They agree a price annually. In order to place an order, Imogen emails Hudson the number of parts that she needs and Hudson processes the order and sends the parts the next day.

In this case, Hudson's action of delivering the goods the next day is his acceptance of Imogen's offer and it is effective when he delivers the goods (in other words, she cannot refuse to pay for those goods). The terms of the contract formed between them by Imogen's email and Hudson's delivery of the goods are set by the established usage between them.

If Hudson did not deliver the goods the next day, but failed to deliver them for a week, then his acceptance by an act would not be valid, and Imogen would be entitled not to accept the goods as there would be no contract between them.

Test your understanding 8

Define 'acceptance' according to the rules laid out in the Convention.

Test your understanding 9

Define 'counter-offer' according to the rules laid out in the Convention.

Test your understanding 10

Acceptance is not effective if the indication of assent does not reach the offeror:

A before a notice of revocation reaches the offeree

B before the time fixed by the offeror

C in reasonable time of the offer being made (assuming no fixed time was specified)

D by the same method that the offeror dispatched the offer

Acceptance: other timing issues

A period of time for acceptance fixed by the offeror begins to run:

- (telegram) when the telegram is handed in for dispatch
- (letter) the date shown on the letter, or, if none appears, the date on the envelope
- (telephone/telex/other instantaneous communication such as email) the moment that the offer reaches the offeree.

The period of acceptance includes:

- official holidays
- non-business days.

However, if a notice of acceptance cannot be delivered on the last day of the stated period because it is an official holiday or a non-business day, the period is extended until the first business day which follows.

Withdrawal of acceptance

Acceptance may be withdrawn if the withdrawal reaches the offeror before or at the same time as the acceptance would have become effective (Article 22).

8 Modification or termination of the contract

A contract may be modified or terminated by the mere agreement of the parties (Article 29(1)).

A contract in writing which contains a provision requiring any modification or termination by agreement to be in writing may not be otherwise modified or terminated by agreement. However, a party may be precluded by his or her conduct from asserting such a provision to the extent that the other party has relied on that conduct (Article 29(2)).

9 Offer and acceptance: summary

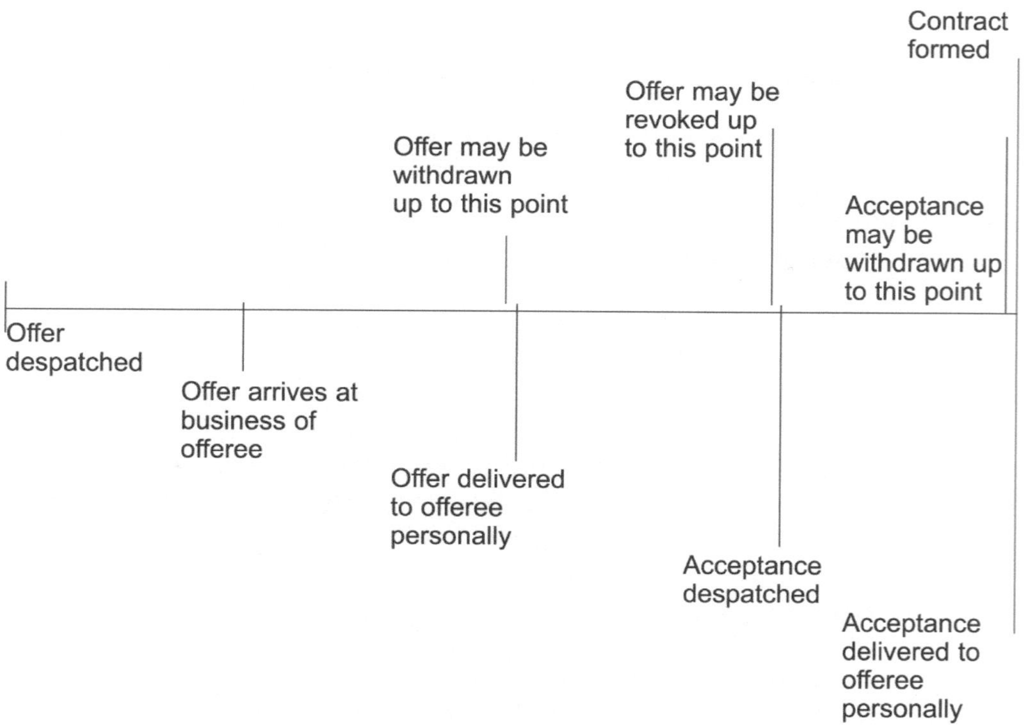

10 Chapter summary

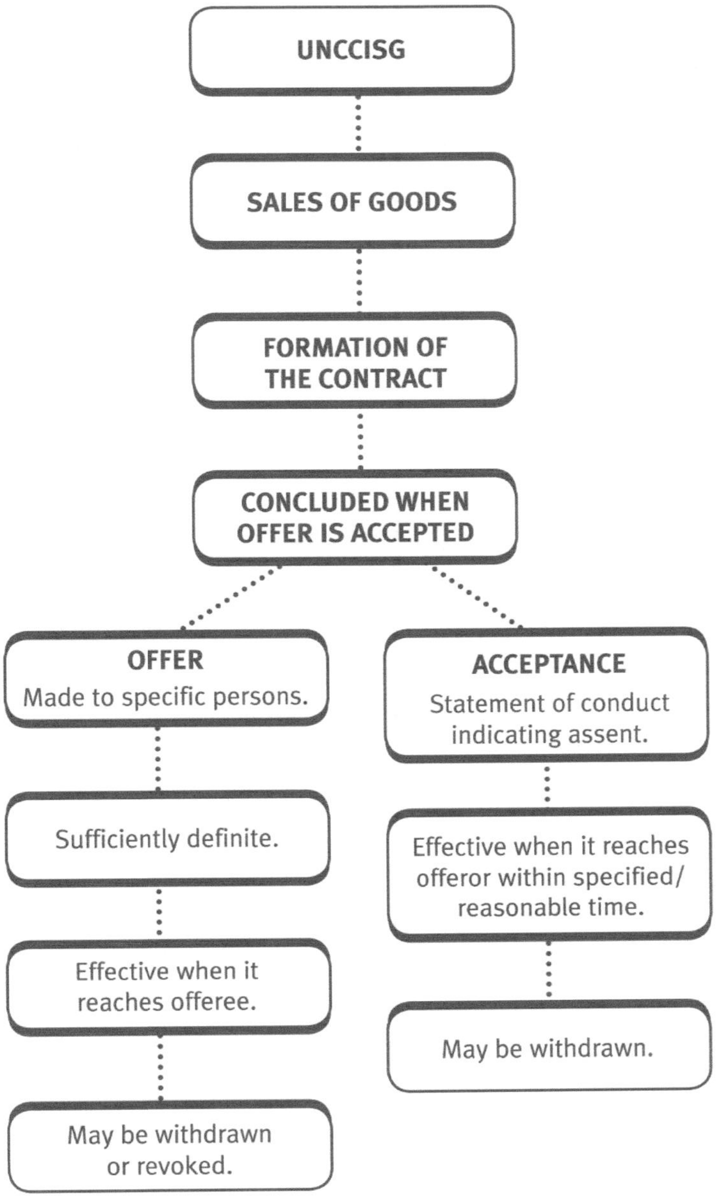

Test your understanding answers

Test your understanding 1

1 C. D is untrue. A and B are incorrect because both parties have to be subject to the Convention for the Convention to apply or the parties have expressly chosen the Convention to apply.

2 True. This is true because both Edwin and Chet are in countries which are contracting states.

3 D. Alison is going to manufacture saucepans. The key raw material of these will be the metal that is being provided by Edwin. Therefore the contract is predominantly for the supply of labour making the saucepans.

4 False. Therefore, as the contract is not for the sale of goods, it does not come within the scope of the Convention.

Test your understanding 2

1 **Contract with Celeste**

The places of business of both parties to the contract are in contracting states. This means that the contract potentially falls within the scope of the Convention.

However, Adele is going to use the goods for her own personal use. Ordinarily contracts to purchase goods for personal use are excluded from the scope of the Convention.

In this case, Adele has not made her intention clear to Celeste and, given that the previous transactions between the parties have not involved the goods being used for personal use, Celeste has no reason to know Adele's intentions. Therefore, this contract will fall within the scope of the Convention despite the goods being for personal use, due to the seller not being made aware of that fact.

Contract with Estelle

Although Binaria is a contracting state, Finisterre is not, and therefore the contract between Adele and Estelle will not come within the scope of the Convention unless the parties expressly have chosen the Convention to be their applicable law.

Contract with Gracia

Whether the contract between Adele and Gracia falls within the scope of the Convention depends on whether Adele is doing business with Gracia's business in Hinland or her business in Idistan. As Idistan is not a contracting state, if the contract were most closely connected with this place of business, then it would not fall within the scope of the Convention.

However, Gracia's manufacturing operations are in Hinland, and the purpose of the Idistan business appears to be to source raw materials for the Hinland operations. Therefore it seems most likely that Adele's contract for goods will be with the business in Hinland.

As Hinland is a contracting state, the contract falls within the scope of the Convention.

As Gracia will manufacture the goods and source the materials herself, this is a contract for the sale of goods, not manufacture only, and therefore it falls within the scope of the Convention.

2 **Terms of the contract with Celeste**

The terms of the contract will be that Celeste will provide 200 units of the goods, as this is what Adele and Celeste have explicitly agreed on the telephone.

In addition, as there is established practice between the parties because they have contracted for similar goods on a number of occasions in the past, the other terms of the contract, relating to delivery and payment, e.g. will be implied from their established practice. Therefore Celeste will be required to deliver the goods in the same way as she usually does and Adele will be required to pay the same price as she usually does, and by the same method.

3 **Form of the contract**

The Convention states that a contract of sale need not be concluded in or evidenced by writing and is not subject to any other requirement as to form, unless the contracting states have made provision to the contrary.

In this case, as there is no indication that Binaria, Doman or Hinland have made any such provision, the contracts may be in any form. Therefore both the contracts are appropriate per the Convention with regard to form, even though one is in writing and the other is not.

As Finisterre is not a contracting state and the Convention does not apply, the form of the contract will depend on the private laws of Binaria and/or Finisterre.

Test your understanding 3

This stands for Free Carrier. This means that the seller has discharged his or her obligations when he or she delivers the goods, cleared for export, to a carrier or other agent named by the buyer.

Test your understanding 4

The most appropriate Incoterm would be DDP (Delivered duty paid), as this represents the lowest responsibility and cost for the buyer.

Test your understanding 5

An offer is a proposal for concluding a contract. It must be:

- addressed to one or more specific persons
- indicate intention to be bound in contract with those persons
- indicate the goods in question
- fix or make provision for determining the quantity of goods
- fix or make provision for determining the price of the goods.

Test your understanding 6

An invitation to treat is a mere proposal that does not meet the requirements of an offer.

Test your understanding 7

An offer reaches the offeree when:

- it is made orally to him or her
- it is delivered to him or her personally (at his or her business or mailing address).

Test your understanding 8

Acceptance is a statement made by the offeree, or some other conduct of the offeree, indicating assent to an offer. Silence and inactivity cannot constitute acceptance.

Test your understanding 9

Counter-offer is a statement purporting to be acceptance, but containing modifications (which are more than minor) causing it not to be acceptance.

Test your understanding 10

Acceptance is not effective if the indication of assent does not reach the offeror:

- before the time fixed by the offeror
- in reasonable time of the offer being made (assuming no fixed time was specified).

A notice of revocation has to reach the offeree before the offeree dispatches the acceptance to be effective. The offeree does not have to use the same method of dispatch as the offeror, but the acceptance must reach the offeror within reasonable time, and method of dispatch will be taken into account when determining whether acceptance has arrived within reasonable time.

Chapter

4

International business transactions: obligations

Chapter learning objectives

Upon completion of this chapter you will be able to:

- explain and be able to apply the rules relating to the obligations of the seller under the United Nations Convention on Contracts for the International Sale of Goods 1980 (UNCCISG): (i) delivery of the goods and handing over documents, (ii) conformity of the goods and third party claims, (iii) remedies for breach of contract for the seller
- explain and be able to apply the rules relating to the obligations of the buyer under UNCCISG: (i) payment of the price, (ii) taking delivery, (iii) remedies for breach of contract by the buyer
- explain and be able to apply the rules relating to the provisions common to both the seller and the buyer under UNCCISG: (i) anticipatory breach and instalment contracts, (ii) damages, (iii) interest, (iv) exemptions, (v) effects of avoidance, (vi) preservation of the goods.

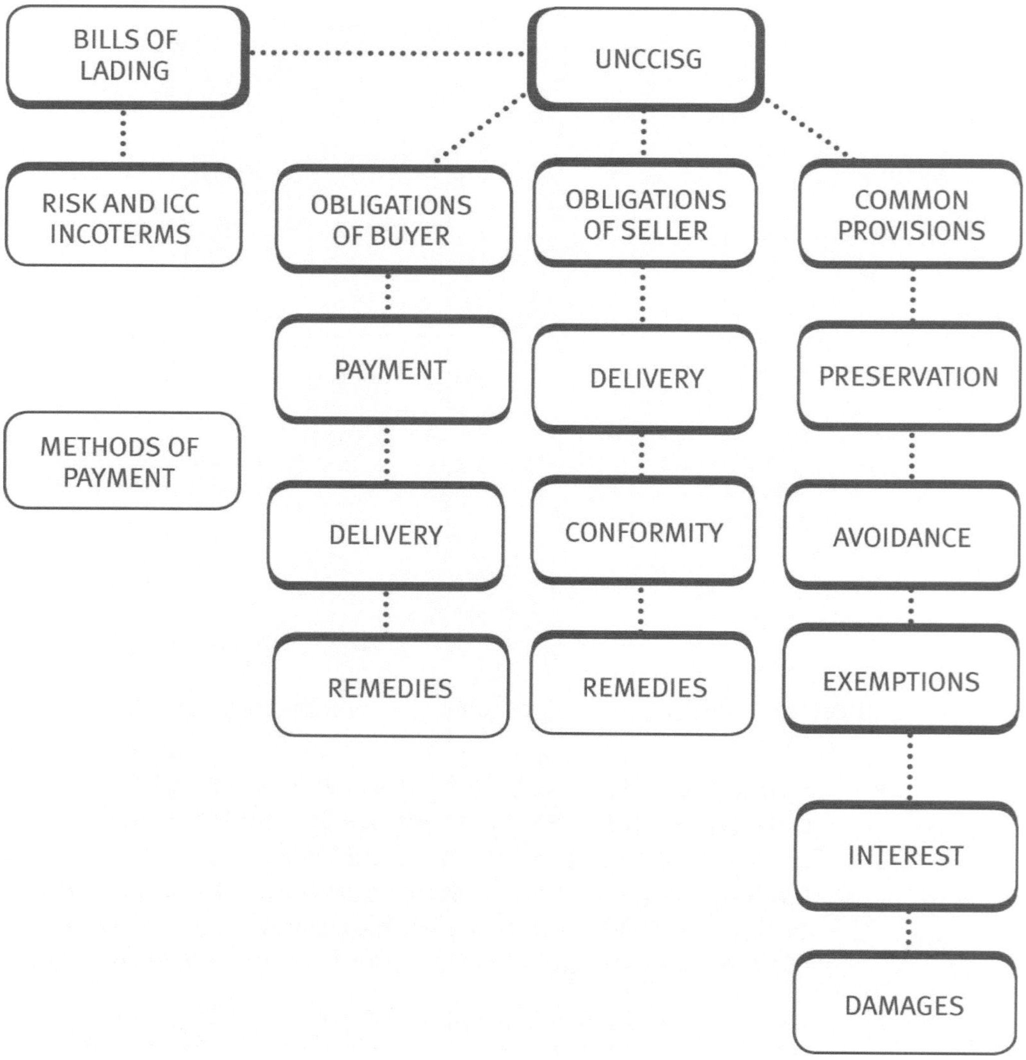

1 Obligations of the seller: delivery

The seller must deliver the goods, hand over any documents relating to them and transfer the property in the goods, as required by the contract and UNCCISG.

Delivery

There are two issues relating to delivery:

- place
- time.

Delivery: basic points

If the contract specifies the place that the goods should be delivered to and when, then the seller must ensure that he or she delivers the goods at that place and time.

If the contract does not specify, the following rules apply:

1 If the contract involves carriage of the goods, the seller must hand over the goods to the first carrier for transmission to the buyer (Article 31(a)).

2 If the contract does not involve carriage and does relate to specific goods, or unidentified goods to be drawn from a specific stock, or relates to goods to be manufactured or produced, and at the time they made the contract the parties knew where the goods would be or would be produced, the seller must place the goods at the buyer's disposal at that place (Article 31(b)).

3 In other cases, the seller must place the goods at the buyer's disposal at the place where the seller had his or her place of business when the contract was made (Article 31(c)).

Unidentified goods drawn from a specific stock are usually goods which cannot easily be identified from the overall batch of goods.

Illustration 1 – Obligations of the seller: delivery

Say, for example, that Karl wants to buy some coal from Leanne. Leanne owns stocks of coal at two storehouses. Storehouse A contains 200 tonnes of coal. Storehouse B contains 100 tonnes of coal. If Karl wanted to buy 100 tonnes of coal, he could buy the stock held at Storehouse B. This would therefore be specific goods, as he knows that every lump of coal in that Storehouse will be sold to him. If he were buying coal from Storehouse A, he would be buying unidentified goods from a specific stock. He would know that 100 of the 200 tonnes in Storehouse A will be sold to him, but he does not know exactly which lumps of coal he is going to purchase.

Test your understanding 1

Look back to the rules on delivery set out above and identify which ICC Incoterm will equate to each transaction given in the example above.

Test your understanding 2

Give an example of goods which may be identified from a specific stock other than coal.

Delivery involving carriage: additional points

If the contract involves carriage, the seller must:

- clearly identify the goods to the contract when handing the goods over to the carrier (by shipping documents, or by marking the goods) (Article 32(1))
- make relevant contracts for the carriage of the goods to the relevant place by appropriate transportation and according to the usual terms applying to that transportation (Article 32(2))
- provide insurance for the goods if the contract so provides (Article 32(3)) by implication
- if the contract does not provide for insurance, the seller must provide the buyer with all relevant information in sufficient time to enable the buyer to insure the goods while they are in transit (Article 32(3)).

e.g

Illustration 2 – Obligations of the seller: delivery

Mohammed and Nigel have a contract for the sale of international goods. Mohammed is delivering the goods to Nigel by sea. The goods are in three metal containers, on which Mohammed has painted Nigel's name, business address, telephone details and unique contract number. This fulfils Mohammed's obligations to identify the goods to the contract when they are handed over to the shipper.

Test your understanding 3

State what ICC Incoterm will equate to the transaction in the example above.

Delivery: time

If the contract specifies the date on which the seller must deliver the goods, the seller must deliver the goods on that date (Article 33(a)) If the contract does not so specify:

- but specifies a period within which the goods must be delivered, the seller must deliver the goods within that period (Article 33(b)).
- In other cases, the seller must deliver the goods within a reasonable time after the contract has been formed (Article 3(c)).

e.g

Illustration 3 – Obligations of the seller: delivery

Olumgbenga and Patience have a contract for Patience to buy 10 tonnes of fresh fish. In this case, while no period for delivery is specified, reasonable time will be a matter of days, otherwise the fish will deteriorate and go off.

Test your understanding 4

Identify factors which might affect the 'reasonable time' for delivery of goods.

Handing over of documents (Article 34)

The following points relate to the handover of documents:

- If the seller is required to hand over documents relating to the goods, he or she must hand them over at the time and place and in the form required by the contract.
- If the seller has handed over documents before the time required by the contract, he or she may correct any lack of conformity in those documents up to the time that he or she was required to hand them over by the contract (provided this does not put the buyer to unreasonable inconvenience or expense). The buyer retains the right to claim damages for this inconformity. (Issues relating to damages will be outlined later.)

2 Obligations of the seller: conformity

The seller must deliver goods which are of the quantity, quality and description required by the contract and which are contained or packaged in the manner required by the contract.

Conformity (Article 35)

Unless the parties have made different agreements in their contract, UNCCISG states that goods do not conform with the contract unless they:

- are fit for the purposes for which goods of the same description would ordinarily be used
- are fit for any particular purpose expressly or implied made known to the seller at the time of the conclusion of the contract, except where the circumstances show that the buyer did not rely, or that it was unreasonable for him or her to rely, on the seller's skill and judgement
- possess the qualities of goods which the seller has held out to the buyer as a sample or model
- contained and packaged in the manner usual for such goods or, where there is no such manner, in a manner adequate to preserve and protect the goods.

The seller is not liable for goods not meeting this description if at the time of the contract:

- The buyer knew that the goods did not conform.
- The buyer could not have been unaware that the goods did not conform.

These rules on conformity are all found in Article 35 UNCCISG, which the examiner might well refer to by name in the examination. It is an important article, which was examined regularly in the old syllabus.

The seller is liable for lack of conformity when:

- it exists at the time that risk passes to the buyer (even if it only becomes apparent afterwards)
- it occurs after the time when risk passes to the buyer if it is due to a breach of the seller's obligations (including, e.g. a breach of any guarantee that the goods will remain fit for their purpose for a period of time).

During the course of this and the following chapters you will see various references to CLOUT cases. CLOUT stands for 'Case law on UNCITRAL texts'. Currently over 2/3 of the world's trade is governed by CISG and every year new States ratify the Convention. There are substantial differences in legal systems and customs in those countries and accordingly full uniformity in such context is impossible. Nevertheless, Art.7 (1) of the Convention specifies that States when interpreting the Convention must have regard to its international character and to the need to promote uniformity in its application and the observance of good faith in international trade. Art 7 (2) requires all questions concerning matters governed by this Convention which are not expressly settled in it to be settled in conformity with the general principles on which it is based or, in the absence of such principles, in conformity with the law applicable by virtue of the rules of private international law.

To further this objective the UNCITRAL Secretariat has devised a system called CLOUT for collecting and disseminating information on court decisions and arbitral awards which relate to the application and interpretation of the United Nations Convention on Contracts for the International Sale of Goods and other Conventions devised by the Commission.

The purpose of the system is to promote international awareness of the relevant legal texts and to facilitate uniform interpretation and application of those texts. The reporting of the decision and awards will enable judges, legal practitioners and in-house lawyer to refer to them in order to determine the possible application and interpretation of the Convention and determine their contractual relationships accordingly. The system aims at court decision and arbitral awards which refers to specific provision of the Convention as well as at those which deal with the relevant issues indirectly (without any direct reference to any specific provisions).

The CLOUT system currently collects cases relating to the following Conventions:

- United Nations Convention on Carriage of Goods By Sea (Hamburg, 1978)
- United Nations Convention on Contract for International Sale of Goods (1980)
- UNCITRAL Model law for International Commercial Arbitration (1985)

- United Nations Conventions on International Bills of Exchange and International Promissory Notes (New York, 1988)
- UNCITRAL Model law on International Credit Transfers (1992)
- United Nations Convention on Independent Guarantees and Stand-by letters of credits (New York, 1995)
- UNCITRAL Model law on Electronic Commerce (1996)
- UNCITRAL Model law on Cross-Borders Insolvency (1997)

e.g

Illustration 4 – Obligations of the seller: conformity

The principles of conformity were tested in CLOUT Case No. 84, in which a Swiss company sold New Zealand mussels to a German company. The German Federal Health Office found the mussels to be 'generally not safe' because they contained a cadmium level in excess of the German statutory limit. However, the court held that the statutory limit expressed an optimum situation of food limits and was not a binding maximum limit. The court also found that the cadmium level in the mussels was in line with the regulations of the exporting country. The mussels were still fit for eating, and as such there was no lack of conformity.

In other words, the Swiss company were not required to be experts in German food law. They sold the German company mussels that were fit to eat in Switzerland and in New Zealand. The German company should have made the Swiss company aware of their special requirements.

Had Swiss law had the same requirements in relation to cadmium content of mussels, then the court probably would have found in favour of the German company. This is because if Swiss law required the cadmium content to be lower, then the Swiss company would have sold the German company mussels that according to their own law were not fit for the purpose – which they should have been aware of.

Test your understanding 5

Adam, from Germany, is buying mussels from Bernard, from France, Catriona, from the UK and Del from Denmark, to be delivered to his place of business. Adam knows that French and UK law is the same as Germany regarding cadmium content of mussels. Adam makes no reference to cadmium content in any of his contracts. Mussels are always delivered chilled.

Bernard's mussels contain a level of cadmium higher than permitted by German law.

Catriona's mussels are not delivered in a refrigerated vehicle.

Del's mussels contain a level of cadmium higher than permitted by German law.

1 **Adam is likely to succeed in a claim for non-conformity against Bernard.**

True

False

Not enough information

2 **Explain your answer to 1.**

3 **Adam is likely to succeed in a claim for non-conformity against Catriona.**

True

False

Not enough information

4 **Explain your answer to 3.**

5 **Adam is likely to succeed in a claim for non-conformity against Del.**

True

False

Not enough information

6 **Explain your answer to 5.**

Early delivery

If the seller delivers goods earlier than required by the contract:

- the buyer may take the delivery or refuse to take the delivery (Article 52(1)).
- the seller may deliver any missing part or repair any lack of conformity up to the date when the goods were supposed to be delivered, so long as this does not cause the buyer unreasonable inconvenience or expense. The buyer retains any right to claim damages under the convention (Article 37).

Inspection by the buyer (Article 38)

The buyer must inspect the goods (or get someone else to):

- within as short a period as is practicable
- if the contract includes carriage, when the goods have arrived at their destination
- if the goods are to be redirected/immediately dispatched on by the buyer, and the seller is aware of that fact, when the goods arrive at the new destination.

e.g

Illustration 5 – Obligations of the seller: conformity

Heidi is buying some goods from Ibrahim. Ibrahim is shipping the goods to a specified port and is aware that Heidi is shipping them immediately to Jonah, to whom she is selling the goods. When the goods arrive with Jonah, he inspects them and discovers them not to conform to the contract terms between himself and Heidi. The requirements as to quality are the same in the contract between Heidi and Ibrahim as they are in the contract between Jonah and Heidi.

In this situation, Heidi has a claim for the lack of conformity against Ibrahim, provided she gives him appropriate notice of the lack of conformity of the goods as set out below.

Test your understanding 6

Kamran has contracts with a number of other parties. First, he is buying goods from Leroy, which he will ship immediately to Mary. Secondly he is buying some goods from Natasha which he will keep in his stores for a little while before selling them on to Ophelia. Thirdly, he is buying some goods from Ping, which he will be selling on to Quentin.

Leroy is shipping the goods to Kamran. Natasha is shipping the goods to Kamran. Kamran will be collecting the goods for Quentin from Ping's warehouse.

When must the goods be inspected in each case and by whom?

Loss of right to rely on lack of conformity (Article 39)

The buyer loses the right to rely on a lack of conformity of the goods if he or she does not give notice to the seller of the nature of the lack of conformity:

- within reasonable time of the buyer discovering the lack of conformity
- within reasonable time of the time when the buyer ought to have discovered the lack of conformity
- within two years from the date on which the goods were handed over to the buyer, unless this length of time is inconsistent with the terms of the contract or any guarantees under the contract.

The above provisions do not protect the seller if the lack of conformity relates to:

- facts which the seller knew
- facts which the seller could not have been unaware of, and
- the seller did not disclose these facts to the buyer.

Third party claims (Article 41)

The seller must deliver goods that are free from any right or claim of a third party, including rights or claims based on industrial or other intellectual property (provided the claim is based on these under the law of the state where the goods will be resold or used if it was contemplated by the parties at the time of the contract that the goods would be sold/used in that state, or under the law of the state where the buyer has his or her place of business):

- unless the buyer agreed to take the goods subject to that right or claim
- unless the buyer knew or could not have been unaware of the right or claim of intellectual property
- unless the right or claim (in respect of industrial or intellectual property) results from the seller's compliance with technical drawings, designs, formulae or other such specifications furnished by the buyer.

The right to rely on these provisions is lost when:

- Buyer does not give notice to the seller specifying the nature of the right or claim of the third party within a reasonable time after he or she has become aware or ought to have become aware of the right or claim. (However, he or she retains the right to claim damages (except for loss of profit) if he or she has a reasonable excuse for his or her failure to give the required notice.
- Seller knew of the right or claim of the third party and the nature of it.

e.g

Illustration 6 – Obligations of the seller: conformity

Ritu has agreed contracts with two parties, Shahid and Tabitha. Under the terms of the first contract, Ritu is purchasing 100 't'-shirts from Shahid, which are printed with a slogan, using the Coke registered device. Under the terms of the contract with Tabitha, Ritu is buying 100 special child-friendly cups. Tabitha intends to supply Ritu with the cups she had left over from a production for a well-known child-friendly cup retailer, Tommi Tipu, which are made to their patented design.

Once the contracts have been completed, Ritu discovers that both sets of goods are subject to a third party claim. She is seeking advice whether she can claim against either Shahid or Tabitha.

In the case of Shahid, it is likely that he will be able to claim that Ritu knew, or ought to have done, that the design used the Coke registered device (which is internationally well-known) and therefore he is not liable for the third party claim from Coke against her.

In the case of Tabitha, Ritu could not necessarily have been expected to recognise that the cups she was buying were subject to patents from Tommi Tipu. However, Tabitha was fully aware of this and therefore Ritu is likely to have a successful claim against Tabitha.

Test your understanding 7

In the following scenarios, identify whether the buyer or seller will be responsible for any third party claim.

1. Umar is buying goods from Victoria. They are both aware that a third party claim could arise in respect of the goods.
2. William is buying goods from Xavier. Xavier is aware that a third party claim could arise in respect of the goods.
3. Yvonne is buying goods from Zara. The goods contain an internationally-recognisable slogan, which is subject to trade marks registered in the countries both businesses operate in.

3 Remedies for breach of contract by the seller

Breach of contract is when the seller fails to perform any of his or her obligations under the contract or UNCCISG.

Fundamental breach of contract is when a party is substantially deprived of what they are entitled to expect under the contract and the result of the breach must be foreseeable (Article 25). Both conditions must be satisfied before the breach can be classified as fundamental, e.g. when the seller provides no goods, or goods that do not conform to the point where they are worthless.

Illustration 7 – Remedies for breach of contract by the seller

The obligations of the seller under UNCCISG are set out at the start of this chapter. So, e.g. if in a contract including carriage, the seller fails to deliver the goods to the first carrier, he or she has breached the contract. If the seller does not provide goods that are fit for the purpose for which they were bought, he or she has breached the contract.

In addition, the seller may breach the contract if he or she fails to keep to terms which were specifically agreed in the contract between the two parties, e.g. that goods would be packaged in a certain way, or delivered on a particular date.

If the seller breaches the contract, the buyer is entitled to:

- claim damages (we shall look at the details relating to damages later) (Article 74 – 77)
- require specific performance of the contract by the seller (Article 46)
- declare the contract avoided (Article 49 (this requires notice (Article 26))
- reduce the price (Article 50)
- give additional period for performance (Articles 47 – 48).

The remedy claimed will depend on the nature of the seller's breach. If the buyer exercises his or her right to remedies other than damages, this does not deprive him or her of the right to claim damages also. Once the buyer has resorted to a remedy for breach of contract, a court or arbitral tribunal has no right to grant the seller a period of grace.

Performance

The buyer may demand that the seller performs his or her obligations under the contract. The rules are:

- The buyer cannot require performance by the seller if the buyer has already resorted to a remedy which is inconsistent with this requirement (Article 46(1)).
- If the goods do not conform with the contract, the buyer may request substitute goods (but only if the lack of conformity constitutes a fundamental breach of contract and the buyer has inspected the goods in reasonable time and given the seller notice of the lack of conformity) (Article 46(2)).
- If the goods do not conform with the contract, the buyer may request that the seller repairs them (if this request is reasonable, the buyer has inspected the goods within reasonable time and given the seller notice of the lack of conformity) (Article 46(3)).
- The buyer may fix a reasonable additional time period for the seller to perform his or her obligations (Article 47(1)).
- During that additional period, the buyer may not resort to other remedies unless the seller informs the buyer of his or her intention not to perform (Article 47(2)).
- The seller may remedy any failure to perform his or her obligations, even after the date of delivery, unless this puts the buyer to unreasonable expense or delay (Article 48(1)).
- If the seller asks the buyer if he or she may put right his or her failure to perform and the buyer does not reply, the seller may perform his or her obligations in the time period set out in his or her request and the buyer may not resort to other remedies in that period (Article 48(2)).

- Such a notice of the seller's intention is deemed to include a request that the buyer make known his or her decision (Article 48(3)).
- Such notices are only valid if they are received by the buyer (Article 48(3)).
- If only part of the goods conform or have been delivered, the above rules apply to the non-conforming or undelivered part.

Avoidance

The buyer may declare the contract avoided, and therefore be absolved of obligations arising under the contract (e.g. to pay the contract price). The contract may be avoided only if:

- the seller commits fundamental breach of contract (Article 49(1)a)
- the seller has not delivered the goods and also fails to deliver the goods during the additional time set for performance by the buyer (Article 49(1)b)
- due to late delivery if the buyer declares the contract avoided within a reasonable time after he or she is aware the goods have been delivered (Article 48(2)a)
- regardless of delivery if the buyer declares it avoided within reasonable time after he or she knew of the breach (or ought to have done) (Article 48(2)b(i)) or after additional time periods for performance have expired (Article 48(2)b(ii))
- if only part of the goods conform or have been delivered, the above rules apply to the non-conforming or undelivered part.

Reduction of the price (Article 50)

The buyer may reduce the price due under the contract (whether it is paid or unpaid at the time) in the same proportion as the value that the goods actually delivered had at the time of delivery bears to the value that conforming goods would have done at the time:

- if the goods do not conform to the contract
- unless the seller remedies his or her failure to perform his or her obligations
- unless the buyer refuses to accept performance by the seller (as set out above).

Early delivery or extra delivery (Article 52)

If the seller delivers the goods early:

- the buyer may take delivery or refuse to take delivery until the appropriate date.

If the seller delivers too many goods:

- the buyer may take delivery of the excess or refuse to accept the excess.
- if the buyer accepts the excess, he or she must pay for it at the contract rate.

If there are additional storage costs they may be recovered by the buyer making a claim for damages in accordance with Article 45(1)(b), unless the acceptance of the early tendered goods amounts to an agreement to modify the delivery date.

e.g

Illustration 8 – Remedies for breach of contract by the seller

These principles were tested in CLOUT Case No. 165, in which an Austrian company sold a leather seating arrangement to a German company. The German company sold the seating arrangement to a third party client, who discovered that the goods did not conform to the contract. The German company requested that the Austrian company repair the goods so that they would conform. The Austrian company repaired the goods, but the German company found them still not to conform to the contract, and declared the contract avoided. The Austrian company claimed that their general terms and conditions stated that the lack of conformity had to be declared to them within five days.

The court found that the lack of conformity after repair was a fundamental breach of contract and that the German company were entitled to declare the contract avoided. It also found that the terms and conditions requiring notification within five days did not apply after the company had already been asked to repair a lack of conformity, and that the German company had declared the contract avoided within reasonable time (five weeks).

e.g

Illustration 9 – Remedies for breach of contract by the seller

The above case is in contrast to CLOUT Case No. 248. In this case a German seller sold frozen meat to a Swiss buyer, to be delivered to Egypt and Jordan. The buyer claimed a lack of conformity of the goods and refused to pay the contract price (declared the contract avoided).

The court held that the difference in quality between the contract specification and actuality was not significant enough to merit the buyer declaring the contract avoided (even though specialists discovered the loss in value of the goods to be 25%). The court held that a buyer should only be able to declare a contract avoided in exceptional circumstances as it is the buyer's most serious remedy. All the circumstances in the case should be taken into account. In this case, the buyer had alternative solutions available to him or her, e.g. demanding a 25% reduction in the contract price.

Test your understanding 8

Explain the buyer's remedy of specific performance.

Test your understanding 9

Coral has delivered 25 machines to Daniel. The terms of the contract between them state that she should deliver 20 machines. Daniel may

A **Accept the extra machines free.**

B **Accept the extra machines but pay for them at the contract price.**

C **Reject the extra machines and declare the contract avoided.**

D **Reject the extra machines and ask that Coral reduces the overall contract price.**

4 Obligations of the buyer: payment

The buyer is obliged to pay the price agreed in the contract and to take relevant steps and comply with necessary formalities to do so, without prompting from the seller.

Fixing the price

The price will be as set by the contract, unless the contract does not fix a specific price for the goods, when the following rules apply:

- the parties are deemed to have impliedly made reference to the price generally charged when the contract was formed for goods sold in comparable circumstances (Article 55)
- if the price is to be determined by weight, the relevant weight is the net weight (Article 56).

Illustration 10 – Obligations of the buyer: payment

These principles were set out in CLOUT Case No. 106, in which an Austrian buyer ordered 249 chinchilla pelts of 'middle or better quality' at a price between 35 and 65DM each. The Austrian buyer sold the pelts immediately to a buyer who rejected a number of the pelts as being lower quality than the contract between them stated. The Austrian buyer listed the pelts that were lower quality and refused to pay the German seller the purchase price in respect of them. However the court found that the Austrian buyer should pay the price, given that the quality was as stated in the contract, and that the price, which, being unspecific, was deemed to have been set with reference to the prevailing market price.

Illustration 11 – Obligations of the buyer: payment

In contrast, in Case No. 139, the court found that the rules deeming that where price was unspecified, prevailing market rate would apply did not apply in this case because it was clear from the contract between the parties that specific agreement about price was required.

Test your understanding 10

Edith and Frazier have a contract for Edith to purchase a quantity of rolled metal. Rolled metal costs $450 per tonne. Frazier delivers the metal to Edith's premises, where it is weighed. The total weight is 23 tonnes, the net weight, 22.45 tonnes.

Calculate the contract price.

Place

The place where the price is to be paid will be as set by the contract, unless the contract does not fix a specific place, when the following rules apply:

- The price shall be paid at the seller's place of business (if the seller changes his or her place of business after the contract has been formed, he or she must bear extra incidental costs to the buyer of paying him or her there) (Article 57(1)(a)).
- The price shall be paid where the goods or associated documents are handed over to the buyer or the buyer's agent (Article 57(1)(b)).

Illustration 12 – Obligations of the buyer: payment

In CLOUT Case No. 25, a Spanish buyer collected goods from a French seller a number of times over a period. The Spanish buyer alleged that the goods were defective and did not pay. The court determined that the price should have been paid at the French seller's premises where the buyer bought the goods (and therefore presumably inspected them to ensure the quality was suitable).

Test your understanding 11

Gary and Helga have a contract for Gary to collect goods from Helga's business premises in Almanistan. Since the contract was formed, Helga has moved her operations to Boumania. It is still possible, but more difficult, for Gary to collect the goods. As he will have to set up special bank arrangements to pay Helga in the new country, it will cost him $20 more to pay the contract price of $59,487.

As a result:

I Helga must deliver the goods to her previous premises in Almanistan.

II Gary must collect the goods from Boumania.

III Gary must pay Helga $59,487.

IV Helga must pay the extra cost of $20.

Which of the statements is correct?

A **I**

B **I, III, IV**

C **II, III, IV**

D **II, III**

Test your understanding 12

Ingrid and Jasper have a contract for Ingrid to deliver goods to Jasper. She will place the goods with the first carrier at Newtown Port, and they will be collected by Jasper's business associate at Oldtown Port.

Where must the price be paid?

Time

When the price is to be paid will be as set out in the contract, unless the contract does not specify, in which case the following rules apply:

- The price shall be paid when the seller places the goods or documents at the buyer's disposal. The seller may make payment a condition of handing over the goods (Article 58(1)).
- In a contract involving carriage, the seller may make a condition that the goods are not handed over to the buyer before payment is made (Article 58(2)).
- The buyer is entitled to examine the goods before he or she makes payment (Article 58(3)).

5 Obligations of the buyer: taking delivery

The buyer must carry out all the acts that would reasonably be expected of him or her (i) in order to enable the seller to make delivery and (ii) in taking the goods (Article 60).

Illustration 13 – Obligations of the buyer: taking delivery

Michael has contracted with Nanette to buy 200,000 jars of honey. Nanette has agreed to transport the honey to the port of Danhaig, where Michael will collect them and pay the price on collection. On the day that Michael is due to collect and pay for the goods, there is a transport strike and Michael is unable to get a suitable vehicle to the docks to collect the honey. However, an associate of his has a warehouse in the docks which the associate has put at his disposal. It is reasonable to expect Michael to take advantage of this offer so that the goods may be collected and Nanette can be paid the price.

Test your understanding 13

Odette is due to deliver goods to Padraig at his place of business on 29 June. On the 26 June, Padraig's workforce declared a strike and the premises are not operational, but Odette's journey will take four days and she has already left.

Should Padraig engage casual staff to ensure the premises are open to Odette and the goods can be unloaded from her vehicle?

6 Remedies for breach of contract by the buyer

If the buyer breaches the contract, the seller is entitled to:

- claim damages (we shall look at the details relating to damages later) (Article 74 – 77)
- require specific performance of the contract by the buyer (Article 62)
- declare the contract avoided (Article 64 requires notice to be given)
- produce goods to the seller's own specification (Article 65(1))
- give additional time for performance of the contractual obligation (Article 63).

The remedy claimed will depend on the nature of the buyer's breach. If the seller exercises his or her right to remedies other than damages, this does not deprive him or her of the right to claim damages also. Once the seller has resorted to a remedy for breach of contract, a court or arbitral tribunal has no right to grant the buyer a period of grace.

Performance

The seller may demand that the buyer performs his or her obligations (pay the price/accept delivery/other obligations) under the contract. The rules are:

- The seller may fix an additional time period of reasonable length to enable the buyer to perform (Article 63(1)).
- Unless the buyer notifies the seller he or she is not going to perform in that time, the seller may then not resort to any other remedy for breach of contract during the additional period (Article 63(1)).
- The seller may not exercise the right to claim specific performance if he or she has already resorted to a remedy inconsistent with specific performance (Article 62).

Avoidance

The seller may declare the contract avoided (and therefore absolve himself of any commitments under that contract) only:

- if the buyer commits fundamental breach of contract (Article 64(1)(a))
- if the buyer does not perform his or her obligations during the additional time period fixed by the seller for performance (or notifies the seller that he or she will not do so) (Article 64(1)(b))
- unless the buyer has paid the price, although the seller may declare the contract avoided in respect of late performance before he or she becomes aware of the performance (Article 64(2)(a))
- for any fundamental breach other than late performance (the buyer having paid the price), so long as it is within reasonable time of the seller knowing about the breach or after the additional time period for performance has expired (Article 64(2)(b)).

Produce goods to own specification (Article 65)

If the buyer is required to specify details relating to the goods under the contract and fails to do so by the date agreed or within a reasonable time after a request from the seller:

- the seller may make the specification of the goods (in accordance with the buyer's needs as far as they are known)
- the seller must inform the buyer of the details of the specification
- the seller must fix a reasonable time for the buyer to make a different specification if he or she chooses
- if the buyer fails to make a different specification after receiving such a communication then the specification of the seller is binding.

e.g

Illustration 14 – Remedies for breach of contract by the buyer

In CLOUT Case No. 83, a Swedish seller of coke delivered to a company in the former Yugoslavia sued the German buyer for payment of the price. The buyer counter-claimed that the coke was of an inferior quality, but the court held that this was no justification for the buyer declaring the contract avoided (which in effect he or she was doing by not fulfilling his or her obligations and refusing to pay the price), particularly as the buyer had not done this until four months after payment was due (which would mean that the notice of rejection of goods was not within reasonable time), presumably as a result of the seller suing for the price. The buyer should have claimed a reduction in the price for the inferior quality of the coke, but had failed to do that within reasonable time, and was therefore required to pay the full contract price to the seller.

End of offer

There are many examples of cases where a claim by the seller has resulted in a counter-claim about quality by the buyer. Remember however, that a claim in respect of lack of conformity has to be made in reasonable time. As can be seen in the case above, a seller is protected by the courts from spurious quality claims made once payment is demanded. A genuine claim about quality must be made within reasonable time from discovery, and given that buyers are required to inspect the goods, most problems with conformity should be discovered shortly after the buyer receives the goods.

e.g

Illustration 15 – Remedies for breach of contract by the buyer

In CLOUT Case No. 47, a German seller of electronic ear devices demanded damages from an Italian buyer, who had failed to take delivery of the devices, even after the seller had set an additional time period for delivery to take place. Applying Article 31, the court found that the buyer should have collected the goods from where the seller had manufactured them and that damages were appropriate.

Quinn and Rachel have a contract under which Rachel is to produce 10 machines for Quinn's factory. Quinn provided some detail of what was required at the time the contract was formed but Rachel wants to start work on the machines, and despite repeated requests by her for Quinn to provide a specification for the machines, he has not replied. Rachel is therefore entitled to create her own specification for the machines, according to the details that she already has. However, she will have to give Quinn the opportunity to produce a different specification if he is not in agreement with hers.

Test your understanding 14

Stewart is contracted to sell Titus 300 sheets of metal. The metal was ready for collection on 1 November, but by 10 November, Titus has not collected the metal or paid the price. Stewart wrote to Titus and told him that if the goods had not been collected or the price not paid by 30 November, he would consider the contract at an end.

It is the 27 November and Stewart has not heard from Titus. Ursula has just visited Stewart's premises and seen the sheets of metal and has offered to buy them from Stewart. Is Stewart entitled to accept her offer?

Test your understanding 15

Waqar and Xavier have a contract for Waqar to collect goods from Xavier's premises on 1 July. Waqar does not collect the goods on 1 July but the price for the goods is transferred to Xavier's bank account on 1 July. Xavier needs the goods to be removed from his premises, as they are in the way of operations.

Xavier may:

I Declare the contract avoided.

II Inform Waqar that the goods should be collected in a week.

III Inform Waqar that the goods should be collected in a week or they will be sold to someone else.

Which of the above statements are correct?

A **Statement I**

B **Statement II**

C **Statement III**

D **Statements II and III**

Test your understanding 16

Set out the rules relating to the seller declaring the contract avoided.

7 Common provisions: anticipatory breach and instalment contracts

Anticipatory breach

Anticipatory breach is where a party to the contract informs the other party (expressly or impliedly) that he or she does not intend to perform his or her obligations under the contract or it appears after concluding the contract that a party will be unable to perform a substantial part of his or her obligation (Articles 71 and 72).

Illustration 16 – Common provisions: anticipatory breach
Elijah and Frederica have agreed a contract between them. A month before Frederica is due to commence work, Elijah becomes bankrupt. It is clear that he will be unable to perform his obligations under the contract (that is, pay for any work Frederica carries out under the contract). Elijah is in anticipatory breach of contract.

UNCCISG states that one party to the contract may suspend the performance of their obligations under a contract if, once the parties have agreed the contract, it is clear that the other party will not be able to perform due to:

- a serious deficiency in his or her ability to perform or his or her creditworthiness (Article 71(1)(a))
- his or her conduct in preparing to perform/performing the contract (Article 71(1)(b)).

If a party suspends performance he or she:

- must give notice to the other party and must continue with performance if the other party gives satisfactory assurance that he or she will be able to perform (Article 71(3))
- may prevent the buyer taking over possession of the goods if he or she has dispatched them, regardless of what documents the buyer possesses, entitling him or her to the goods (Article 71(2)).

(Unless the party in breach has declared that he or she will not perform his obligations) if the party in anticipatory breach is committing a fundamental breach of contract:

- the injured party may declare the contract avoided (Article 72(1)).
- if time allows, the injured party must give reasonable notice to the party in breach that the contract is avoided (Article 72(2)).

Test your understanding 17
Define anticipatory breach.

Test your understanding 18

John and Keira have agreed the terms of their contract. Keira is due to start work on the contract on 30 June. On 31 May, Keira informs John that she will not be able to commence work on the contract.

1 **Keira has committed:**

Anticipatory breach

Avoidance of contract

Delay

Nothing

2 **John is entitled to:**

Demand performance

Set an additional time frame for Keira to perform the contract

Declare the contract avoided

Seek damages

3 **John must give Keira reasonable notice if he declares the contract avoided.**

True

False

Instalment contracts

An 'instalment contract' is where the contract contains a number of separate parts, e.g. a contract to deliver goods in separate chunks over a long period of time.

In an instalment contract:

- If one party fails to perform any of his or her obligations in respect of any instalment and this is a fundamental breach of contract with respect to that instalment, the other party may declare the contract avoided with respect to that instalment (Article 73(1)).
- If one party fails to perform any of his or her obligations in respect of any instalment and this causes the other party reasonable grounds for a belief that a fundamental breach of contract will occur in respect of future instalments, he or she may declare the contract avoided (within reasonable time) (Article 73(2)).
- If the buyer declares the contract avoided in respect of one delivery, he or she may declare it avoided in respect of past and/or future deliveries if those deliveries are interdependent and could not be used for the purpose both parties were aware of at the outset of the contract (Article 73(3)).

Illustration 17 – Common provisions: anticipatory breach

Consider the following situations:

Graham is in contract with Helen to deliver fruit and vegetables to her every week for six months. In month three, week one, the fruit and vegetables have deteriorated and are not fit to sell. Helen does not pay for that instalment, and in month three, week two, the goods are fit for the purpose again and the instalment contract continues.

Indira is in contract with Jaitinder to deliver raw materials to her factory on a monthly basis over the period of a year. The goods are delivered late three months in a row, causing major problems to production, and Indira does not give satisfactory assurance that the goods will be delivered on time in the future. Indira declares the remainder of the contract avoided.

Kieran is in contract with Lysander to deliver the components for a crane over the course of production. Lysander has given Kieran a schedule of production. Each part is critical to the overall production of the crane, and the production process is time-sensitive.

The crane is 75% complete when Kieran delivers some metal parts which do not meet Lysander's quality control standards and which cannot be used in production. Lysander informs Kieran that the entire contract is avoided as soon as tests have been completed on the faulty metal parts.

Test your understanding 19

Define instalment contracts.

8 Common provisions: damages

Damages for breach of contract by one party consist of a sum equal to the loss, including loss of profit, suffered by the other party as a consequence of the breach.

Under (Article 74) damages may not exceed:

- the loss foreseen by the parties as a result of possible breach of contract at the outset of the contract
- the loss which ought to have been foreseen at the outset of the contract.

Under (Article 75) if the contract is avoided and:

- if the buyer has in a reasonable manner and within a reasonable time bought replacement goods
- or, if the seller has resold the goods in a reasonable manner and within a reasonable time

then

- the party claiming damages may recover the difference between the contract price and the price in the substitute transaction
- the party claiming damages may also recover additional damages subject to what was reasonable foreseeable at the time of the contract
- if a purchase or resale has not taken place and there is a current price for the goods in the place where the goods should have been delivered, the party claiming damages may recover the difference between the contract price and the current price in the country of delivery at the time of avoidance. If, however, the party claiming the damages has avoided the contract after taking over the goods, the current price at the time of such taking over shall be applied instead of the current price at the time of avoidance (Article 76(1))
- if a purchase or resale has not taken place, there is a current price for the goods, and the contract was avoided after one party had taken over the goods, the current price at the time of taking over will be relevant instead of the price at the time of avoidance (Article 76(2))
- if there is no current price for the goods at the place where the goods should have been delivered, then a reasonable substitute price should be used, taking account of the cost of delivery to the place where the goods should have been (Article 76(2)).

e.g

Illustration 18 – Common provisions: damages

Paradorn and Queenie are in contract. Paradorn has delivered fabric designed to Queenie's specification to Queenie. Queenie has inspected the fabric and notified Paradorn that it does not conform to the design and that she will therefore not pay the purchase price. Because the fabric does not conform to the design, Queenie cannot use the material for her client, and incurs a penalty cost that is set out in the contract between Queenie and her client. Queenie also has to engage Rodrigo to produce new fabric quickly, which costs her a premium. Unfortunately, there is an unexpected shortage of the silk thread required to make the fabric, and this causes the cost of the new material to rise even further.

Queenie is seeking damages from Paradorn. She may include the penalty cost in the cost of damages, provided she made Paradorn aware at the time of their concluding the contract that she was subject to such a penalty if she defaults. She may also include the cost of obtaining substitute goods from Rodrigo, as it would have been foreseeable at the time of the contract that if Paradorn failed to provide suitable goods then she would have to pay a premium to obtain substitute goods quickly. However, given that the shortage in silk thread is unexpected, she cannot claim for the more expensive thread, as this additional cost would not have been foreseeable at the time she and Paradorn entered into contract.

Illustration 19 – Common provisions: damages

Sajeeda and Thomas are in contract with one another. Sajeeda, whose place of business is A, is required to deliver 20 sheets of aluminium to Thomas, whose place of business is B, on 30 June. She delivers the goods and Thomas refuses to accept them. Sajeeda was unable to sell the aluminium to any other parties. The contract price was $5,000.

On 30 June, the price of aluminium sheets in A is $240 per sheet and in B is $275. Sajeeda is therefore entitled to damages of $500 (the price of sheets in B multiplied by 20, minus the contract price).

Test your understanding 20

Define damages.

Test your understanding 21

Damages may not exceed the loss which was foreseen (or ought to have been) at the time of the contract.

True

False

Mitigation

Any injured party who relies on breach of contract (and therefore the right to claim damages) must take reasonable measures to limit the loss he or she incurs (including loss of profit) that arise from the breach (Article 77).

Illustration 20 – Common provisions: damages

Seller produces goods for buyer, who declares in advance of seller delivering the goods that he or she does not want to accept the goods and will not pay for them. Buyer is in anticipatory breach, and seller is entitled to claim damages. However, seller must mitigate his or her loss, e.g. by selling the goods to someone else, even if at a lower price than he or she would have obtained from buyer. If seller does not mitigate his or her loss, then buyer will have the right to reduce the damages he or she has to pay by the amount that seller could have obtained by selling the goods to a third party.

Test your understanding 22

Lolita and Mikhail have a contract. Lolita has manufactured the goods due under the contract, but before she delivers them, Mikhail announces his intention not to accept the goods or pay for them.

I Lolita may claim damages, but she must try and sell the goods to a third party to mitigate her loss.

II Lolita is entitled to claim the cost of delivering the goods to Mikhail as part of her damages.

III Lolita is entitled to claim the cost of delivering the goods to the third party as part of her damages.

Which of the above statements is true?

A **I**

B **I and II**

C **I and III**

D **None of the statements**

9 Common provisions: interest (Article 78)

If a party fails to pay:

- the price
- any other sum in arrears
- the other party is entitled to interest on the outstanding balance
- interest will be determined at an appropriate rate, depending on the applicable law.

Illustration 21 – Common provisions: interest (Article 78)

In CLOUT Case No. 220, where there was a dispute between an Italian company and a Swiss company. The court determined that the Swiss company should pay interest on the purchase price and that the interest rate would be determined according to Italian law. However, it further concluded that the interest period would be determined according to Swiss law, which states that interest is payable after a reminder has been given by the seller.

Test your understanding 23

Under UNCCISG, a party owing any amounts to another party may be required by a court to pay interest on that sum, the amount of interest being calculated by the court applying what they deem to be applicable law.

True

False

Test your understanding 24

Umberto and Vanessa have a contract. Vanessa was due to pay the contract price on 30 June. Umberto sent a copy invoice to Vanessa on 7 August. When Vanessa continued to fail to pay, Umberto referred the matter to arbitration on 31 August. On 9 November, the arbitral tribunal stated that Vanessa should pay the price and pay interest. The applicable law states that interest is due from date the relevant party was reminded about the payment.

Interest will be due from:

A **30 June**

B **7 August**

C **31 August**

D **9 November**

10 Common provisions: exemption

A party is not liable to pay damages for a failure to perform his or her obligations if he or she proves:

- Failure was beyond his or her control (or beyond the control of a third party he or she engaged to perform the whole or part of the contract) and he or she could not reasonably have taken the impediment into account at the time the contract was agreed or to have avoided or overcome its consequences (Article 79(1)).

This article only has effect while the impediment exists (Article 79(3)).The party subject to the impediment:

- must notify the other party within reasonable time (Article 79(4))
- may be liable to damages if the other party does not receive the notification within reasonable time
- may be liable to a different remedy requested by the other party, e.g. reduction of the price if the goods were defective (Article 79(5)).

Illustration 22 – Common provisions: exemption

UNCCISG does not define 'impediment' further, but from the general description of an impediment given, it is reasonable it would include things often set out more clearly in domestic laws, such as 'force majeure' or 'Act of God'.

Illustration 23 – Common provisions: exemption

The principles were tested in CLOUT Case No. 140, in which a German company had contracted to buy chemicals from a Russian company. The Russian company failed to deliver the chemicals in accordance with the contract, and the German company contacted the Russian company repeatedly to insist on performance of the contract, and extending the time-period of the contract to enable the Russian company to do so. Finally the German company purchased the chemicals from a different source and claimed damages from the Russian company, being the difference between the contract price and the price of chemicals from the third party.

The Russian company claimed that it had suffered an impediment because an emergency production stoppage at the factory had made it impossible to produce the goods.

The court decided that damages should be paid as the Russian company could not prove the facts relating to the impediment and were unable to establish that it could not be expected to take such emergency stoppages into account at the outset of the contract. Also, the Russian company could have purchased the required chemicals from a different source in order to fulfil its contractual obligations.

In addition they decided that the measure of damages (contract price less the price of chemicals from a third party) was reasonable as the Russian company could not establish that the buyer could have bought the replacement chemicals more cheaply.

Test your understanding 25

Anil and Brigit have a contract with one another. Anil is contracted to produce plastic parts and supply them to Brigit. The day before the goods are delivered, lightening strikes Anil's premises, which are badly burnt and the plastic parts are significantly damaged.

Which of the following remedies Brigit can claim?

I **Damages**

II **Performance within a specified time period**

III **Avoidance of the contract**

A **I**

B **I and II**

C **I or III**

D **II or III**

11 Common provisions: effects of avoidance

The remedy of avoidance has been discussed above.

Avoidance:

- releases both parties from their obligations under the contract, subject to damages due (Article 81(1))
- does not affect any provision in the contract relating to settlement of disputes (Article 81(1))
- does not affect any provision in the contract setting out provisions in the event of avoidance (Article 81(1)).

If the contract is partly completed when is it declared avoided

- a party may claim restitution of whatever has been supplied/paid under the contract (Article 81(2))
- if both parties owe restitution it must be carried out at the same time (Article 81(2)).

e.g

Illustration 24 – Common provisions: effects of avoidance

An instalments contract between Carlotta and David is declared avoided when David has made one delivery out of 12. Carlotta paid a 50% deposit prior to the deliveries commencing. As the contract has been avoided, Carlotta is entitled to be repaid her 50% deposit and David may have his single delivery returned. They should arrange to perform both these returns on the same day.

The right to declare the contract avoided or for the buyer to demand substitute goods is lost if:

- It is impossible for the goods to be returned in substantially the same condition in which they were received (Article 82(1)).

Unless:

- the impossibility is not the fault of the party in possession of the goods (Article 82(2)(a))
- the goods have deteriorated as a result of the buyer's inspection which he or she is required to make (Article 82(2)(b))
- the goods have been sold or used in the normal course of business before the lack of conformity was discovered (Article 82(2)(c)).

Additional points:

- The buyer may pursue all the other remedies set out in UNCCISG or the contract (Article 83).
- If the seller has to refund the price, he or she must pay interest on it (Article 84(1)).
- If the buyer has benefited from possessing the goods before the contract is avoided and he or she cannot restore the goods, he or she must account to the seller for those benefits (Article 84(2)).

Illustration 25 – Common provisions: effects of avoidance

Elspeth was delivered some goods by Fidel under a contract by which Fidel is to deliver three further consignments. Due to Elspeth's failure to meet the contract term of payment of the whole contract price on receipt of the first delivery or within the additional time period set by Fidel, Fidel has now declared the contract avoided. Elspeth cannot return the goods to Fidel because she sold them immediately to Gurinder for a profit of 5%, so she must not only pay the percentage of the purchase price applicable to that delivery, but also account to Fidel for the 5% profit she made on the goods.

12 Common provisions: preservation of the goods

Under Article 85 the seller must take appropriate, reasonable steps to preserve the goods:

- if the buyer is in delay in accepting the goods
- where payment of the price and delivery of the goods are to be at the same time and the seller is in control of the goods
- where the seller is retaining the goods until the buyer in breach has reimbursed the buyer's reasonable expenses for preserving them.

Under Article 86 the buyer must take appropriate, reasonable steps to preserve the goods:

- if the buyer has received the goods and intends to reject them in accordance with UNCCISG provisions
- if the buyer has rejected the goods in accordance with UNCCISG and intends to retain them until the seller has reimbursed the buyer's reasonable expenses
- if the goods have been placed at the buyer's disposal and the buyer exercises the right to reject them (in which case he or she must take possession of them so long as this does not cause unreasonable inconvenience and expense).

According to Article 87 a party who is required to preserve the goods may:

- deposit the goods in a warehouse of a third party at the expense of the other party assuming the cost is not unreasonable
- sell the goods to a third party if there has been unreasonable delay by the other party to take possession of the goods or pay the price or cost of preservation if reasonable notice of the sale is given to the other party (unless the goods are subject to deterioration in which case notice is only required if possible)
- retain reasonable expenses for preserving the goods out of the sale proceeds, although he or she must account for the balance to the other party.

Illustration 26 – Common provisions: preservation of the goods

Harvey has a contract to deliver 20 boxes of frozen meat to Newport, where Imogen will collect them. Imogen inspects the goods at Newport and rejects them because they do not conform to the contract specification. Harvey cannot collect the goods from Newport for two days. Imogen therefore arranges for the goods to be kept in frozen in a storage at Newport on Harvey's behalf.

Test your understanding 26

In the above scenario Imogen is entitled to reimbursement from Harvey for the costs of the frozen storage.

True

False

13 Chapter summary

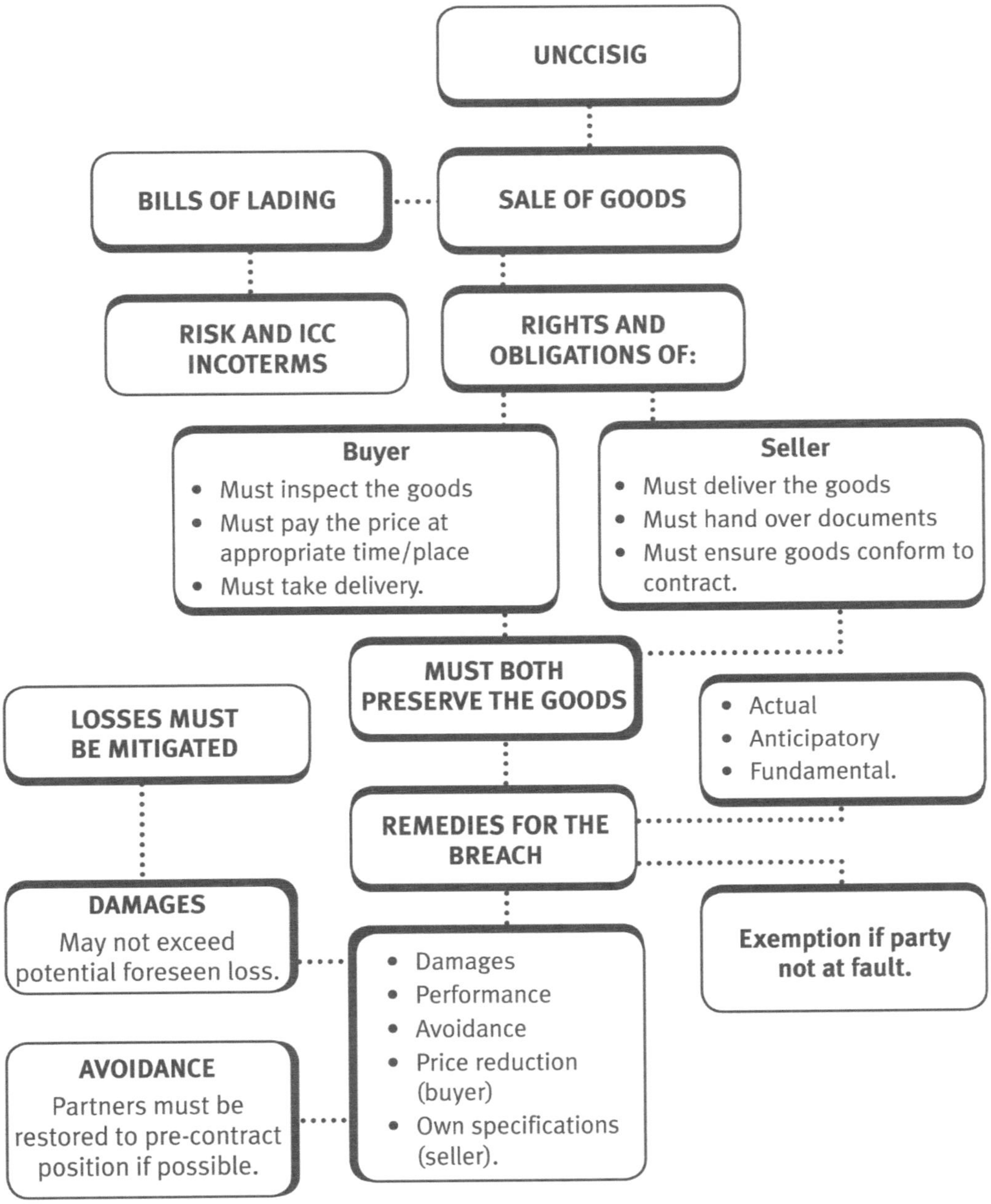

Test your understanding answers

Test your understanding 1

1 This equates to FCA (free carrier) unless carriage is to be by ship, in which case it equates to FOB (free on board). This is because it represents the requirement for the seller to simply place the goods with the first carrier.

2 & 3 These equate to EXW (ex works) because it represents the minimum requirement on the seller, simply to make the goods available to the buyer where the goods are/at the seller's premises.

Test your understanding 2

A mill might have a stock of 50 tonnes of flour. 20 tonnes of the flour from that mill would constitute identified goods from a specific stock provided they are clearly marked or separated from the other goods.

Test your understanding 3

The relevant Incoterm would be either CFR (cost and freight) or CPT (carriage paid to) depending on when the risk transfers. (The passing of risk will be outlined later in this chapter.)

Test your understanding 4

- Whether the goods are perishable or not.
- The method of transport used for the goods.
- The time such goods usually take in production.
- The customary availability of raw materials.

Test your understanding 5

1 True.

2 German and French law have the same requirement as regards cadmium content in mussels. Therefore Bernard has sold Adam mussels that are unfit to eat in France and Germany. Bernard should have met the requirement of his own country, therefore Adam will have a case against him.

3 True.

4 Mussels are always delivered chilled, therefore it is a requirement that they are delivered in refrigerated vehicles. Catriona has neither delivered the mussels packaged in the customary way, nor in a way that will preserve the goods.

5 Not enough information.

6 It is unclear whether Del should have met the requirement of German law without being told as this will depend on the law in Denmark. If Danish law has the same requirement or a higher one, then Adam will have a case against Del.

Test your understanding 6

1 Goods from Leroy

Mary must inspect the goods as soon as is practicable after they arrive with her. This is because the goods are being shipped directly to her without stopping at Leroy's premises.

2 Goods from Natasha

Kamran must inspect the goods as soon as is practicable after they arrive at his premises.

3 Goods from Ping

Kamran must inspect the goods at Ping's premises, because this is where Kamran is taking over the goods.

Test your understanding 7

1 Umar

2 Xavier

3 Yvonne

Test your understanding 8

The buyer may request that the seller performs his or her obligations under a contract. So, e.g. if the contract is for Seller to deliver two cupboards to Buyer, and he or she does not deliver them, the Buyer may request that he or she does so, and specify an additional time period within which performance should take place.

Alternatively, if Seller's breach of contract is a lack of conformity of the goods, Buyer may request that the seller repairs the goods, or delivers substitute goods, and set an additional time period within which Seller may do so.

Buyer may not resort to any other remedy during the extra time period he or she has set for performance.

Seller may also volunteer performance to remedy a breach of contract, unless this puts the buyer to unreasonable delay or expense.

Test your understanding 9

B Alternatively Daniel may reject the excess, but as Coral has delivered the other 20 machines in accordance with the contract, he may not declare the contract avoided or reduce the price. If Daniel accepts the excess machines, he must pay for them.

Test your understanding 10

The contract price is $10,102.50 (22.45 × 450 = 10,102.50).

Test your understanding 11

C Gary must collect the goods from Helga's existing premises and must pay the price. Helga must bear the extra costs.

Test your understanding 12

Oldtown Port.

Test your understanding 13

Yes, because Padraig is required to take reasonable steps to ensure that delivery can take place.

Test your understanding 14

No Stewart has extended an additional time period to Titus in which to perform his contract obligations. Stewart is barred from taking any other action in relation to those goods until the time period is up on 1 December. On 1 December, he may declare the contract avoided and will therefore be entitled to sell the metal to another party.

If Titus had declared that he has no intention of fulfilling his contract obligations during the fixed time period, then Stewart would be entitled to sell the metal.

Test your understanding 15

D Xavier may not declare the contract avoided until he has set a reasonable additional time period for Waqar to collect the goods. There is no reason to assume that a week is not a reasonable time in this case. If Waqar fails to collect the goods during the additional time period, then Xavier may declare the contract avoided (and sell the goods to someone else). Therefore statements (ii) and (iii) are correct. The effects of avoidance will be dealt with later. It suffices to say at this stage that if Xavier did, in the fullness of time, declare this contract avoided, he would be required to repay the purchase price to Waqar.

Test your understanding 16

The seller may declare the contract avoided:

- if the buyer commits fundamental breach of contract
- if the buyer does not perform his or her obligations during the additional time period fixed by the seller for performance (or notifies the seller that he or she will not do so).

The seller may not declare the contract avoided if the buyer has paid the price, unless

- the buyer has performed his or her obligations under the contract late and the seller was unaware of that performance
- it is for any breach other than late performance, so long as it is within reasonable time of the seller knowing about the breach or after the additional time period for performance has expired.

Test your understanding 17

Anticipatory breach is where a party to the contract informs the other party (expressly or impliedly) that he or she does not intend to perform his or her obligations under the contract or it appears after the conclusion of the contract that a party is unable to perform a substantial part of his or her obligation.

Test your understanding 18

1 Keira has committed anticipatory breach of contract.

2 John is entitled to any of the remedies listed. However, depending on the circumstances of Keira's breach, demanding performance and giving additional time for such performance may be pointless.

3 False. John does not need to give notice as Keira has declared her own anticipatory breach.

Test your understanding 19

An 'instalment contract' is where the contract contains a number of separate parts, e.g. a contract to deliver goods in separate chunks over a long period of time.

Test your understanding 20

Damages for breach of contract by one party consist of a sum equal to the loss, including loss of profit, suffered by the other party as a consequence of the breach.

Test your understanding 21

True

Test your understanding 22

C Lolita has not incurred the cost of delivering the goods to Mikhail, but if she sells the goods to a third party, she will have incurred these costs as a result of Mikhail's breach.

Test your understanding 23

True

Test your understanding 24

B

Test your understanding 25

D Brigit may not claim damages as Anil has suffered an impediment beyond his control and beyond the scope of what could have been reasonably foreseen. However, as Anil has fundamentally failed to supply the goods, she may declare the contract avoided, or set an additional time for him to perform his obligations, once the factory is operational again.

Test your understanding 26

True

Chapter

5

International business transactions: risk and payment

Chapter learning objectives

Upon completion of this chapter you will be able to:

- explain and be able to apply the rules relating to the passing of risk under the United Nations Convention on Contracts for the International Sale of Goods 1980 (UNCCISG)
- define and explain the operation of bills of lading
- explain the operation of (i) bank transfers, (ii) bills of exchange, (iii) letters of credit, (iv) letters of comfort
- explain and be able to apply the rules of UNCITRAL Model Law on International Credit Transfer
- explain and be able to apply the rules of the United Nations Convention on International Bills of Exchange and Promissory Notes.

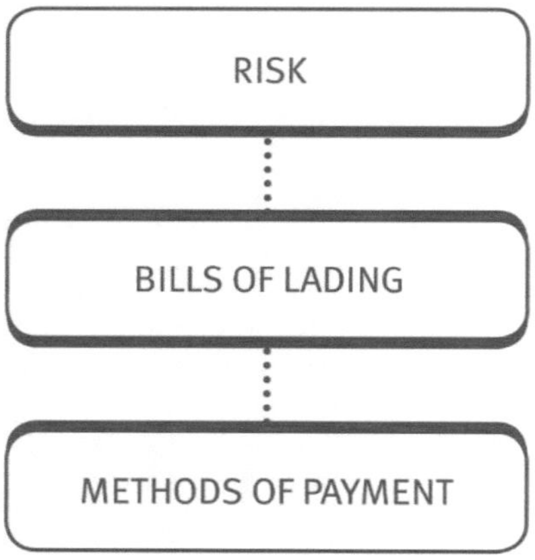

1 Passing of risk

Risk in goods means the responsibility for them, particularly if things go wrong and, e.g. insurance is required.

Illustration 1 – Passing of risk

Javine and Katrina had a contract for the sale of goods. Katrina put the goods on a ship to be delivered to Javine, who was going to collect them at the port at the other end of the journey. During the voyage, there was a storm and the ship containing the goods was sunk. The key question is who was responsible for the goods at the time they were sunk and therefore who bears the cost of the loss. The ICC Incoterms discussed earlier help determine when risk passes. E.g. if Javine and Katrina had a FOB or a FAS contract, then Javine would have been responsible for the goods when the ship sank. However, if they had a CIF or a CIP contract, it is likely that Katrina would have been responsible.

Test your understanding 1

Define the following types of contract:

I **FOB**

II **FAS**

III **CIF**

IV **CIP**

Test your understanding 2

Explain why the passing of risk is important.

Contracts involving carriage

- If the contract does not specify a place where the seller is going to hand over goods to the buyer, the risk passes to the buyer when the goods are given to the first carrier (Article 67(1)).
- If the contract specifies the place at which the seller is going to hand over the goods to the first carrier, the risk passes to the buyer when the goods are given to the first carrier at that place (Article 67(1)).
- In the above cases, risk only passes to the buyer if the goods are clearly identified to the contract (by markings or by shipping documents) (Article 67(2)). In UK, identification of goods usually involve appropriation of the goods to the contract.
- Goods may only be appropriated to the contract if they are clearly identified and separated from other goods.

e.g

Illustration 2 – Passing of risk

Leo and Michelle have a contract for Leo to deliver goods to Michelle by sea and road. Leo places goods with Dolphin Shipping, at Newtown on 24 June to be delivered to London port. The goods will be transferred to Truckers Ltd after they reach the port.

The contract between Leo and Michelle makes no reference to when risk passes. Risk passes on 24 June when the goods are placed with Dolphin Shipping (the first carrier), assuming that the goods are clearly appropriated to the contract.

If the contract between Leo and Michelle had made reference to which port the goods should have been shipped from, then risk would pass when the goods were placed with the first carrier at that place. So for instance, if Michelle had specified that the goods be shipped from Oldtown, then Leo would have had to ship the goods from there, and if he shipped them from Newtown, risk would have remained with him.

Test your understanding 3

Peter and Quinine have a contract for Peter to deliver goods to Quinine by ship. As the route is unusual, the goods will be transported by three shippers: Marine Enterprises, who will collect the goods from Peter and deliver them to the next carrier, Swift Shipping Co, who will accept the goods from Marine Enterprises and ship them to a named destination, then Caribbean Carriers Co will collect the goods from that destination and deliver the goods to Quinine.

When will risk pass to Quinine?

Goods sold in transit (Article 68)

- Risk in goods in transit passes to the buyer when the contract is concluded.
- If circumstances indicate, risk passes to the buyer when the goods were handed to the carrier who issued the documents relating to the contract of carriage.
- If at the time of the sale the goods were lost or damaged and the seller knew or ought to have known this, risk remains with the seller.

e.g

Illustration 3 – Passing of risk

Rashid and Sam are contracting for Rashid to buy a consignment of kitchen utensils from Sam. Sam has recently bought the utensils and they are in transit from Country A to Country B by sea. Sam has not had a chance to inspect the goods and will not have the chance to inspect them until he arrives in Country B on 5 June. Rashid wants to collect the 20 boxes that he has bought on 4 June. Rashid and Sam agree terms on 1 June. Risk in the goods therefore passes to Rashid on 1 June, as Sam has not had a chance to inspect the goods and therefore could not know if the goods were damaged. Rashid should make suitable arrangements to insure the goods from 1 June.

Test your understanding 4

When does risk pass to the buyer in a contract to buy goods in transit?

Other cases

- In other cases, risk passes to the buyer when he takes over the goods (Article 69(1)).
- If the buyer does not take over the goods at the appropriate time, the risk passes when the goods are placed at his or her disposal and in not collecting them, he or she is in breach of contract (Article 69(1).
- If the buyer is due to collect the goods from somewhere other than the seller's premises, risk passes when delivery is due and the buyer is aware that the goods are placed at his or her disposal at that place (Article 69(2)).
- If the goods are not appropriated to the contract, then risk does not pass until the goods are clearly appropriated to the contract (Article 69(3)).

Illustration 4 – Passing of risk

Wilfred and Xylon have a contract for Wilfred to provide Xylon with 1,000 leather bags. The contract states that the goods should be made available for Xylon to collect from Wilfred's factory on 1 June.

Risk will pass to Xylon when he collects the goods from Wilfred's factory on 1 June. If Xylon is late in collecting them, risk will still pass to him on that date. So, e.g. if Xylon cannot collect the goods until 2 June and the factory burns down on the evening of 1 June, Xylon must still pay for the goods and bear the loss of the goods, because risk had passed to him.

Test your understanding 5

Yazmina and Zara have a contract for Zara to sell Yazmina 1,000 metres of a fabric made to Yazmina's design. Yazmina is due to collect the goods from a third party within a week of Zara making Yazmina aware that the goods are available there. Zara delivers the fabric to the third party premises on 1 June. She telephones Yazmina to tell her the goods are available there on 2 June. Yazmina inspects the fabric on 5 June, but as she wants to transport it in a different vehicle, she does not collect the fabric until 6 June.

Risk passes to Yazmina on:

A **6 June**

B **5 June**

C **2 June**

D **1 June**

2 Bills of lading

A bill of lading is a document which is issued by a carrier to the shipper acknowledging that they have received the shipment of goods and that they have been placed on board a particular vessel which is bound for a particular destination. It states the terms on which the goods are to be carried.

The bill of lading can therefore be an important document in determining when risk has passed from buyer to seller.

There are four types of bills of lading:

- Inland bill of lading: this is a contract for transporting goods overland to an exporter's international carrier.
- Ocean bill of lading: this is a contract for transporting goods from an exporter to a specified foreign market overseas.
- Through bill of lading: this is a contract that covers both the inland and the international transport of goods.
- Airway bill: this is a contract for both international and domestic flights to a specified destination. This is a non-negotiable document that only serves as a receipt for the shipper.

Illustration 5 – Bills of lading

This is an example of an airway bill.

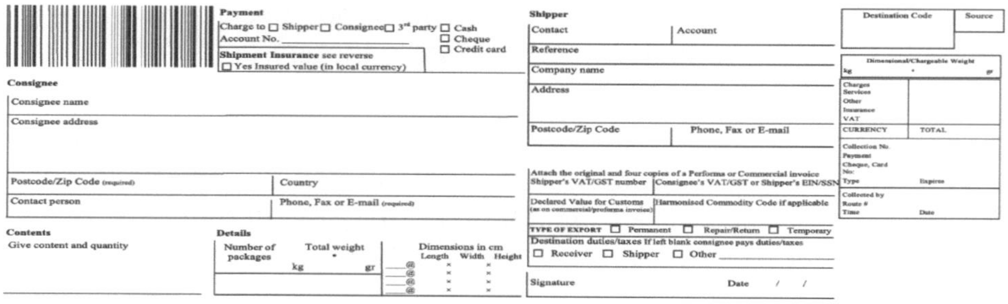

Payment
Charge to ☐ Shipper ☐ Consignee ☐ 3rd party ☐ Cash
Account No. ☐ Cheque
☐ Credit card
Shipment Insurance see reverse
☐ Yes Insured value (in local currency)

Consignee
Consignee name
Consignee address
Postcode/Zip Code (required) | Country
Contact person | Phone, Fax or E-mail (required)

Contents
Give content and quantity

Details
Number of packages | Total weight kg • gr
Dimensions in cm: Length × Width × Height

Shipper
Contact | Account
Reference
Company name
Address
Postcode/Zip Code | Phone, Fax or E-mail

Attach the original and four copies of a Performa or Commercial invoice
Shipper's VAT/GST number | Consignee's VAT/GST or Shipper's EIN/SSN
Declared Value for Customs (as on commercial/proforma invoice) | Harmonised Commodity Code if applicable
TYPE OF EXPORT ☐ Permanent ☐ Repair/Return ☐ Temporary
Destination duties/taxes If left blank consignee pays duties/taxes
☐ Receiver ☐ Shipper ☐ Other
Signature Date / /

Destination Code | Source
Dimensional/Chargeable Weight kg • gr
Charges
Services
Other
Insurance
VAT
CURRENCY | TOTAL
Collection No.
Payment
Cheque, Card No:
Type Expires
Collected by
Route #
Time Date

A bill of lading has three purposes:

- It is a formal receipt by the ship owner for the goods.
- It is evidence of the contract of carriage between the original parties to the bill of lading and a contract of carriage between the carrier and a third party.
- It can be a document of title to the goods.

There are two general types of bills of lading:

A **non-negotiable bill of lading** requires the carrier to deliver the goods to the consignee (buyer) named in the bill of lading. The person to whom the goods are being sent normally needs to show the bill of lading to obtain the release of the goods. An airway bill is an example of a non-negotiable bill of lading.

A **negotiable bill of lading** gives the person who has legal ownership of the bill the ownership of the goods and the right to re-route the shipment. These are issued to shipper's order rather than to a named consignee (the buyer). The carrier will therefore hold the goods until it receives the original bill of lading that has been endorsed by the seller. The seller must endorse the bill of lading and deliver it to the bank in order to receive payment if the payment is made by the letter of credit.

Think back to the seller's obligation (set out in chapter 3) to hand over the appropriate documents to the buyer. The seller needs to ensure that the buyer has the bill of lading to obtain the goods.

Test your understanding 6

Define a bill of lading.

Test your understanding 7

Define a non-negotiable bill of lading.

Test your understanding 8

Define a negotiable bill of lading.

Test your understanding 9

Ahmed (seller) is sending goods to Beatrice (buyer) by sea under a negotiable bill of lading. The shipper is Carriage Inc.

Answer the following questions relating to this shipment.

1 **Carriage Inc has heard that there are shipping delays on the proposed route due to bad weather. The company has recommended that the goods be shipped by a different route. Who has authority to confirm the re-route of the goods?**

Ahmed

Beatrice

Carriage Inc

2 **Beatrice will be able to collect the goods from the docks with no further action from Ahmed.**

True or False

3 **Ahmed must endorse the bill of lading and present it to the bank to receive payment.**

True or False

3 Methods of payment

Paying for goods in international transactions can pose difficulties where people come from nations with different banking practices, and even making bank transfers across national boundaries is more difficult than for domestic bank transfers. We shall look at the following types of payment:

- bank transfers
- bills of exchange
- letters of credit
- letters of comfort.

The United Nations (UN) has two further conventions/model laws on payments which we shall also look at:

- UNCITRAL Model Law on International Credit Transfer 1992.
- UN Convention on International Bills of Exchange and International Promissory Notes 1988.

4 Bank transfers

The UNCITRAL Model Law on International Credit Transfers defines a credit transfer as 'the series of operations, beginning with the originator's payment order, made for the purpose of placing funds at the disposal of a beneficiary. The term includes any payment order issued by the originator's bank, or any intermediary bank intended to carry out the originator's payment order' (Article 2(a)).

Originator means the issuer of the first payment order in a credit transfer.

Intermediary bank means any receiving bank other than the originator's bank and the beneficiary's bank.

e.g

Illustration 6 – Bank transfers

You are probably familiar with domestic bank transfers. Many people are now paid by direct bank transfer from their company's bank account to their own. In these days of internet banking, many people make direct bank transfers from their own accounts to pay bills. In principle, international bank transfers are the same as these domestic ones, with certain added complications resulting from the fact that the transfer is being made across national borders.

5 UNCITRAL Model Law on International Credit Transfers

Categories of transaction covered by the Model Law

The Model Law covers credit transfers where:

- The sending bank and receiving bank are in different states (Article 1(1)).
- The credit transfer involves other entities that execute payment orders in the same way as banks as a normal part of their business (Article 1(2)).
- For the purpose of determining the sphere of application of this law, branches and separate offices of a bank in different states are separate banks (Article 1(3)).
- Note that the Model law allows the parties to a credit transfer to vary their rights and obligations under this Model Law by agreement (Article 4).

The definition of credit transfer was given above. The following definitions will also be useful:

- Payment order is an unconditional instruction by a sender to a receiving bank to place at the disposal of a beneficiary a fixed or determinable amount of money if the receiving bank is to be reimbursed by the sender and the instruction does not provide that the payment is to be made at the request of the beneficiary (i.e. the seller) (Article 2(b)).
- Sender means the person who issued a payment order (i.e. the buyer), but includes the sending bank (Article 2(e)).

Obligations of sender of payment order – Chapter III, Art.5

The key obligation of the sender is to pay the receiving bank for the payment order when the bank accepts it. Problems arise if:

- the person sending the payment order did not have authority to do so
- the payment order was forged.

There are three steps in the Model Law to prevent this happening:

- The sender is only bound by the payment order if the sender issued it himself or it was issued by another person who had authority to bind the sender (Article 5(4)(a) and (b)).
- A purported sender is bound if the payment order is subject to authentication procedures agreed between the sending and receiving banks, and the receiving bank had carried out this authentication (Article 5(2)(b)).
- A sending and receiving bank cannot agree between themselves that the purported sender is bound in this way if the authentication process is not commercially reasonable (Article 5(2)(a) by implication).

Bank transfers

Most banks have authentication procedures to ensure that bank transfers are valid, e.g. they might require pre-registration by a company in order to enable that company to make bank transfers, and as part of that process, might require a list of signatures from all the people authorised to initiate bank transfers, so that the signature can be verified when the bank transfer is requested.

The Model Law in effect says that people are entitled to rely on these procedures and, if having gone through the procedures, the bank accepts the bank transfer, then the sender is bound by the transfer and must honour it, even if it was incorrectly made.

The only way that a sender can avoid this situation is if it proves that the payment order resulted from the actions of someone who was:

- not a present or former employee of the purported sender
- not a person who had such a relationship with the purported sender that enabled that person to access the authentication procedure, unless it can be shown that the sender was at fault in allowing the authentication procedure to be found out through his or her own carelessness.

In other words, if a former employee requested a bank transfer because he or she was aware of the authentication process, the sender is liable, because the authentication process should have been able to cope with former employees.

Sender's payment to receiving bank

For the purpose of UNCITRAL Model Law on International Credit Transfers, payment of the sender's obligation under art.5(6) to pay the receiving bank occurs:

A if the receiving bank debits an account of the sender with the receiving bank, when the debit is made

e.g **Illustration 7 – UNCITRAL Model Law**

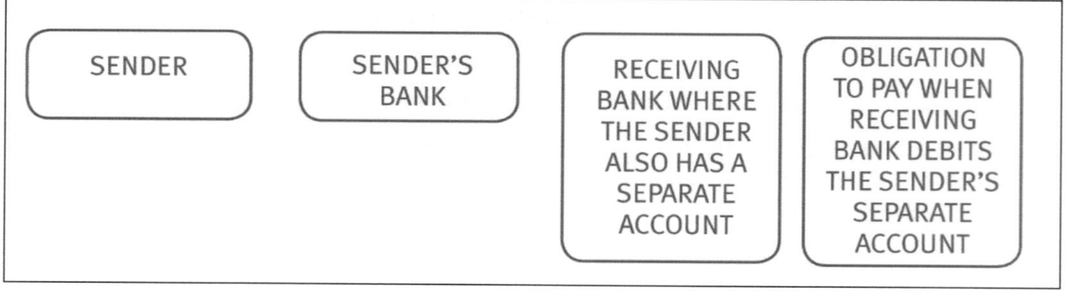

B if the sender is a bank and the above does not apply:

C I when the sender has already caused a credit to be entered on account of the receiving bank and this credit is used or if not used, on the banking day following the day on which the credit is available for use and the receiving bank is aware of the availability of the credit to use, or

II when the sender has already caused a credit to be entered on account of the receiving bank but in a third bank and this credit is used or, if not used, on the banking day following the day on which the credit is available for use and the receiving bank is aware of this fact, or

III when a final settlement is made in favour of the receiving bank at a central bank at which the receiving bank maintains an account, or

IV when final settlement is made in favour of the receiving bank in accordance with the applicable rules.

e.g **Illustration 8 – UNCITRAL Model Law**

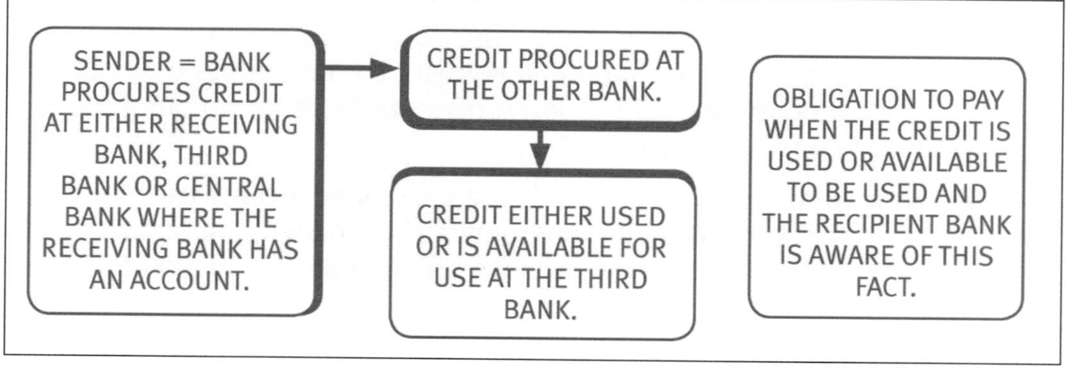

Obligations of receiving bank other than the beneficiary's bank

The receiving bank is required to execute a payment order that it accepts. Acceptance is indicated by:

- issuing a payment order to the beneficiary's bank to carry out the payment order received (Article 72(c))
- (in a funds transfer system that requires all payment orders received from other banks in the same system must be executed) by receiving such a payment order (Article 72(a))
- debiting the sender's account at the receiving bank for the value of the payment order (Article 72(d))
- giving notice of intention to the sender of acceptance (Article 72(b))
- failing to give notice that it does not accept the payment order within the required time (within one banking day of receipt) (Article 72(e)).

Execution is by:

- placing funds at the disposal of the beneficiary (i.e. in his or her bank account) (Article 10(1)), or
- if the receiving bank is not the beneficiary's bank, the receiving bank issuing a payment order to the beneficiary's bank, which is then obliged to place funds at the beneficiary's disposal (Article 8(2)).

Problems may arise with credit transfers, e.g. if there are inconsistencies in the payment order (e.g. the amount given in words and numbers do not match) (Article 8(3), (4) and (5)). When this happens, the receiving bank is obliged to:

- notify the sender of the problem (Article 11)
- seek the assistance of the next receiving bank to complete the bank transfer if the problem arose at the receiving bank (Article 13)
- repay the sending bank the amount credited to it, with interest, if the credit transfer fails (Article 14).

Bank's liability for failure to perform one of its obligations

In addition to the money back (+ interest) guarantee outlined above, a bank may also have liability to pay additional interest if the credit transfer is delayed through its fault (Article 17(1)).

Completion of credit transfer and its consequences

A credit transfer is completed when the beneficiary's bank accepts a payment order for the benefit of the beneficiary (Article 19). At this point:

- the matter becomes a private banking issue between the beneficiary and his or her bank
- the other banks in the process have fulfilled their obligations.

Test your understanding 10

Define international credit transfer.

Test your understanding 11

Define payment order, in the context of international credit transfer.

Test your understanding 12

On 7 May, Adrienne entered into a contract to buy some goods from Bailey and has agreed to pay by international credit transfer. She uses the National Bank of Caru (NBC) and Bailey uses the National Bank of Dentur (NBD).

Adrienne instructs NBC to initiate a payment order to NBD for the benefit of Bailey on 4 June. NBC sends the appropriate paperwork to NBD on that date. NBD has an account at NBC. NBC credits that account with the amount due to Bailey on 5 June. NBD transfers the money to Bailey's account at NBD on 6 June.

I **The credit transfer is initiated on:**

A 7 May

B 4 June

C 5 June

D 6 June

II **The credit transfer is accepted by NBD on:**

A 7 May

B 4 June

C 5 June

D 6 June

III **The credit transfer is completed on:**

A 7 May

B 4 June

C 5 June

D 6 June

6 Bills of exchange

A bill of exchange is an unconditional order in writing by one person to another to pay a specified sum to a specified person or bearer on a particular date (s1 (1) Bills of Exchange Act 1882). In essence, a bill of exchange is therefore an IOU used in international trade.

Illustration 9 – Bills of exchange

A common example of a bill of exchange used by individuals which you may be familiar with is a cheque. The piece of paper itself has no value, but the cheque will be cashed by the payee and the banker will pay the amount stated on it, on demand.

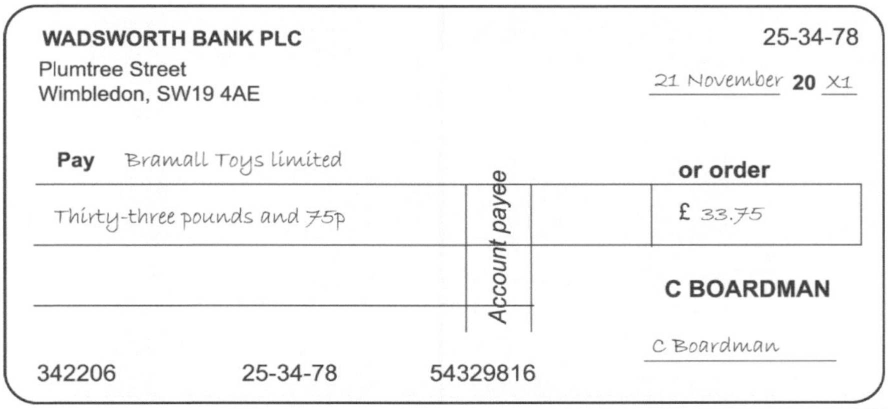

There are various terms associated with bills of exchange that help us see more clearly what one is. These are:

Definitions associated with bills of exchange:

- Drawer – the person who makes the order and draws up the bill.
- Drawee – the party on whom the bills is drawn, usually a bank.
- Payee – the person to whom the bill is payable.
- Acceptor – the drawee once he or she has assented to the bill. The drawer must accept in writing with a signature, a simple signature by the drawee is sufficient.
- Holder – the person who holds the bill (this might be the payee, the drawer or the drawee). There are three different types of holders: holders in due course, holders for value and mere holders.
- Endorsee – anyone to whom the bill is transferred to make them the beneficiary of the bill.

e.g

Illustration 10 – Bills of exchange

Returning to our simple illustration of the cheque (above), you can see some of these terms in action. The drawer is the person who has drawn up the bill. On a cheque, you can see their name printed below the box showing the numerical total. The drawer has to sign the cheque in order to validate it. The drawee is the bank who has originally issued the cheque to the drawer. The name of this bank is shown clearly on the top of the cheque. Once the drawer has written out the cheque and signed it, the bank becomes liable to pay the sum from the drawer's bank account. The payee is written in by the drawer on the first line, where the cheque says 'pay'.

e.g

Illustration 11 – Bills of exchange

Here is an example of an international bill of exchange

> *INTERNATIONAL BILL OF EXCHANGE (UNCITRAL CONVENTION)*
>
> *DRAWN BY Daneco Industries Inc, UNITED STATES OF AMERICA*
>
> *ON 1 June 2006*
>
> *IN FAVOUR OF EasyLife Co, UNITED KINGDOM*
>
> *ON FUNDS AT National Bank, UNITED STATES OF AMERICA*
>
> *TO THE SUM OF $257,994.06*
>
> *TO BE PAID AT London, United Kingdom*
>
> *Signature on behalf of DaneCo Industries* ....
>
> *Signature on behalf of National Bank* ....

Once the drawee has signed the bill and thus accepted it:

- the drawee becomes the principal debtor on the bill
- the drawee is primarily liable to pay for it
- therefore the drawee will ensure prior to acceptance that the drawer has sufficient funds to pay the drawee the value of the bill of exchange.

A bill of exchange is a transferable and negotiable asset.

- The payee may sell the bill of exchange to another party.
- To entitle the other party to benefit from the bill (in effect, become the new payee) the payee must endorse the bill of exchange in favour of the new owner.
- This can be achieved by writing the new owner's name on the bill with the signature of the former payee.

Test your understanding 13

Define bill of exchange.

Test your understanding 14

Define payee in the context of bills of exchange.

Test your understanding 15

Define drawee in the context of bills of exchange.

Test your understanding 16

Define drawer in the context of bills of exchange.

7 UN Convention on International Bills of Exchange and International Promissory Notes

Scope of application and form of the instrument

As defined by the Convention, a bill of exchange is a written instrument which contains an unconditional order whereby the drawer directs the drawee to pay a definite sum of money to the payee or to his or her order, which is payable on demand or at a definite time, is dated and is signed by the drawer (Article 3).

Per the Convention, a promissory note is a written instrument which contains an unconditional promise whereby the maker undertakes to pay a definite sum of money to the payee or to his or her order, is payable on demand or at a definite time, is dated and is signed by the maker.

The Convention applies to international bills of exchange and promissory notes that contain certain required elements:

- The instrument must contain the words 'International bill of exchange (UNCITRAL Convention)' (Article 1(1)) or 'International promissory note (UNCITRAL Convention)' (Article 1(2)) whichever is relevant, in its heading and text.
- The bill of exchange must specify at least two of the following places and indicate that any two of them are situated in different states: the place where the bill is drawn, the place next to the signature of the drawer, the place next to the name of the drawee, the place next to the name of the payee, the place of payment (Article 2(1)).
- The promissory note must specify at least two of the following places and indicate that any two of them are situated in different states: the place where the note is made, the place indicated next to the name of the maker, the place indicated next to the name of the payee, the place of payment (Article 2(2)).

Interpretation of the Convention

The sum payable by an instrument is:

- deemed to be definite (although the instrument might state that it is to be paid with interest, or in instalments, according to a rate of exchange indicated in the instrument, or in a currency other than the one in which it is expressed in) (Article 7)
- the sum expressed in words if there is a discrepancy between the sum expressed in numbers and the sum expressed in words (Article 8(1))
- deemed to be expressed in the currency of the state where the payment is to be made if the exact currency is not specified and the currency specified is in general use (e.g. 'dollars', which is a different currency in the US, Canada, Hong Kong, New Zealand and Australia) (Article 8(3)).

Interest payable under an instrument:

- is deemed to run from the date of the instrument, unless otherwise specified (Article 8(4))
- is deemed to be payable only if the rate at which it is to be paid is specified (Article 8(5))
- may be fixed rate or variable rate (the instrument may specify maximum and minimum rates if the rate is variable) (Article 8(6)).

An instrument is:

- payable on demand if it states so or if no time of payment is expressed (Article 9(1)(a) and (b))
- payable at a definite time if it states that it is payable on or after a stated date; at a fixed period after the date of the instrument; by instalments at successive dates or by instalments at successive dates with the stipulation in the instrument that upon default payment of any instalment the unpaid balance becomes due (Article 9(3)).

An instrument may be made by several parties and may be payable to several parties, in which case:

- it is payable to all of them (together) (Article 10(3))
- unless the instrument is clear that it is payable to any one of the payees (Article 10(3))
- the rights of a holder may be exercised only by all of them (Article 10(3))
- unless the instrument is clear that it is payable to any of them in possession of the instrument may exercise the rights of a holder (Article 10(3)).

Transfers of the instrument

An instrument may be transferred:

- by endorsement (written on the instrument and signed) and delivery to the endorsee (Article 13(a))
- by delivery only if the last endorsement is in blank (a signature only) (Article 13(b)).

A holder is (i) the payee in possession of the instrument, (ii) a person in possession of an instrument that has been endorsed to him or her, even if the endorsement was forged (Article 1(a) and (b)).

A protected holder is the holder of an instrument which was complete when he or she took it (or incomplete when he or she took it, but it contained the words 'international bill of exchange (UNCITRAL Convention)' in the heading and was signed and has since been completed with authority) provided that he or she is not aware of any problems associated with the bill. Holders are assumed to be protected unless the reverse is true (Article 29).

If the endorsement is in blank (a signature alone, or a signature stating that the bill is payable to the person in possession of it) the holder may:

- further endorse it in blank or by a special endorsement (signature accompanied by an indication of to whom the bill is endorsed) (Article 16(a))
- convert the blank endorsement to a special endorsement in his or her own favour (Article 16(b))
- transfer the instrument by delivery to another person (Article 16(c)).

Under Article 17(1) a bill cannot be transferred if the bill or an endorsement on the bill contains words such as:

- not negotiable
- not transferable
- not to order
- pay X only.

An endorsement:

- must be unconditional (or it will be deemed to be, even if it appears to contain conditions) (Article 18(1))
- must relate to the entire sum of the bills or it is ineffective (Article 19)
- is deemed to arise in the order in which it appears on the instrument (relevant if there are two or more endorsements) (Article 20).

Under Article 21(1) an endorsement containing the words 'for collection', 'for deposit', 'value in collection', 'by procuration', 'pay any bank':

- authorises the endorsee to exercise all rights of the instrument (Article 21(1)(a))
- may endorse the instrument only for the purposes of collection (Article 21(1)(b))
- makes the endorsee subject only to the claims and defences which may be set up against the endorser (Article 21(1)(c))
- makes the endorsee not liable on the instrument to any subsequent holder (Article 21(2)).

Under Article 22(1) an endorsement containing the words 'value in security', 'value in pledge', or any other words indicating a pledge:

- authorises the endorsee to exercise all rights of the instrument (Article 22(1)(a))
- allows the endorsee to endorse the instrument only for the purposes of collection (Article 22(1)(b))
- makes the holder subject to particular claims and defences set out in Article 28 or 30 of the Convention (see below) (Article 22(1)(c))
- makes the endorsee not liable on the instrument to any subsequent holder (Article 22(2)).

Transfer warranties

Unless otherwise agreed, a person who transfers an instrument makes an implied representation that:

- the instrument is of a good quality (i.e. it does not bear any forged or unauthorised signature and has not been materially altered) (Article 45(1)(a) and (b))
- there are no facts that could impair the right of the transferee to payment of the bill (Article 45(1)(c)).

A holder has rights to the instrument unless:

- he or she took the instrument with knowledge of a valid claim by another person (Article 45(2) by implication)
- he or she obtained the instrument by fraud
- he or she obtained the instrument by theft.

Liabilities of the parties

The following rules apply with respect to liability in relation to a bill of exchange:

- A person is generally not liable on a bill of exchange unless he or she signs it (Article 33(1)).
- If someone signs a bill with a different name he or she is still liable as if he or she had signed his or her own name (Article 33(2)).
- If a person's signature is forged, that person is not liable on the bill unless he or she consented to the forgery (Article 34).
- If a bill is materially altered, the person who signs it after the alteration is liable according to the terms of the altered text (Article 35(1)(a)).
- A bill may be signed by an agent (so long it is clearly stated that he or she is signing on behalf of a principal, the agent will not be liable, and the principal will) (Article 36).
- The drawer undertakes to pay the bill if it is dishonoured (Article 38(1)).
- The drawer may limit his or her liability for acceptance or payment by an express stipulation in the bill (Article 38(2)).
- The maker undertakes to pay the promissory note under Article 39(1) and may not limit his or her liability under Article 39(2).
- The drawee is not liable on the bill unless he or she accepts it (Article 40(1)).
- Once the drawee has accepted the bill (which must be unqualified and written on the bill) he or she is liable on it (Article 40(2)).
- The endorser undertakes to pay the instrument to the holder if it is dishonoured (Article 44(1)).
- The endorser may limit his or her liability for acceptance or payment by an express stipulation in the bill (Article 44(2)).

Guarantees and avals

Payment of an instrument may be guaranteed under Art.46(1):

- The guarantee must be written on the instrument or attached to it (Article 46(2)).
- By writing the words 'guaranteed', 'aval' or 'good as aval' or words of similar import (Article 46(3)).

Presenting the bill for payment

Under Article 55, to obtain payment of the bill it must be duly 'presented for payment'.

An instrument is duly presented for payment if it is presented in accordance with the following rules:

(a) The holder must present the instrument to the drawee or to the acceptor or to the maker on a business day at a reasonable hour

(b) A note signed by two or more makers may be presented to any one of them, unless the note clearly indicates otherwise

(c) If the drawee or the acceptor or the maker is dead, presentment must be made to the persons who under the applicable law are his or her heirs or the persons entitled to administer his or her estate

(d) Presentment for payment may be made to a person or authority other than the drawee, the acceptor or the maker if that person or authority is entitled under the applicable law to pay the instrument

(e) An instrument which is not payable on demand must be presented for payment on the date of maturity or on one of the two business days which follow

(f) An instrument which is payable on demand must be presented for payment within one year of its date

(g) An instrument must be presented for payment

   (i) At the place of payment specified on the instrument

   (ii) If no place of payment is specified, at the address of the drawee or the acceptor or the maker indicated in the instrument; or

   (iii) If no place of payment is specified and the address of the drawee or the acceptor or the maker is not indicated, at the principal place of business or habitual residence of the drawee or the acceptor or the maker

(h) An instrument which is presented at a clearing-house is duly presented for payment if the law of the place where the clearing-house is located or the rules or customs of that clearing-house so provide.

Dishonour for non-payment

Under Article 58, a bill is dishonoured by non-payment:

(a) If payment is refused upon due presentment or if the holder cannot obtain the payment to which he or she is entitled under this Convention

(b) If presentment for payment is dispensed with and the instrument is unpaid at maturity.

Other practical issues

The Convention allows a number of provisions to benefit modern commercial practice.

- Instruments with floating rates of interest: instruments are allowed to carry a variable rate of interest without losing negotiability.
- Rates of exchange outside instrument: reference may be made to a rate of exchange not specified in the instrument (e.g. the bank exchange rate in X country on X date).
- Instruments payable in instalments: instruments are allowed to specify payments in instalments on successive dates. These may contain an acceleration clause stating that in the event of a default in payment, the entire unpaid balance becomes payable.
- Instruments denominated and payable in a monetary unit of account: i.e. a currency other than the official currencies of nation states, such as the European Currency Unit (ECU) or the Unit of Account of the Preferential Trade Area for Eastern and Southern African States (UAPTA).
- Foreign currency obligations: except where the instrument indicates a specified currency in which the payment must be made, payment must be made in the currency in which the bill is expressed.

Further notes:

- Rules on lost instruments: a party from whom payment of a lost instrument is claimed may require the person claiming payment to give security in order to indemnify it for any loss which it may suffer by reason of the subsequent payment of the lost instrument (Article 78).
- Protest: the Convention allows four business days for protest to be made.
- Limitation on actions: the Convention sets the limitation on actions period at four years (Article 84(1)).

Test your understanding 17

Define international bills of exchange within the context of the UN Convention on such instruments.

Test your understanding 18

Define international promissory notes within the context of the UN Convention on such instruments.

Test your understanding 19

Emil has drafted a bill of exchange in favour of Fernando. There is a discrepancy between the sum written in numbers, which is '$30,000' and the written sum, which is 'thirteen thousand dollars'. Fernando will receive:

A **$30,000**

B **$13,000**

Test your understanding 20

Julio has drawn up an international bill of exchange in favour of Kathleen, which has been accepted by Julio's bank. Kathleen endorses the bill in favour of Leander, who in turn endorses the bill 'for collection' in favour of Mary. Mary in her turn, endorses the bill 'for collection' in favour of Nathan.

Which of the following is potentially liable on the bill.

A **Julio**

B **Julio's bank**

C **Kathleen**

D **Leander**

E **Mary**

F **Nathan**

8 Letters of credit

A letter of credit is an undertaking by a bank to make a payment to a named beneficiary within a specified time, against the presentation of documents which comply strictly with the terms of the letter of credit.

There are four parties to a letter of credit:

- The buyer, who is known as the applicant.
- The buyer's bank, which is known as the issuer or issuing bank.
- The seller/payee, who is known as the beneficiary.
- The beneficiary's bank. This will be the correspondent bank which may be advising only or confirming.

e.g

Illustration 12 – Letters of credit

Letter of Credit (Irrevocable)

_______________ [Bank]
_______________ [Address]
_______________ [County]
_______________ [Date]

Irrevocable Credit

All drafts drawn must indicate credit number.

Gentlemen: You are hereby authorised to value on the _____ [bank], of the City of ______________________________, County of________________, for any sum or sums up to the aggregate of ________________ ($) US Dollars

For the account of____
Available by your drafts at ________________ [specify] day's sight.

Drafts are to be accepted only against delivery of the following documents:

Documents of title must be dated not later than __________, 20_____.

All drafts against this credit are to be drawn and negotiated before ______ [date].

We hereby agree with the drawers, endorsers, and bona fide holders of drafts drawn in compliance with the terms of this credit that they shall be honoured on presentation.

Yours truly,

Your Name

A letter of credit:

- ensures that the seller has performed all the requirements of the underlying sales contract before payment is made
- is an autonomous transaction. According to the principle of autonomy of credits any conditions in the underlying contracts are irrelevant. Any condition, which the buyer wants to ensure is satisfied before payment is made, must be stipulated in the letter of credit itself
- provides security for the seller, as it promises that if the appropriate documents are presented to the bank, the seller will receive payment
- provides security for the buyer, as it undertakes to examine the documents to ensure that all appropriate documents are tendered

- transfers the risk of non-payment to the buyer's bank, so long as the seller fulfils all his or her obligations, as the bank is bound to pay the money on presentation of the documents, even if the buyer does not pay the bank
- is therefore the most secure form of payment for the seller other than cash in advance.

Procedures

To create and use a letter of credit, the following steps would be taken:

- The exporter (seller) and importer (buyer) agree the terms of their contract.
- The buyer applies to their bank for a letter of credit.
- The buyer's bank (issuer) issues the letter of credit and sends it to the seller's bank (advising bank).
- The advising bank informs the seller that the letter of credit has been opened in his or her favour.
- The seller ships the goods.
- The seller presents the information required or the letter of credit (such as invoice, bill of lading) to the advising bank.
- The advising bank checks that the documents are the correct ones and, if so, pays the seller.
- The advising bank forwards the documents to the issuing bank.
- The issuer checks that the documents are the correct ones and, if so, pays the seller's bank.
- The issuer debits the buyer and releases the documents to the buyer, including the bill of lading so that the buyer can obtain the goods from the carrier.

Types of letters of credit

There are numerous types of letters of credit:

- Revocable: these can be amended or cancelled at any time prior to the payment being made by the buyer without the seller's consent. These therefore offer little protection to the seller and are rare.
- Irrevocable: these cannot be amended or cancelled without the agreement of all relevant parties (buyer, seller, banks). The ICC Uniform Customs and Practice for Documentary Credits states that all letters of credit falling within its scope are irrevocable unless otherwise stated (Article 6(c)).
- Unconfirmed: these are sent by the advising bank directly to the seller without guarantee that the bank will make payment, but confirming that the letter is valid.

- Confirmed: these contain an added confirmation by the advising bank that payment will be made so long as the compliant documents are presented by the seller. The confirming bank usually makes an additional charge for this service.
- Standby: this is a letter of credit used as support when a different, less secure method of payment has been agreed between the parties, so that if payment fails, the seller may claim payment by letter of credit.
- Revolving: this is used where there are regular shipments of the same commodity to the buyer so that a different letter does not have to be issued each time. The letter must state that it is revolving (either by time, until a set level of credit runs out, or by value, so that the same value is used each time).
- Transferable: this is one where the seller has the right to request that the paying bank make the payment to a third party (e.g. the person from whom the seller has bought the goods in question).
- Back-to-back: this is slightly more complex than a transferable letter of credit, and is where the original letter of credit is used as security to establish a second letter of credit in favour of the seller's supplier.

Test your understanding 21

Define letters of credit.

Test your understanding 22

An irrevocable letter of credit gives security to:

A The buyer

B The seller

Test your understanding 23

Explain the difference between a confirmed and an unconfirmed letter of credit.

Test your understanding 24

Alice, the buyer, is setting up a letter of credit to pay Bernard, the seller, for goods he is shipping to her. What steps must Alice take?

9 Letters of comfort

A letter of comfort is a tool used assure a creditor that a third party will ensure payment of its debtor's debts.

Letters of comfort are generally used by parent companies to encourage potential lenders or clients to extend credit to their subsidiary companies by stating their intention to provided financial backing for those subsidiary companies.

As such letters of comfort do not normally amount to actual promises, remaining mere statements of intention, they cannot be accepted so as to constitute a binding contractual agreement. As a consequence the holders of letters of comfort have no legal recourse if the parent company subsequently fails to recognise and give effect to them.

Kleinwort Benson Ltd v Malaysia Mining Corporation Berhad (1989)

Facts: Kleinwort Benson lent £5m to a Malaysian mining company and were provided with a letter of comfort from Malaysia Mining Corporation.

Held: The Court of Appeal held that the specific letter of comfort in this case, was not binding, apparently for the reason that the plaintiff was aware of the risky nature of letters of comfort and charged additional interest on the loan. Nonetheless the court held that in different circumstances a letter of comfort could form the basis for an action in breach of contract.

In effect, it is a reference to the bank from a third party on behalf of the buyer, who wishes to make the payment.

10 Chapter summary

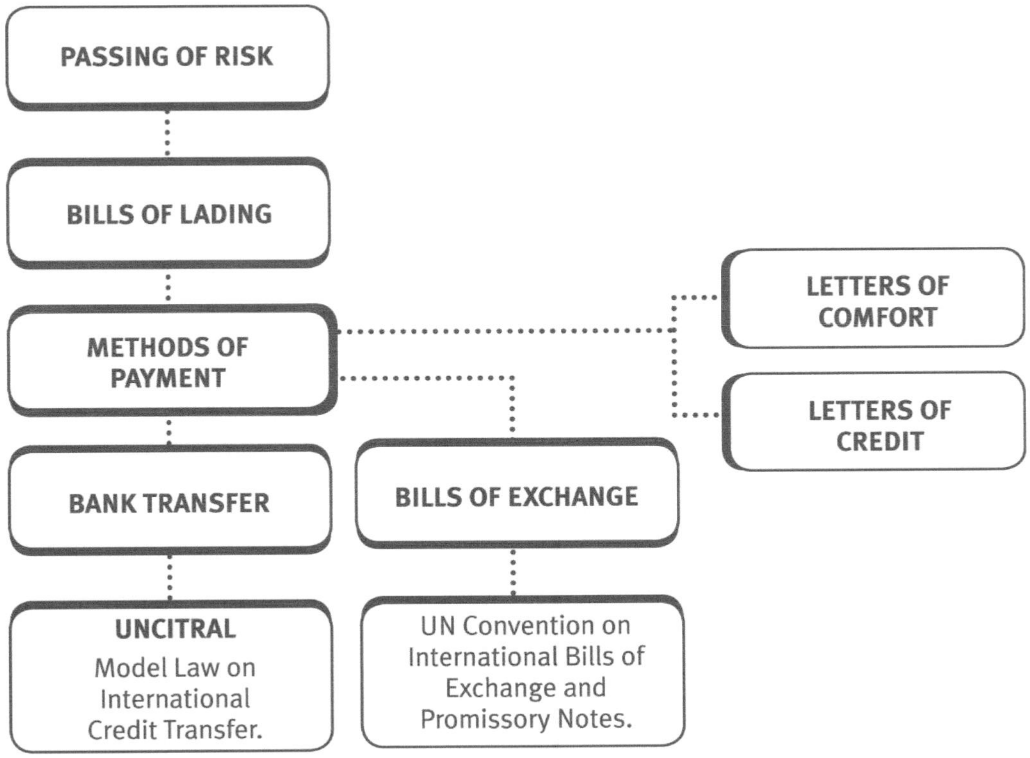

Test your understanding answers

Test your understanding 1

I FOB stands for Free on Board. This Incoterm is specific to delivery by ship. The seller has delivered the goods when they pass the ship's rail at the named port of shipment. The seller bears the responsibility for clearing the goods for export, but the buyer is responsible for the goods from when they are placed on the ship and bears the costs from then on.

II FAS stands for Free Alongside Ship. This term is also specific to delivery by ship. In this case the seller also has to bear export charges, but has delivered the goods once they are standing alongside the ship at the port. The buyer is responsible for getting them on the ship and from them on.

III CIF. This stands for Cost, Insurance and Freight. This means the seller must pay the cost and freight involved in getting the goods to a named destination, but the risk passes to the buyer when the goods are placed on the ship. In addition, the seller must pay for insurance to cover the goods when they are in transit. The seller need only pay for the minimum insurance, so if the buyer wants more comprehensive insurance, the buyer must make arrangements for that. Higher-level insurance may also be stipulated in the underlying contract.

IV CIP. This stands for Carriage and Insurance Paid. This means that the seller pays for the freight of the carriage of the goods to the named destination. The seller is required to clear the goods for export. The risk passes from the seller when the goods are at the named destination. In addition, the seller must pay for insurance for the goods during carriage. Damage to the goods or loss of them after risk has passed to the buyer does not free him or her from the need to pay the price of the goods, unless the loss of damage is the seller's fault (Article 66). It is clear then that when the risk 'passes' is an important issue. UNCCISG sets out the rules in Chapter IV titled 'Passing of risk'.

Test your understanding 2

It is important that the parties to a contract know when risk passes because they need to know when they are responsible for the goods and will bear the cost of loss or damage. It will also be important in order to determine who has the insurable interests in the goods and accordingly who can claim under the insurance policy in case of loss.

Test your understanding 3

Assuming that there is no extra provision in the contract for when risk passes and that the goods are clearly marked to the contract, risk will pass to Quinine when the goods are placed with Marine Enterprises.

Test your understanding 4

Risk passes to the buyer when the contract is concluded.

Test your understanding 5

C Risk passes to Yazmina when the goods are made available to her at the specified place and she is made aware of that.

Test your understanding 6

A document which is issued by a carrier to the shipper acknowledging that they have received the shipment of goods and that they have been placed on board a particular vessel which is bound for a particular destination.

Test your understanding 7

A **non-negotiable bill of lading** requires the carrier to deliver the goods to the consignee (buyer) named in the bill of lading. The person to whom the goods are being sent normally needs to show the bill of lading to obtain the release of the goods.

Test your understanding 8

A **negotiable bill of lading** gives the person who has legal ownership of the bill the ownership of the goods and the right to re-route the shipment. These are issued to shipper's order rather than to a named consignee (the buyer). The carrier will therefore hold the goods until it receives the original bill of lading that has been endorsed by the seller.

Test your understanding 9

1 **Ahmed.** As the bill is negotiable, he is the legal owner of it and has the right to authorise a different shipping route.

2 **False.** Beatrice will not be able to collect the goods until she can show the original bill of lading to the carrier, endorsed by Ahmed.

3 **True.**

Test your understanding 10

The series of operations, beginning with the originator's payment order, made for the purpose of placing funds at the disposal of a beneficiary. The term includes any payment order issued by the originator's bank, or any intermediary bank intended to carry out the originator's payment order.

Test your understanding 11

Payment order is an unconditional instruction by a sender to a receiving bank to place at the disposal of a beneficiary a fixed or determinable amount of money if the receiving bank is to be reimbursed by the sender and the instruction does not provide that the payment is to be made at the request of the beneficiary (i.e. the seller).

Test your understanding 12

I 4 June. The payment order is initiated by the sender's bank when it sends the payments order to the receiving bank.

II 5 June. The payment order is accepted when the credit is made in the receiving bank's account.

III 5 June. The payment order is completed when the beneficiary's bank (NBD) accepts a payment order for the benefit of the beneficiary.

Test your understanding 13

An unconditional order in writing by one person to another to pay a specified sum to a specified person or bearer on a particular date.

Test your understanding 14

The person to whom the bill is payable.

Test your understanding 15

The party on whom the bill is drawn, usually a bank.

Test your understanding 16

The person who makes the order and draws up the bill.

Test your understanding 17

A bill of exchange is a written instrument which contains an unconditional order whereby the drawer directs the drawee to pay a definite sum of money to the payee or to his or her order, which is payable on demand or at a definite time, is dated and is signed by the drawer.

Test your understanding 18

A promissory note is a written instrument which contains an unconditional promise whereby the maker undertakes to pay a definite sum of money to the payee or to his or her order, is payable on demand or at a definite time, is dated and is signed by the maker.

Test your understanding 19

B $13,000

Test your understanding 20

Julio, Julio's bank, Kathleen and Leander. Mary and Nathan cannot be liable to future holders, as they have endorsed the bill for collection only.

Test your understanding 21

An undertaking by a bank to make a payment to a named beneficiary within a specified time, against the presentation of documents which comply strictly with the terms of the letter of credit.

Test your understanding 22

Security is given to both parties. The seller knows that he or she will be paid for the goods and the buyer knows that the seller will have to fulfil the obligations of presenting the relevant documents to the bank before payment will be made.

Test your understanding 23

A confirmed letter of credit is one where the seller's bank has added its guarantee to the letter of credit that the seller's bank will pay the seller on presentation of the appropriate documents. An unconfirmed letter of credit contains no such guarantee from the seller's bank, although the seller's bank does confirm that the letter is genuine.

Test your understanding 24

She must finalise the terms of her agreement with Bernard and then apply to her bank for a letter of credit. Her bank will then issue the letter of credit to Bernard's bank.

Chapter

6

International business forms – agency

Chapter learning objectives

Upon completion of this chapter you will be able to:

- define the role of the agent and give examples of such relationships, paying particular regard to partners and company directors
- explain how the agency relationship is established
- define the authority of the agent
- explain the potential liability of both principal and agent.

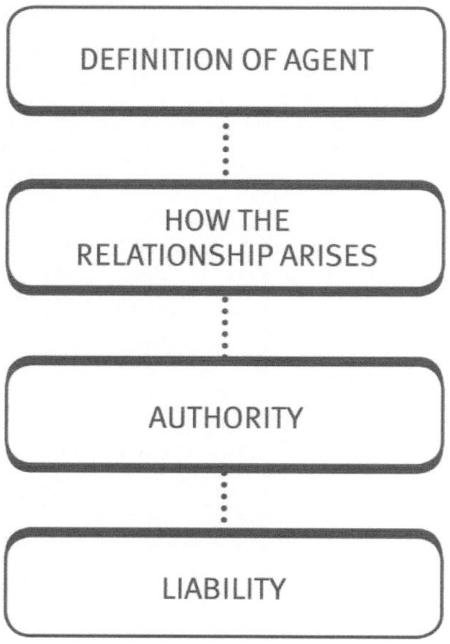

1 Definition of an agent

An agent (A) is a person who has been authorised, either expressly, by conduct or by implication, to act for another party which is called the Principal (P). The agent is making and entering into legal relations with a third party on behalf of the principal. The resulting contracts are therefore made between the Principal and the third party and not directly with the agent.

The role of agency in modern commercial transactions is significant. Commercial life would be very burdensome if every deal had to be done in person. Also, the invention of artificial legal entities such as private and public companies with separate legal personality and limited liability partnerships necessitated the use of agents as the companies or LLP cannot act by themselves.

Illustration 1 – Definition of an agent

An agency relationship exists in lots of situations:

- A director acts as an agent for his or her company.
- A partner acts as an agent for his or her partnership.
- An estate agent is appointed by a seller of a house to find a buyer.
- A travel agent is appointed by a holiday company to make bookings with customers.

2 How the agency relationship arises

Introduction

An agency relationship can be established in one of five ways:

- express agreement
- implied agreement
- necessity
- ratification
- estoppel.

Express agreement

This is where P actually appoints A as his or her agent. The agreement can be made orally or in writing.

Implied agreement

This is where P has not expressly agreed that A should be his or her agent. However, the agreement can be implied from the parties' conduct or relationship.

Necessity

This requires four conditions to be satisfied:

- P's property is entrusted to A
- an emergency arises making it necessary for A to act
- it is not possible to communicate with P
- A acts in the interest of P.

Prager v Blatspeil (1924)

Facts: A bought skins as the agent for P but was unable to send them to P because of prevailing war conditions. Since A was also unable to communicate with P, he sold the skins before the end of the war.

Held: A was not an agent of necessity, because he could have stored the skins until the end of the war. There was no real emergency.

Great Northern Railway v Swaffield (1874)

Facts: There was a contract between the two parties whereby GNR agreed to transport the defendant's horse to a particular railway station from where it would be collected.

When no one arrived to pick it up, the station master, having tried unsuccessfully to contact the defendant, placed the horse in a stable overnight.

Held: GNR was entitled to recover the costs of stabling because it had become the agent of the defendant by necessity.

Ratification

If a properly appointed agent exceeds his or her authority, or a person having no authority purports to act as an agent, the principal has no liability on that contract unless the principal 'ratifies' the contract.

The effect of ratification is to backdate A's authority to act as agent. This requires P to:

- have the contractual capacity to make the contract
- have been in existence both when the contract was made and at the date of ratification
- be identified when the contract is made
- be aware of all the material facts
- clearly signify his or her intention to ratify the whole contract within a reasonable time.

Note that a void or illegal contract cannot be ratified.

Kelner v Baxter (1866)

Facts: The promoters of a company entered into a contract on behalf of a company before it was incorporated, to purchase some property. The other party was not paid.

Held: As the company did not exist at the time the contract was made, the company could not ratify the contract. The promoters were personally liable to the seller.

Fitzmaurice v Bayley (1856)

Facts: A principal in effect said to a third party – I don't know what my agent has agreed to do, but I must support him.

Held: The principal had ratified. Although he did not know that the agent had exceeded his authority he had agreed to take the risk.

Estoppel

This arises where P implies that A is his or her agent even though he or she is not. He or she is then prevented from denying A's authority (see **Freeman & Lockyer v Buckhurst Park Properties** Ltd in section 3).

Test your understanding 1

Peter advertised his car for sale in a local newspaper and then went on holiday leaving his car in the drive. While Peter was away, Tom, having seen the advertisement, went to look at the car and decided to make an offer for it. Peter's neighbour, Alf, pretending to act with Peter's authority, entered into negotiations with Tom and eventually accepted Tom's offer on Peter's behalf.

Alf had no authority to act in this way. When Peter returned from his holiday, he wrote to Tom saying that he was ratifying Alf's act.

Advise Tom whether he is bound by the contract.

3 Authority

The authority of an agent is a central issue in the concept of agency. The question of authority deals with the powers and duties that the agent has on behalf of the principal and it will determine when and for which acts the Principal will be liable and will have to indemnify the agent. If the agent exceeds his or her powers, the principal may still be liable to the third party but he or she may have rights against the agent for breach of contract.

Express actual authority	This is authority that P has explicitly given to A.
Implied actual authority	An agent has implied authority to do things which: • are reasonably incidental to the performance of an expressly authorised act • an agent occupying that position would usually have authority to do • have not been expressly prohibited by P. See **Watteau v Fenwick (1893)** below.

Apparent	Such authority arises where A is held out by P as having authority. The representation by P may arise from previous dealings (allowing A to make contracts in the past is a representation that A has authority to continue to do so in the future). See **Freeman & Lockyer v Buckhurst Park Properties (1964)** below. However, a third party cannot rely on apparent authority when he or she knows of the lack of actual authority.

Watteau v Fenwick (1893)

Facts: The new owners of a business continued to employ the original owner as the manager. In the agency agreement the new owners ordered the agent not to buy certain items, including cigars. The manager still bought cigars from a third party. The owners then refused to pay for the cigars.

Held: The purchase of the cigars was within the usual authority of a manager of a hotel. The contract was binding on the owners. (If a limitation on the usual authority is going to be effective, it must be communicated to the third party before any contract is made).

Freeman & Lockyer v Buckhurst Park Properties Ltd (1964)

Facts: The defendant company had four directors, none of whom had been appointed as the managing director. One director effectively ran the business by himself and entered into a number of contracts with the claimants. On previous occasions, the board on behalf of the company had honoured the contracts and paid the claimants. However, on this occasion, the board refused to pay arguing that the director had no express authority to make the contract because he was not the managing director.

Held: Although the director had no express authority to make the contract, the director had acquired apparent authority. This was because by honouring similar contracts in the past, the company (as the principal) had given the impression that the director had the authority to make this sort of contract. The claimants had relied on this representation by continuing to deal with the director when purporting to act on behalf of the company.

Test your understanding 2

Harry wanted to insure the contents of his house against all loss and damage and appointed Colin to effect a policy, instructing him to 'insure any furniture'. Having obtained quotes from various companies, Colin eventually took out insurance with Hawk Star Limited. Sometime later vandals broke into Harry's house and did substantial damage to his furniture. They did not steal anything. When Harry claimed, Hawk Star refused to pay as the policy covered loss by theft or fire but not damage by vandals.

Advise Harry whether he can recover the value of damaged furniture from Colin.

Breach of warranty of authority

As discussed earlier if an agent has no authority or exceeds it the principal may ratify the contract and become liable. However, if the principal does not ratify, then the agent will be liable to the third party for breach of warranty of authority because he or she warranted or promised that he or she had authority which he or she did not possess.

4 Liability

Where the agent acts for a disclosed principal

A principal is disclosed where the existence of the principal has been made known to the third party. It is not necessary for the principal to be identified to the third party.

As a general rule, the contract is between the principal and the third party. The agent is neither liable nor entitled under the contract. However, the agent will be personally liable in the following exceptional circumstances:

- where the agent showed an intention to undertake personal liability, e.g. by signing a written contract in his or her own name
- trade usage or custom
- where the agent refuses to identify the principal
- where the agent is acting on behalf of a fictitious principal.

Where the agent acts for an undisclosed principal

An undisclosed principal is where the principal's existence has not been made known to the third party. When the third party discovers the existence of P, he or she can elect to treat P or A as bound by the transaction.

Agent's fiduciary duty

An agent has a fiduciary duty to his or her principal: (Please see chapter 8 for the explanation of the meaning of the word fiduciary.)

- A must not allow his or her personal interests to conflict with those of P.
- A must always act in the best interests of P.
- A must not make a secret profit.
- A has a duty to account to P for all money and property received.

Where an agent is in breach of his or her fiduciary duty, the following remedies are available:

- P can repudiate the contract with the third party.
- A can be dismissed without notice.
- P can refuse to pay any money owed to A or recover any money already paid.
- P can recover any secret profit made or any bribe that was given.

Boston Deep Sea Fishing & Ice Co v Ansell (1888)

Facts: Ansell was managing director of the claimant company. He accepted a 'commission' (bribe) from a supplier to order goods from that supplier, on behalf of the company. When the company found out, he was dismissed.

Held: The defendant was in breach of his fiduciary duty as the agent of the company. Therefore the company could recover the commissions paid to him.

Test your understanding 3

Brian instructs Fred to sell his house and agrees to pay him $1,000 on completion of the sale. Fred sells the house and on completion is paid his commission by Brian. Brian subsequently discovers that Fred has also been paid a commission of $500 by the purchaser.

Advise Brian whether he can sue Fred and, if so, what remedies are available to him.

Principal's liability to the agent

The agent has the right:

- To claim remuneration or commission for services performed.

  Usually the amount of remuneration or commission to be paid is stated in the agency agreement. Where it is not specified and it is a commercial agreement, the court will imply a term into the agreement requiring a reasonable amount to be paid.

- To claim an indemnity against P for all expenses reasonably incurred in carrying out his or her obligations.

- To exercise a lien over P's property. The lien allows the agent to retain possession of P's property that is lawfully in A's possession until any debts due to A, e.g. arrears of remuneration, have been paid by P.

5 Chapter summary

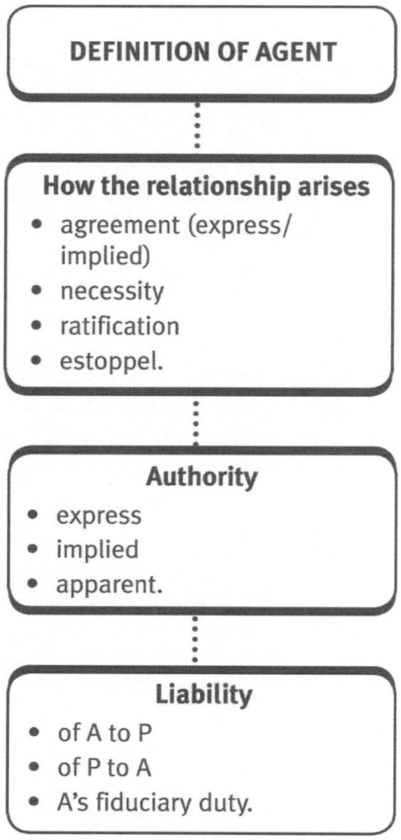

Test your understanding answers

Test your understanding 1

Where a person purports to act as another's agent, even though he or she has no authority to do so, the principal is only bound by the contract if he or she decides to ratify it.

The principal can only ratify the contract if certain requirements are satisfied. The principal must have the contractual capacity to make the contract both at the time the contract is made and at the time of ratification. The principal must have been identified to the third party at the time the contract was made.

The principal must be aware of all material facts and ratify the contract within a reasonable time. The principal must ratify the whole contract.

It would appear that all these requirements can be satisfied in this situation. Therefore Peter is able to ratify the contract.

When the principal ratifies the contract, it is binding on the parties from the date on which it was originally made. Therefore Tom is bound by the contract.

Test your understanding 2

When an agent is appointed, he or she is given express authority to act on behalf of the principal. However, where the terms of authority are ambiguous or where the agent is given discretion to act the law implies authority to enable an agent to carry out his or her express duties. The agent must always act in the best interests of the principal.

Colin's authority is very ambiguous. He or she can decide which policy to take out 'to insure the principal's furniture'.

If Colin can show that when he or she made the decision to take this policy as opposed to any other, that he or she was acting in Harry's best interests, Colin will be acting within his or her authority. Harry will not be able to recover the value of the damaged furniture from Colin.

Test your understanding 3

An agent owes various duties to his or her principal and the most important is the fiduciary duty. This means that the agent must not allow his or her own personal interests to conflict with the interests of the principal. The agent must not make a secret profit from his or her dealings on behalf of the principal or accept any bribes or commissions.

The situation is very similar to **Boston Deep Sea Fishing & Ice Co Ltd v Ansell (1888)** where the managing director, as the agent of the company, was paid a bribe by a supplier to deal with that supplier on behalf of the company. The court held that the agent had acted in breach of his or her fiduciary duty.

As Fred has been paid a commission by the purchaser, Fred is in breach of the fiduciary duty that he owes to Brian. This means that Brian can recover the $1,000 paid to Fred and also the $500 bribe paid by the purchaser.

If the purchaser knew that Fred accepted the $500 in breach of his fiduciary duty, the contract for the sale of the property is voidable at Fred's option.

Chapter

7

Types of Business Organisation

Chapter learning objectives

Upon completion of this chapter you will be able to:

- distinguish between different types of business organisation
- explain the meaning of the different types of partnership
- in relation to general or ordinary partnerships:
  - discuss how they are established
  - explain the authority of the partners in relation to partnership activity
  - outline the liability of the partners for partnership debts
  - explain the ways in which they can be brought to an end.

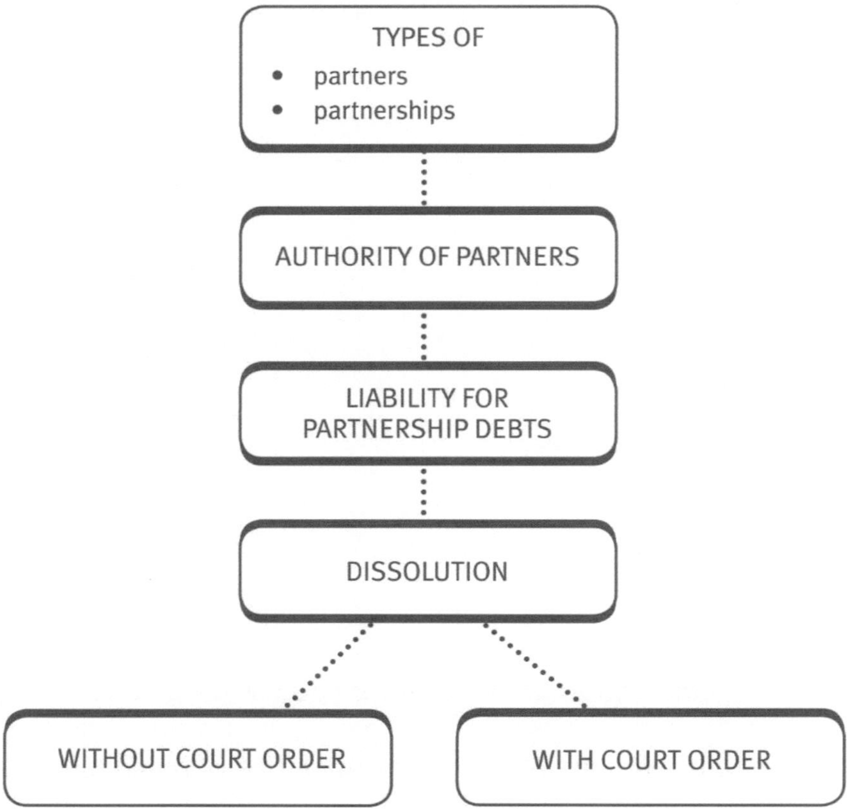

1 Types of Business Organisation

Different forms of business organisation

Sole trader/sole practitionership	• The owner 'is' the business – owns the assets and is liable for all the debts. • No legal formalities are required to set up a sole trader business. • This form of business is inappropriate for large businesses or those involving a degree of risk.
General partnership	Defined by Partnership Act 1890 (PA 1890) as the relationship which subsists between persons carrying on a business in common with a view of profit. (See below.)
Limited partnership	Formed under the Limited Partnership Act 1907. (See below.)

Limited liability partnership (LLP)	• An artificial legal entity with perpetual succession. It can hold property in its own right, enter into contracts in its own name, create floating charges, sue and be sued. • The liability of the members of an LLP is limited to the amount of capital they have agreed to contribute. • The LLP must file annual accounts and an annual report with Companies House.
Company	A corporation is an artificial legal person. (See Chapter 7.)

The rest of this chapter will focus on partnerships.

2 Types of partnership

Definition

A partnership is a relationship which subsists between two or more persons carrying on a business in common with a view to profit: s1(1) Partnership Act 1890 (PA 1890).

A partnership can be a small operation or as with some large firms of solicitors and accountants partnerships with several hundred partners.

Types of partners

General partner	Actively involved in the day-to-day business.
Sleeping partner	Takes no active part in the running of the business. However, is jointly and severally liable for the debts and contracts of the business.
Limited partner in a limited partnership	Contributes a specific amount of capital. Liability limited to that amount. Cannot take part in the management of the firm.
Salaried partner	Will receive a fixed amount in income. Not a real partner unless he or she also receives a share of the profits.

Types of partnership

Partnership	Governed by Partnership Act 1890 – this is the default position if a partnership is not formed under either of the two Acts below.
Limited partnership	Governed by Limited Partnership Act 1907 (LPA 1907).
Limited liability partnership	Governed by Limited Liability Partnerships Act 2000. Limited liability partnership has separate legal personality. It means that it is legally separate from its members.

Characteristics of a partnership

In order for a partnership to exist, a business must be carried on with a view to profit (s1(1) PA 1890). This means that the persons involved in the partnership intend the business to yield a profit and they are all entitled to share in that profit.

The following do not create a partnership:

- joint ownership of property (s2(1) PA 1890)
- the sharing of gross returns (s2(2) PA 1890)
- the sharing of expenses (s2(3) PA 1890).

Cox v Coulson (1916)

Facts: C agreed with M that M would put on a play at C's theatre. C was to have 60% and M 40% of the gross box office receipts. C paid the expenses of running the theatre and M paid the expenses of putting on the play. During a performance the claimant, who was in the audience, was accidentally shot by one of the actors. The claimant sued C alleging that C was M's partner and was jointly liable with M.

Held: C was not M's partner because they merely shared gross box office receipts.

A partnership begins as soon as the partners agree to form a business together. The actual date the partnership starts trading may differ.

The partnership agreement is a contract. Like any contract it may be:

- express (e.g. oral, in writing or by deed) or
- implied.

The partners are contractually bound by the terms they have agreed, even if they conflict with PA 1890.

Limited partnerships under Limited Partnership Act 1907

A limited partnership is a partnership in which the liability of one or more partners is limited to their capital contribution.

A limited partnership must fulfil the following conditions:

- There must be at least one partner with unlimited liability (s4(2) LPA 1907).
- The partnership must be registered with the Registrar of Companies as a limited partnership (s5 LPA 1907).
- Limited partners may not participate in the management of the business. If they do, they forfeit their limited liability (s6(1) LPA 1907).
- A limited partner has no power to bind the firm to contracts, i.e. unlike the unlimited partners, they are not an agent (s6(1) LPA 1907).

Partnership around the world

The models outlined above are:

- UK law based
- used in many countries around the world in those forms.

It is also useful to consider partnerships based in the other types of legal frameworks that were introduced in the first chapter:

- Civil law: société et nom collectif and société en commandite simple (French legal system).
- Sharia law: musharakah and mudaraba.

Civil law partnerships

The société et nom collectif (snc) is a type of limited partnership which exists in French law. It is similar to the English unlimited partnership in every way except the fact that an snc has corporate personality and is therefore a legal person in its own right. However, this does not mean that it is responsible for its own debts and the partners must meet the partnership debts from their own assets in the same way that English partners do. In addition, the 'managers' (gerants) of an snc (defined in the articles signature of which creates the snc) may also be liable for the snc's debts.

There must be at least two partners. Partners are treated as sole traders for tax purposes. All partners are gerants and hold important management rights, most of which can be settled in the articles. The only decisions requiring unanimity are the decision to transfer shares, to remove a partner or to cease trading.

The société en commandite simple is another form of commercial association in French law similar to a limited partnership in the UK. The key difference from the snc is that some partners are given the right to limited liability.

Sharia law partnerships

Musharakah is a form of partnership in Islamic jurisprudence. It is derived from Shirkah, which means 'sharing' and is divided into two different kinds:

- Shirkat-ul-milk – which relates to the owning of property by two or more persons, and
- Shirkat-ul-'aqd – which refers to a joint commercial enterprise, essentially a partnership created by mutual contract.

Shirkat-ul-'aqd is further subdivided into three types of commercial enterprise, one of which is Shirkat-ul-A'mal, which is sometimes known as a Musharakah, a partnership relationship established through a mutual contract. The proportion of profit to be distributed amongst the partners must be determined by that contract, and if it is not, then no Musharakah is deemed to exist by Sharia law. Partners are liable according to the investment they have made into the business (e.g. if they contributed 20% of the capital, they are liable for 20% of the debt). Partners are considered to be agents of one another unless it has been agreed that some partners are to be excluded from management.

Mudaraba is a contract where at least two parties join in a commercial venture, one of whom has finance and the other of whom has no finance but, say, ideas and entrepreneurship. The financier (rabbul-mal) enables the entrepreneur (mudarib) to undertake a business enterprise. The financier is entitled to an agreed share of the profits but has no management rights in the enterprise.

3 Authority of partners under PA 1890

Agency relationship

When entering into a contract to carry out the business, each partner is acting as the agent of all the partners:

- The express authority of a partner is set out in the partnership agreement.
- The implied authority is set out in s5 PA 1890.
- A partner may have apparent authority where the other partners have allowed that partner to enter into certain transactions such that the partner has been held out has having the authority to enter into those transactions.

S5 PA 1890 states that every partner is the agent of the firm and of the other partners. This means that each partner has the power to bind all partners to all business transactions entered into during the course of the partnership's business.

Implied authority

Under s5 every partner is presumed to have the implied authority to:

- sell the firm's goods
- buy goods necessary for, or usually employed in, the business

- receive payments of debts due to the firm
- engage employees
- employ a solicitor to act for the firm in defence of a claim or in the pursuance of a debt.

Trading partnerships

The above implied powers apply to both trading and non-trading partnerships. Partners in trading partnerships have the additional power to borrow money.

In order to be acting within their implied or apparent authority, the individual partner must be acting within the usual scope of a partner's powers in the particular business concerned.

Mercantile Credit Co v Garrod (1962)

Facts: P and G entered into a partnership to let lock-up garages and repair cars. P ran the business and G was a sleeping partner. The partnership agreement expressly stated that the firm would not buy and sell cars. P sold a car to a finance company, M. M sued G to recover the £700 which it had paid to P for the car. G denied liability claiming that P when selling the car had been acting outside the agreed limits of the firm's business and therefore P had no actual or apparent authority to make the contract. Evidence was given that other garage businesses of the type carried on by P and G did deal in cars.

Held: The test of what is the firm's business is not what the partners agreed it should be but 'what it appears to the outside world' to be. Under that test P appeared to M to be carrying on business of a kind carried on by such a firm. This contract was within the apparent authority of P and therefore the contract was binding on G.

Test your understanding 1

Jekyll and Hyde are in partnership providing forensic services to police services. The partnership agreement states that all scientific equipment is to be supplied by James and that neither partner may incur liability of more than $2,000 without consulting the other. Jekyll, although he contributed all the firm's initial capital, does not have any active involvement and visits its premises rarely. Hyde receives a salary, as well as a share of the profits, and works full-time for the firm.

Jekyll now seeks your advice as he has found out that Hyde has ordered $5,000 worth of equipment from Edgar. Advise him.

4 Liability for partnership debts

Is there liability in contract?

The firm is liable for contracts made by a partner if they were acting within their express, implied or apparent authority.

The firm is not bound by the actions of a partner if:

- the third party knows the partner has no authority, or
- the partner has no authority and the third party does not know or believe them to be a partner.

Holding out

Every person who by their words or conduct represents themselves (or knowingly allows themselves to be represented) as a partner, is liable as if they are a partner to anyone who thereby gives credit to the firm: s14 PA 1890.

Martyn v Gray (1863)

Facts: G went to Cornwall to discuss the possibility of investing in a tin mine belonging to X. Nothing came of the discussions, but while G was in Cornwall he was introduced by X to M as 'a gentleman down from London, a man of capital'. M later gave X credit believing he was in partnership with G.

Held: The introduction amounted to a representation that G was in partnership with X, and so G was liable for the debt incurred subsequent to the introduction. He should have made the true position clear by correcting the impression made.

Liability in tort

Where a tort is committed during the ordinary course of the partnership's business, or by a partner acting with the authority of the other partners, the partners are jointly and severally liable to the person who has suffered loss.

Misapplication of money or property

The partnership is liable to make good the loss where a third party's money or property is misapplied:

- after being received by a partner within their express, implied or apparent authority, or
- while it is in the custody of the firm, such as in the partnership bank account.

Which partners are liable?

General rule	Every partner is jointly and severally liable for the debts and contracts of the business. Outsiders can sue one partner alone or the firm. The Civil Liability Act 1978 provides that a judgment against one partner does not bar a subsequent action against the other partners.
New partners	A new partner is not personally liable for debts incurred before they became a partner.
Retiring partners	A retiring partner remains liable for any debts incurred while they were a partner. If no notice of the retirement is given, the firm continues to be bound by their actions as they are still being held out as a partner.
Change in partners	Where a third party deals with a partnership after a change in partners, all of the partners of the old firm are still treated as partners, until the third party receives notice of the change: • Previous customers require actual notice. • Third parties who were not existing customers can be notified by a notice in the Gazette: s36 PA 1890. This is known as constructive notice. Notification must take place prior to retirement if the retiring partner is to avoid liability for contracts entered into after their retirement.
Novation	A creditor agrees with the outgoing, continuing and/or incoming partners that liability for an existing debt will be that of the continuing and incoming partners. (Thus the liability of the outgoing partner is removed and the incoming partner becomes liable for the debt even though it was incurred before he or she became a partner.)
Indemnity	The continuing and incoming partners may agree to indemnify the outgoing partner against debts incurred pre- and/or post-retirement.

Test your understanding 2

Following their earlier dispute, Jekyll and Hyde do not believe that they can continue in partnership. It is proposed that Jekyll will retire and Edgar will be admitted as a partner.

What will be the liability for the firm's debts of (i) Jekyll and (ii) Edgar once these changes have been made?

5 Dissolution

Without court order

The partnership will automatically end in the following situations:

- The expiry of a fixed term or the completion of a specific enterprise (s32(a) PA 1890).
- One of the partners gives notice (unless the partnership agreement excludes this right) (s32(c) PA 1890).
- Death or bankruptcy of a partner (s33 PA 1890).
- Where continuation of the partnership would be illegal (s4 PA 1890).

Hudgell, Yeates and Co v Watson (1978)

Facts: Practising solicitors are required by law to have a practising certificate. One of the partners in a firm of solicitors forgot to renew his certificate which meant that it was illegal for him to practise.

Held: The failure to renew the practising certificate brought the partnership to an end, although a new partnership continued between the other two members.

By court order

Under s35 PA1890, the court can bring a partnership to an end in the following situations:

- Partner has mental disorder or permanent incapacity.
- Partner engages in activity prejudicial to the business.
- Partner wilfully or persistently breaches the partnership agreement.
- Partner conducts himself in a way that it is no longer reasonably practicable for the others to carry on in business with him or her.
- Business can only be carried on at a loss.
- It is just and equitable to do so.

Distribution of assets

In the event of dissolution the assets of the partnership will be used to pay off the debts of the partnership. As a partnership does not have the advantage of limited liability status, if the proceeds on the sale of the assets does not cover the debts then the partners' personal wealth will be called upon to make up the shortfall.

The proceeds from the sale of the assets will be applied in the following order:

(i) paying debts to outsiders

(ii) paying the partners any advance they made to the firm beyond their capital contribution i.e. a loan

(iii) paying the capital contribution of the partners.

If there is a residue remaining this will be divided between the partners in the same proportion in which they share the profits of the partnership.

In the event that the assets are insufficient to meet the debts to outsiders then profits held back from previous years or partners' capital will be used to make good the shortfall. If these are also insufficient then the partners will individually contribute in the proportion to which they shared in the profits.

6 LLPs

A limited liability partnership (LLP) is a corporate body which combines the features of a traditional partnership with a company.

LLPs are covered in the next chapter once we have covered the characteristics of a company.

7 Chapter summary

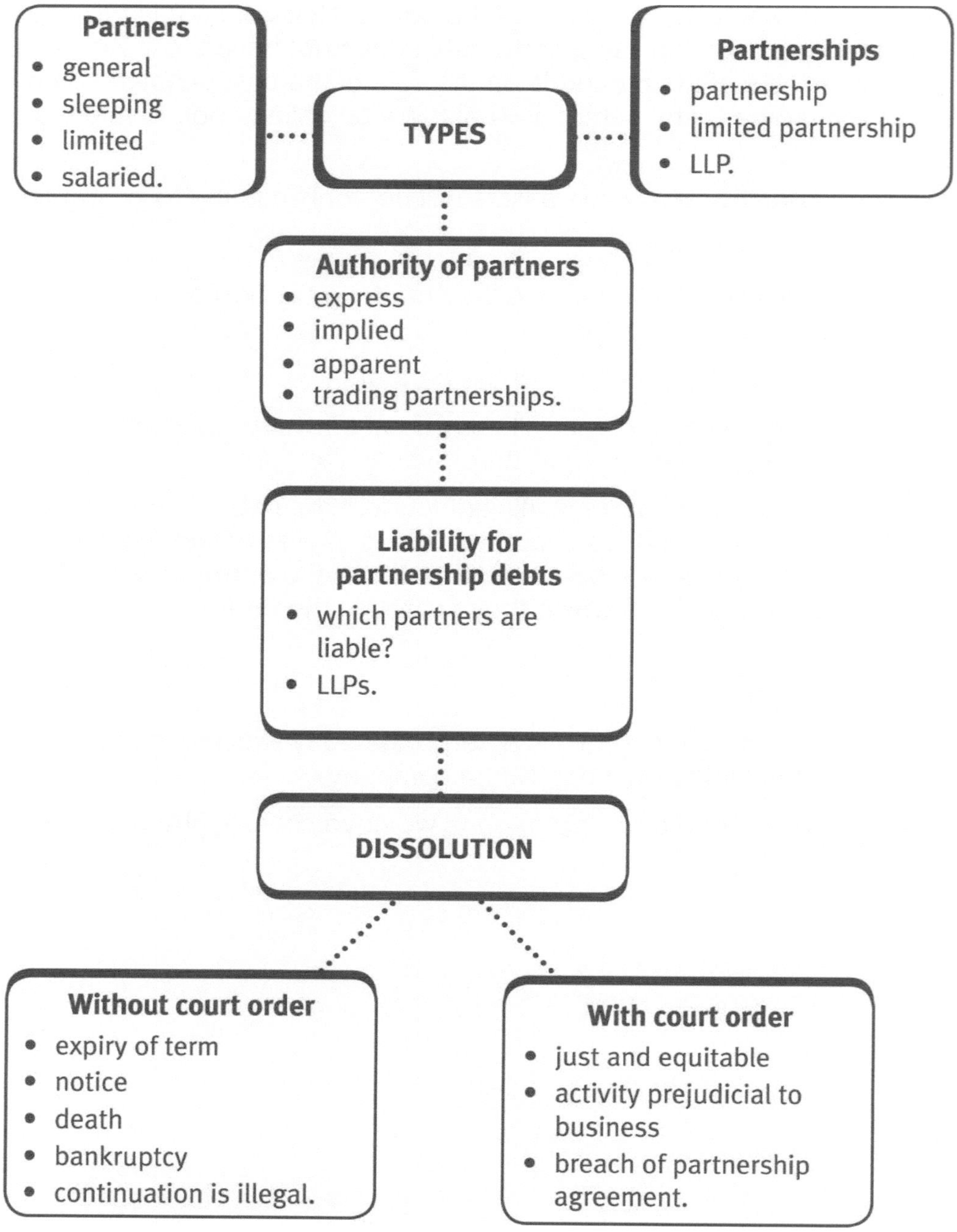

Test your understanding answers

Test your understanding 1

PA 1890 states that a partnership is a relationship which subsists between two or more persons carrying on a business with a view to profit. Each partner is liable for the debts of the firm.

Jekyll is a sleeping partner who takes no part in the running of the business, but he is treated as any other partner with respect to his liabilities.

Hyde is a salaried partner which means that he can run the business. Any act done within the ordinary course of the firm's business is binding on all partners and they are jointly liable for the debts of the business.

When Hyde enters into the contract with Edgar, he is exceeding the authority given him in the partnership agreement. However, the partnership agreement is not a public document and Edgar could not be expected to know of any limitation imposed upon Hyde's authority. In addition to express authority, every partner has implied authority under s5, to enter into contracts on behalf of the business. As long as the equipment could be used in the ordinary course of the business, the contract will be binding on both parties.

When Hyde enters into the contract with Edgar, he is acting in breach of the partnership agreement. Jekyll can sue for breach of agreement and recover damages for any loss he suffers.

Test your understanding 2

A partner who has retired from the firm is not liable for any debts that arise after his or her retirement. He or she must notify the partnership's usual suppliers of his or her retirement and make sure that his or her name is taken off the list of partners.

A notice should also be placed in the Gazette to give notice to the persons who have not previously dealt with the firm that he or she is no longer a partner.

Jekyll will continue to be liable for the debts that arose while he was still a partner. However, it is possible to avoid this by agreement with Hyde, Edgar and the creditors.

An incoming partner is only liable for the debts arising after he or she became a partner. However, if there is an arrangement with the creditors by which the new partners assume the obligations of the old, Edgar will be liable for the old debts as well. This agreement can be express or it can be implied from the conduct of the partnership.

Chapter

8

Corporations and legal personality

Chapter learning objectives

Upon completion of this chapter you will be able to:

- explain the meaning and effect of limited liability
- explain meaning of LLPs and compare companies and partnerships
- analyse the different types of companies, especially public and private companies
- illustrate the effect of separate personality
- recognise instances where separate personality will be ignored
- explain the role and duties of company promoters
- describe the procedure for registering companies, both public and private
- describe the contents of model articles of association
- analyse the effect of a company's articles
- explain how articles of association can be changed
- describe the statutory books, records and returns that companies must keep or make.

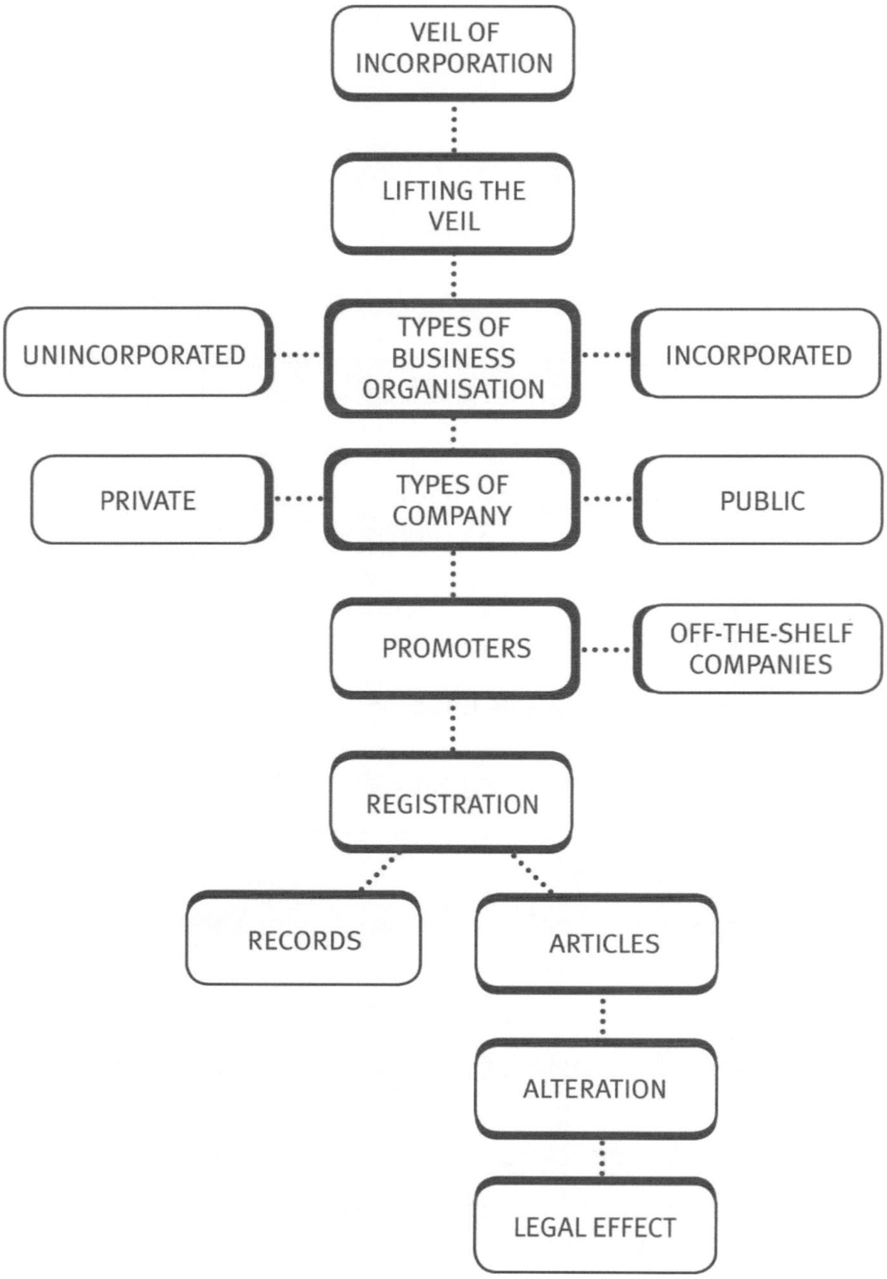
VEIL OF INCORPORATION
LIFTING THE VEIL
UNINCORPORATED
TYPES OF BUSINESS ORGANISATION
INCORPORATED
PRIVATE
TYPES OF COMPANY
PUBLIC
PROMOTERS
OFF-THE-SHELF COMPANIES
REGISTRATION
RECORDS
ARTICLES
ALTERATION
LEGAL EFFECT

1 The doctrine and veil of incorporation

Meaning

The company is separate legal entity (i.e. separate from its shareholders, the part owners and its directors, the managers).

Salomon v Salomon & Co Ltd (1897)

Facts: S transferred his business to a limited company. He was the director and majority shareholder and a secured creditor. The company went into liquidation and the other creditors tried to obtain repayment from S personally.

Held: S as shareholder and director had no personal liability to creditors, and he could be repaid in priority as a secured creditor. This enshrined the concepts of separate legal personality and limited liability in the law.

Lee v Lee's Air Farming Ltd (1960)

Facts: This case concerned an aerial crop-spraying business. Mr Lee owned the majority of the shares (all but one) and was the sole working director of the company. He was killed while piloting the aircraft.

Held: Although Lee was the majority shareholder and sole working director of the company, he and the company were separate legal persons. Therefore he could also be an employee of the company for the purposes of the relevant statute with rights against it when killed in an accident in the course of his employment.

Macaura v Northern Life Assurance (1925)

Facts: M owned a forest. He formed a company in which he beneficially owned all the shares and sold his forest to it. He, however, continued to maintain an insurance policy on the forest in his own name. The forest was destroyed by fire.

Held: He could not claim on the policy since the property damaged belonged to the company, not him, and as shareholder he had no insurable interest in the forest.

Consequences of incorporation

There are a number of consequences of being a separate legal entity:

- Limited liability. A company is liable for its own debts. If a company fails, the liability of the shareholders is limited to any amount still unpaid on their share capital (or any amount they have agreed to contribute if the company is limited by guarantee). The consequence that a company's members have limited liability for its debts gives protection to the members from the company's creditors and from the risk of the business collapsing.

- A company enters into contracts in its own name and can sue and be sued in its own name.
- A company owns its own property.
- A company has perpetual succession, irrespective of the fate of shareholders.
- The management of a company is separated from its ownership.
- A company is subject to the requirements of the Companies Act 2006 (CA06) and the Small Business, Enterprise and Employment Act 2015 (SBEEA 2015).
- Where a company suffers an injury, it is the company itself that must take the appropriate remedial action. This is known as the rule in **Foss v Harbottle**.

Foss v Harbottle (1843)

Facts: Two minority shareholders initiated legal proceedings against, among others, the directors of the company. They claimed that the directors had misapplied the company's assets.

Held: The court dismissed the claim and held that when a company is wronged by its directors it is only the company that has standing to sue.

2 Lifting the veil of incorporation

Meaning

The phrase 'lifting the veil of incorporation' means that in certain circumstances the courts can look through the company to the identity of the shareholders.

The usual result of lifting the veil is that the members or directors become personally liable for the company's debts.

Statutory examples

There are a number of occasions on which statute will intervene to lift the veil:

- S399 of CA06 requires accounts to be prepared by a group of related companies, therefore recognising the common link between them.
- Under the Insolvency Act 1986 (IA 1986), members and/or directors liable for wrongful or fraudulent trading may be personally liable for losses arising as a result. (See chapter 13).
- If a public company starts to trade without first obtaining a trading certificate, the directors can be made personally liable for any loss or damage suffered by a third party: S767 CA06.
- Under the Company Directors Disqualification Act 1986, if a director who is disqualified participates in the management of a company, that director will be jointly or severally liable for the company's debts.

Case law examples

Sham companies

The veil will be lifted only where '**special circumstances** exist indicating that it is a mere facade concealing the true facts': **Woolfson v Strathclyde Regional Council (1978)**.

For example:

Gilford Motor Co Ltd v Horne (1933)

Facts: An employee had a covenant in his contract of employment which stated that he would not solicit his former employer's customers. After he left their employment he formed a company to solicit those customers and claimed it was the company approaching the customers and not him.

Held: The court held that the company could be restrained from competition, as the previous employee had set it up to evade his own legal obligations. An injunction was granted against him and the company.

Jones v Lipman (1962)

Facts: Mr. Lipman contracted to sell his land and thereafter changed his mind. In order to avoid an order of specific performance he transferred his property to a company.

Held: The veil was lifted in order to prevent the seller of a house evading specific performance. An order of specific performance was granted against him and the company to transfer the property to the buyer.

Nationality

In times of war it is illegal to trade with the enemy. It may be possible to lift the veil of incorporation so as to impute to a company the same nationality as its members.

Daimler v Continental Tyre & Rubber Co (1916)

Facts: The defendant, a UK incorporated company, was owned by five individuals and a company incorporated in Germany. Only one individual was British and he held one share.

Held: The claimants need not discharge their debt to the defendants since effective control of the latter was in enemy hands and hence to do so would be to trade with the enemy.

Groups

Although each company within a group is a separate legal entity, there have been a number of cases where the courts have lifted the veil between a holding company and its various subsidiaries. This has generally been done in order to:

- benefit the group by obtaining a higher compensation payment on the compulsory purchase of premises
- benefit creditors of an insolvent company by making other companies within the group liable for its debts.

DHN Food Distributors v London Borough of Tower Hamlets (1976)

Facts: DHN carried on business from premises owned by a subsidiary. The subsidiary itself had no business activities. Both companies had the same directors. The local authority acquired the premises compulsorily but refused to pay compensation for disturbance of the business since the subsidiary, which owned the premises, did not also carry on the business.

Held: The companies were, in economic terms, mutually interdependent on each other and therefore they should be regarded as a single economic entity. Thus there was a valid claim for disturbance since ownership of the premises and business activity were in the hands of a single group.

The above case can, however, be contrasted with the more recent case of **Adams v Cape Industries (1990)** which represents the current position:

Adams v Cape Industries (1990)

Facts: Cape was an English registered company. One of its subsidiaries, CPC, a company incorporated and carrying on business in the United States, had a court judgement against it.

Held: It was unsuccessfully argued that the veil should be lifted between the companies so as to enable the judgement to be enforced against Cape. The Court of Appeal said there were no special circumstances indicating that CPC was a mere facade for Cape such as was the situation in Jones v Lipman. There was no agency as CPC was an independent corporation under the control of its chief executive, and the DHN doctrine of economic reality would not be extended beyond its own facts to facts such as these where the effect would be to make a holding company liable for its subsidiary's debts.

Test your understanding 1
In the context of company law explain:
A **what is meant by, and the consequences of, the 'veil of incorporation'**
B **under what circumstances the 'veil' will be lifted.**
(ACCA June 2003)

3 LLPs

Ordinary partnerships lack the characteristics of a company in the sense that they do not have limited liability or separate legal personality. Over the time the government was pressurised to recognise the needs of some partnerships (especially professional partnership such as solicitors, accountants and auditors) to limit their liability and have separate legal personality without having to form a company. This trend resulted in a key development in the form of the Limited Liability Partnerships Act 2000. The Limited Liability Partnerships can be formed since 6 April 2001 and have similar features to a private limited company. The members of an LLP are not directly responsible for the debts of the partnerships and the law relating to ordinary partnership does not apply to them.

Incorporation	• Incorporation document must be delivered to registrar stating name of LLP, location and address of registered office, names and addresses of members (minimum two) (s2(1)(a) and (b)). • Must send a Declaration of Compliance that LLP satisfies requirements of the Limited Liability Partnerships Act 2000 (s2(1)(c)). • Registrar issues a certificate of incorporation (s3(1)(b)).
Membership	• First members sign incorporation document (s4(1)). • Later members join by agreement with the existing members (s4(2)). • Membership ceases on death, dissolution or in accordance with agreement with other members (s4(3)). • Rights and duties are set out in membership agreement (s5(1)(a)). • If no agreement, governed by Limited Liability Partnership Regulations 2001 (s5(1)(b)). • Each member acts as an agent of the LLP (s6(1)).

Designated members	• Perform the administrative and filing duties of the LLP. • Incorporation document specifies who they are (s8(1)). • Must be at least two designated members. If there are none, all members will be designated members (s8(2)).
Name	• Must end with Limited Liability Partnership, llp or LLP (Schedule, Part 1, para 2(1)). names and registered office. • Rules on choice are the same as for companies – schedule: names and registered office (Schedule, Part 1 para 3).
Taxation	Members are treated as if they are partners carrying on business in a partnership, i.e. they pay income tax not corporation tax.
Registers	The LLP must maintain the following registers: • Register of members • Register of members usual residential addresses • Register of people with significant control. The LLP can keep these registers at its registered office or choose to send the information to the Registrar of Companies to be kept on the public register at Companies House.
Liability for debts	• The liability of a member of an LLP to contribute to its debts is limited to his or her capital contribution. However, there is no requirement for a capital contribution, and any contribution made can be withdrawn at any time. • If an LLP goes into liquidation, the court can order the members to repay any drawings made in the previous two years if it can be shown that the member knew or had reasonable grounds to believe that the LLP: – was unable to pay its debts at the date of withdrawal, or – would become unable to pay its debts because of the withdrawal: s214A Insolvency Act 1986 (IA 1986). The fraudulent and wrongful trading provisions of IA 1986 apply to members of LLPs in the same way as they apply to directors of companies **(see chapter 13)**.

Differences between LLP and partnership	• The liability of the members of an LLP is limited to the amount of capital they have agreed to contribute (s1(4)). • The LLP must file annual accounts and an annual report with Companies House. • LLP is an artificial legal entity with perpetual succession. It can hold property in its own right, enter into contracts in its own name, create floating charges, sue and be sued.

Company versus partnership

Company and LLP	Ordinary partnership under the PA 1890
Created by registration – with a written constitution.	No special formality required for creation.
Separate legal person, i.e. can own property, sue or be sued, and contract in own name.	Not a separate legal person – the partners own any property, are liable on contracts and are liable if sued.
Shares are transferable.	Limits on transfer of shares (may require dissolution of partnership or consent of other partners to enable partners to realise their share).
Can create both fixed and floating charges as security for borrowing.	Can only create fixed charges as security for borrowing.
Managed by directors, who may or may not also be shareholders.	Managed by partners, who are also the owners of the business.
The company cannot usually return capital to its members (except on dissolution).	Partners may withdraw their capital.
The company is liable for its debts. (No personal liability for shareholders beyond any unpaid portion of the price of their shares or the amount they have agreed to contribute.)	The partners are personally liable for the debts of the firm. Their liability is joint and several.
Must make information about financial affairs and ownership publicly available.	Private business. No disclosure of results.
The business is run by the directors. Members have no right to participate.	Every partner has the right to take part in the management of the business.

Must comply with Companies Act requirements concerning meetings.	No administrative requirements regarding meetings.
Formal dissolution procedure (known as liquidation). Death/bankruptcy of any member/ director does not dissolve the company.	May dissolve by agreement. Automatically dissolved on the death/bankruptcy of any partner.
Companies pay corporation tax.	Partners pay income tax.

Test your understanding 2

1 **X Ltd, Y Ltd and Z Ltd have formed the XYZ partnership. If the partnership should become insolvent, which of the following statements is correct?**

A The shareholders of each company are fully liable for the firm's debts.

B X Ltd, Y Ltd and Z Ltd are fully liable for the firm's debts.

C The directors of each company are fully liable for the firm's debts.

D The liability of X Ltd, Y Ltd and Z Ltd for the firm's debts is limited to the amount of their capital contributions.

2 **In relation to E Ltd, a company limited by shares, which one of the following statements is correct?**

A The liability of the company and its shareholders is limited, but the directors are fully liable for the company's debts.

B The liability of the company and its directors is limited, but the shareholders are fully liable for the company's debts.

C The liability of the company, its directors and shareholders is limited.

D The liability of the directors and shareholders is limited, but the company is fully liable for its own debts.

3 Mr X owns shares in Y Ltd. This means that Mr X:

I is a part-owner of Y Ltd

II is a part-owner of Y Ltd's property.

Which of the above is/are correct?

A I only

B II only

C Both I and II

D Neither I nor II

4 Types of company

Introduction

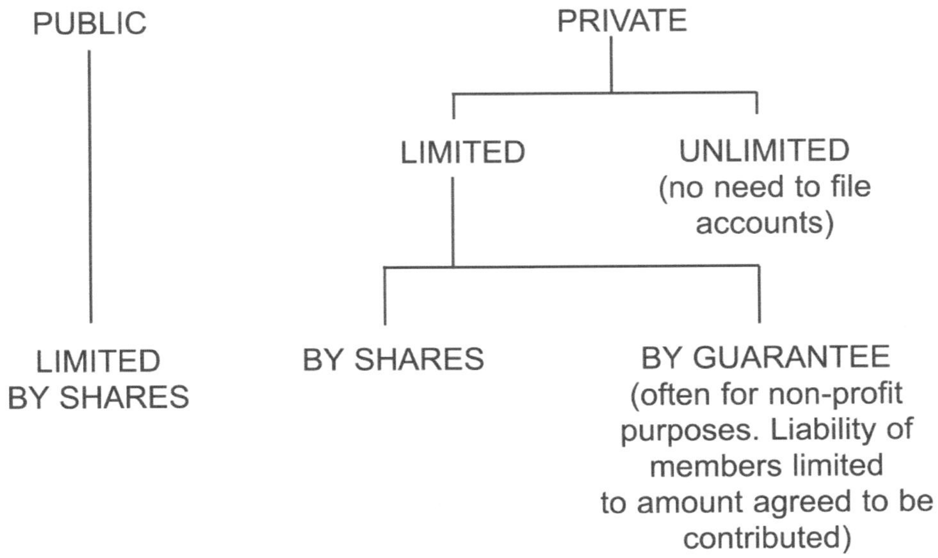

Private company versus public company

	Public companies	Private (limited) companies
Definition	Registered as a public company.	Any company that is not a public company.
Name	Ends with plc or public limited company.	Ends with Ltd or limited.
Capital	In order to trade, must have allotted shares of at least £50,000 of which at least ¼ of the nominal value should be paid up.	No minimum (or maximum) requirements.
Raising capital	May raise capital by advertising its securities (shares and debentures) as available for public subscription.	Prohibited from offering its securities to the public.
Start of trading	Must obtain trading certificate from registrar before commencing trading.	Can begin from date of incorporation.
Directors	Minimum two.	Minimum one.
Secretary	Must have one. Must be qualified.	Need not have one.

Accounts	Must file accounts within 6 months.	Need not lay accounts before general meeting. Must file within 9 months.
Audit	Accounts must be audited.	Audit not required if meets exemption criteria.
AGM	Must be held each year.	Need not hold an AGM.
Resolutions	Can't pass written resolutions.	Can pass written resolutions.

Unlimited companies

An unlimited company is a separate legal entity and, if it has assets, it will have the benefits arising from separate legal personality. However, if the company's assets are insufficient to meet its liabilities, all members are liable to contribute without limit towards paying its debts and the cost of liquidation.

Such companies do have the advantage that they need not have their accounts audited, and need not deliver annual copies to the Registrar of Companies.

Community interest companies

Since 2004 it has been possible to form a 'Community Interest Company' for those wishing to establish social enterprises. The company's object must be considered by a reasonable person to be of benefit to the community and any surpluses made by the company should be reinvested for the purposes of the company.

Such a company must first be registered as a company limited by guarantee or as a company limited by shares and then apply to the Regulator of Community Interest Companies for Community Interest Company status.

These companies may be used as vehicles for community interests such as a local crime prevention group. The company name must end in C.I.C.

Small companies and micro-entities

A company will be 'small' if it meets any two of the following criteria:

- turnover of £10.2 million or less
- £5.1 million or less of net assets on its balance sheet
- 50 employees or less

If a company is small it can use the exemption to not have its accounts audited. It can also choose whether or not send a copy of the director's report and profit and loss account to Companies House and submit abridged accounts.

A company will be a micro-entity if it meets any two of the following criteria:

- turnover of £632,000 or less
- £316,000 or less of net assets on its balance sheet
- 10 employees or less

If a company is a micro-entity it can prepare simpler accounts than those required by statutory minimum requirements and choose to send only a balance sheet with less information to Companies House. It can also benefit from the same exemptions available to a small company.

Test your understanding 3

1 **Which one of the following statements is incorrect in relation to a public company limited by shares?**

A The company must have at least one director.

B The company must have a qualified company secretary.

C The company must have an allotted share capital of at least £50,000.

D The company must be registered as a public limited company.

2 **What is the main requirement of the Companies Act 2006 relating to a private company?**

A The allotted capital must not exceed £50,000.

B It must not have more than 50 members.

C The liability of its members must be limited.

D It must not invite the public to subscribe for its shares.

Test your understanding 4

Spencer and his brother Trevor have decided to leave their employment as software engineers and set up a consultancy. Spencer has come to you for advice; he is unsure about the type of business organisation he should commence trading as.

A **Fill in the gap, delete as appropriate and complete the sentence.**

The term 'partnership' is defined in .... People can form such organisations informally or formally but they need/do not need written agreements.

The definition of a partnership is ...

(Your answer must not exceed 20 words)

B **Fill in the gaps, delete as appropriate and complete the sentence.**

The major advantage of incorporating a business is that the .... of the .... is

.... On company insolvency, the amount the shareholders/directors can be obliged to contribute to the company's assets is ....

(Your answer must not exceed 10 words)

C **Delete as appropriate and fill the gap.**

The formalities required to form a company are less/more onerous than for other types of business organisation. In addition there is less/more regulation in relation to the officers of a company compared to partners. Partnerships are also less/more private in that they do/do not have to publish annual accounts.

D **Spencer and Trevor may one day wish to become a public company. What are the main characteristics of this business entity?**

(Your answer must not exceed 20 words.)

5 Promoters

Definition

There is no statutory definition of a promoter.

According to case law, a promoter is a person who 'undertakes to form a company and who takes the necessary steps to accomplish that purpose': **Twycross v Grant (1878)**.

The definition excludes people just acting in a professional capacity, such as accountant or solicitor.

Duties

Duties

It has long been established in Equity that certain relationships place one party in a vulnerable position versus the other by virtue of the nature of the relationship. This usually occurs when one party has the power to deal with the affairs of the other party without being subjected to the full control of the other either due to impossibility or impracticality. Such persons will be treated as being in a fiduciary relationship with the weaker party.

To prevent the stronger party from benefiting from such a position, Equity developed a set of strict rules which are consistently applied to prevent a fiduciary from abusing their position of power.

> The most common examples of fiduciary relationships are:
> - trustees and beneficiary
> - director and the company
> - principal and agent
> - partners in partnership
> - promoters and the company.

A promoter is under a fiduciary duty to:

- disclose any interest in transactions to the company and not to make a 'secret profit'
- disclose any benefit acquired to an independent board and/or to the shareholders.

If a promoter does make a secret profit, the company may:

- Rescind the contract – but this is not always possible, e.g. if a third party has acquired rights under the contract.
- Obtain damages – but this requires the company to prove loss.
- Recover the profit – the company must prove that the promoter has failed to disclose his or her profit from a transaction.

Erlanger v New Sombrero Phosphate Co (1878)

Facts: Erlanger bought the lease of an island for phosphate mining for £55,000. He then set up the New Sombrero Phosphate Co. Eight days after incorporation, he sold the island to the company for £110,000 through a nominee. After eight months, public investors found out the fact that Erlanger had bought the island at half the price the company had paid for it. The company sued to rescind the contract and recover its money.

Held: The contract could be rescinded. The promoters of a company stand in a fiduciary relationship to investors, meaning they have a duty of disclosure.

Pre-incorporation contracts

A pre-incorporation contract is a contract made by a person acting on behalf of an unformed company.

The position at common law is that a company, prior to its incorporation, does not have contractual capacity and the promoter is therefore personally liable. (This is because a company does not legally exist until it is incorporated.)

Kelner v Baxter (1866)

Facts: A, B and C entered into a contract with the claimant to purchase goods on behalf of the proposed Gravesend Royal Alexandra Hotel Co. The goods were supplied and used in the business. Shortly after incorporation the company collapsed.

Held: As the Gravesend Royal Alexandra Hotel Co was not in existence when the contract was made it was not bound by the contract and could not be sued for the price of the goods. Neither could it ratify the contract after incorporation.

S51 CA06 reinforces the common law position by providing that, subject to any agreement to the contrary, the person making the contract is personally liable. Clear and express words are needed in order to negate liability: **Phonogram Ltd v Lane (1981)**.

The promoter can protect his or her position by:

- including a term in the contract giving the company the right to sue under the Contracts (Rights of Third Parties) Act 1999
- postponing finalising contracts until the company is formed
- entering into an agreement of novation (this involves discharging the original contract and replacing it with a new one) or assigning (transferring) the contract
- agreeing with the company that there is no personal liability for the promoter
- buying an 'off-the-shelf' company, so it is ready to contract without waiting for incorporation.

Off-the-shelf companies

An 'off-the-shelf' company is one that has already been formed. Buying off the shelf has a number of advantages as follows:

- cheap and simple
- can trade immediately
- no problem of pre-incorporation contracts.

Test your understanding 5

1 **Which of the following statements is true in respect of a promoter in breach of their duty not to make a secret profit?**

A The company can always sue the promoter for damages.

B The company can only rescind the contract with the promoter when the promoter owned the property before the promotion began.

C The company can always rescind the contract with the promoter.

D The company can only rescind the contract with the promoter when the promoter acquired the property after the promotion began.

2 **Which of the following are correct?**

I Purchasing an 'off-the-shelf' company enables a business to commence more quickly.

II It is generally cheaper to purchase an 'off-the-shelf' company than to arrange for a solicitor or accountant to register a new company.

III Incorporating a company by registration enables the company's documents to be drafted to the particular needs of the incorporators.

A I and II only

B II and III only

C I and III only

D I, II and III

3 **A company's contractual capacity before incorporation is limited in that it may:**

A only make contracts necessary to form the company

B only ratify, once formed, contracts necessary to form the company

C only make or ratify, once formed, contracts necessary to form the company

D not make or ratify, once formed, any contract even if necessary to form the company

Test your understanding 6

Alfred and Betty have carried on a business as a partnership for some years. They have now decided to incorporate their business.

A **Explain the difference in liability for business debts between partners and shareholders.**

(Your answer must not exceed 25 words)

B **Fill in the gaps, delete as appropriate and complete the sentence.**

Alfred bought some stationery on credit before the date of incorporation. Alfred is/is not personally liable for the debt because

....

(Your answer must not exceed 10 words)

The company can/cannot unilaterally adopt the contract. A range of better solutions might have included

....

(Your answer must not exceed 25 words)

6 Registration

Documents to Registrar

The following must be submitted to the Registrar in order to form a company:

Memorandum of association	• Used to be a more important document under previous company legislation. • Signed by all subscribers (first shareholders) and stating that they wish to form a company and agree to become members of the company. • In relation to a company limited by shares, the memorandum provides evidence of the members' agreement to take at least one share each in the company. • Is not possible to amend or update the memorandum of a company formed under CA06.

Application for registration	S9 CA06 sets out the information that must be delivered to the Registrar when an application for registration is made. In all cases, the application form must include: • the proposed name of the company • whether the members will have limited liability (by shares or guarantee) • whether the company is to be private or public • details of the registered office.
Statement of capital and initial shareholdings	Essentially is a 'snapshot' of a company's share capital at the point of registration. This must state: • the total number of shares to be taken by the subscribers to the memorandum • their aggregate nominal value • the class of shares and the rights which attach to them • the aggregate amount unpaid on the total number of shares • a contact address for each subscriber.
Statement of guarantee (if applicable)	This states the maximum amount each member undertakes to contribute.
Statement of consent to act	The company confirms that the director or secretary has given their consent to act.
Statement of compliance	This provides confirmation that CA06 has been complied with. It may be made in paper or electronic form.
Registration fee	Currently £20.

Note: As the model articles will apply if no articles are supplied, it is not a requirement that articles must be sent, although all companies will have articles.

The Streamlined Company Registration Service, which was set up as a collaboration between Companies House and HRMC, allows for new businesses to register their company and also register for tax at the same time. The purpose of the service is to make it easier for new businesses to fulfil their legal obligations by registering with Companies House and HMRC in one go and dispense with the requirement to send duplicate information to both.

Registrar's duties

On receipt of the above documents the Registrar must:

- **Inspect the documents** and ensure that Companies Act requirements are fulfilled.
- **Issue certificate of incorporation** which is conclusive evidence that Companies Act requirements have been fulfilled: s1 5 CA06. The company exists from the date on the certificate of incorporation.

Trading certificate – public companies only

A plc cannot commence trading until the Registrar has issued a trading certificate.

In order to obtain a trading certificate, an application must be made to the Registrar which states:

- The nominal value of allotted share capital ≥ £50,000.
- That at least a quarter of the nominal value and all of the premium have been paid up.
- The amount of preliminary expenses and who has paid or is to pay them.
- Any benefits given or to be given to promoters.

If it trades before the certificate is issued:

- The company and any officers in default are liable to a fine.
- It is a criminal offence to carry on business, but any contracts are still binding on the company.
- Any transactions are valid. However, if the company fails to comply with its obligations 21 days after being called upon to do so, the directors become jointly and severally liable for those obligations.
- It is a ground for winding up if not obtained within one year: s122 IA 1986.

Test your understanding 7

1 Bob and Mike decided to form a company. On 1 March 20X6, they sent the necessary documents to the registrar. On 10 May 20X6, they received the certificate of incorporation dated 1 May 20X6. Subsequently they discovered that the company was registered on 1 June 20X6.

What was the date of incorporation?

A 1 March 20X6

B 1 May 20X6

C 10 May 20X6

D 1 June 20X6

2 **The effect of a public company trading without a trading certificate is that:**

A the contracts are valid

B the contracts are voidable at the option of the company

C the contracts are voidable at the option of the third party

D the contracts are void

3 **Which of the following documents need not be submitted to register a company limited by shares?**

A A memorandum of association

B Articles of association

C A statement of the first directors and secretary

D A statutory declaration of compliance with the requirements of the Companies Acts

Test your understanding 8

Adam and Ben have carried on business together in partnership for a number of years. They have now decided to operate their business through the medium of a private company limited by shares called AB Ltd.

A **Complete this sentence.**

As partners, the liability of Adam and Ben for the firm's debts was

....

(Your answer must not exceed 3 words.)

B **In order to register a private company limited by shares the partners will need to submit the following documents to the Registrar of companies.**

I

II

III

IV

V

VI

C	**Complete this sentence:** If the Registrar of Companies is satisfied with the documents submitted to him for registration, he will issue a .... which enables the company to commence trading immediately.	
D	**Explain the liability of Adam and Ben in the event of AB Ltd becoming insolvent.**	
(Your answer must not exceed 20 words.)		

Name of company

The name of the company must comply with the following rules:

- It must have limited (Ltd) or public limited company (plc) at the end as applicable.
- It cannot be the same as another in the index of names.
- It cannot use certain words which are illegal or offensive.
- It must have the Secretary of State's consent to use certain words (e.g. England, Chartered, Royal, National, University, Insurance, etc.) or any name suggesting a connection with the government or any local authority.
- It must avoid the tort of passing off (see **below**).

A company can voluntarily change its name by passing a special resolution under s77 CA06 or by any other means provided for in the articles.

The Secretary of State requires a company to change its name in the following circumstances:

Reason	**Period**
The name is the same as, or too like, an existing registered name.	12 months
The name gives so misleading an indication of the nature of the company's activities as to be likely to cause harm to the public.	No time limit
Misleading information or undertakings were given when applying for a name that required approval.	5 years

If a company feels than another company has a name which is too similar to its own, it may object to the Company Names Adjudicator under CA 06. The Adjudicator will consider the case and then make their decision. In most cases the Adjudicator will require a name change, and in some cases the Adjudicator may state the new company name.

The tort of passing off

The tort of passing off arises:

- where one business uses a name which is similar to that of an existing business, and
- it misleads persons into believing that they are the same business, and
- it causes actual damage to that business or will probably do so.

Ewing v Buttercup Margarine Co Ltd (1917)

Facts: Ewing who traded under the name Buttercup Dairy Company sued to restrain a newly registered company called Buttercup Margarine Company Ltd from using the name on the grounds that the general public might reasonably believe that there was a link between the two businesses.

Held: The court held that the word 'Buttercup' was so closely associated with Ewing dairy products as to be likely to cause confusion if used by the similar margarine business. An injunction was granted to prevent the defendant company from trading under its name.

If passing off is proved, the court may restrain the business from trading under that name and order that damages be paid to the person whose business has suffered loss.

Test your understanding 9

1 **Which of the following names could not without further consent be a permissible name under the Companies Act for a company, the main object of which is to contract refuse collection services for Westminster City Council?**

A Westminster City Refuse Services Ltd

B Council (Refuse Collection) Services Ltd

C Refuse Collection (Westminster) Ltd

D City Waste Disposal Ltd

2 **Which of the following statements is correct?**

I It is not possible to register a company limited by shares with the same name as a company already on the register.

II Once on the register, a company limited by shares cannot change its registered office.

A I only

B II only

C Both I and II

D Neither I nor II

3 **A business has been registered under the name 'The Mark Jones Partnership Co Ltd'. What type of business organisation must this be?**

A A partnership

B A private limited company

C A public limited company

D Any of the above as this is a business name

7 Articles of association

Introduction

The articles of association form the company's internal constitution.

They:

- set out the manner in which the company is to be governed and
- regulate the relationship between the company and its shareholders.

There are no mandatory contents.

Model articles

For companies incorporated under Companies Act 2006, model articles have been prescribed by the Secretary of State.

There are three model articles which cover the following companies:

- private companies limited by shares; or
- private companies limited by guarantee; or
- public companies.

These model articles will apply where a company is formed without registering articles or where the articles registered do not exclude or modify the model articles.

A company:

- may adopt the model articles in full or in part
- is deemed to have adopted the model articles if there is no express or implied provision to exclude them; or
- may draft its own unique articles.

Companies Act 2006 states that the articles should be contained in a single document which is divided into consecutively numbered paragraphs.

Articles should contain rules on a number of areas, the most important of which are as follows:

- Appointment and dismissal of directors
- Powers, responsibilities and liabilities of directors
- Director's meetings
- Member's rights
- Dividends
- Communication with members
- Issue of shares
- Documents and records.

8 Legal effect of company's constitutional documents

S33 CA06 states that the provisions of a company's constitution bind the company and its members to the same extent as if there were covenants on the part of the company and of each member to observe those provisions. This means that the articles form a contract between the company and its members, and the members between themselves, even if they do not sign them.

1 **The articles are in all respects enforceable by the company against its members.**

Hickman v Kent or Romney Marsh Sheepbreeders' Association (1915)

Facts: The company's articles included a clause to the effect that all disputes between the company and its members were to be referred to arbitration. A member brought court proceedings against the company.

Held: The proceedings were stopped. The company could enforce the arbitration clause against a member.

2 **The articles are enforceable by the members against the company.**

Pender v Lushington (1877)

Facts: The articles provided for one vote per ten shares, with no member to have more than 100 votes. A member with more than 1,000 shares transferred the surplus to a nominee and directed him how to vote. The chairman refused to accept the nominee's votes.

Held: The right to vote was enforceable against the company.

3 **The articles also operate as a contract between individual members in their capacity as members.**

Rayfield v Hands (1958)

Facts: The articles required the directors to be members, i.e. to hold qualification shares and to purchase shares from any member who wished to sell.

Held: This was enforceable against the directors in their capacity as members.

However, the articles do not bind the company to non-members nor do they bind the members in any other capacity.

Ely v Positive Government Security Life Assurance Co (1876).

Facts: The articles provided that Eley should be solicitor to the company for life.

Held: This was not a right given to him as a member and he could not rely on the articles as a contract for professional services. The right to be a director of a company has also been held to be an outsider right (i.e. a non-membership right).

Beattie v EF Beattie (1938)

Facts: The company's articles contained an arbitration clause. B, a member and director of the company, was in dispute with the company concerning his rights as director. He brought court proceedings against the company.

Held: He was not bound by the arbitration clause since he was acting in his capacity as director, not a member.

However, even where the articles are not a relevant contract for this purpose they may be evidence of another contract made independently.

New British Iron Co, ex parte Beckwith (1898)

Facts: The articles stated that directors were entitled to be paid £1,000 on taking office.

Held: The contract was implied from the directors' action in taking office. The provision in the articles was merely evidence of that separate contract.

The articles also operate as a contract between individual members in their capacity as members. It is important in an examination question to check the capacity in which the person is claiming. Is it as a member, or in some other capacity, such as a director or an accountant? Obviously the articles have no effect as a contract between the company and a person who is not a member even if they are named in them and given apparent rights against the company. In Eley's case above, Eley's membership was irrelevant to his claim; as solicitor he had no claim – he was attempting to enforce a non-member's right.

Test your understanding 10

Which of the following statements is/are correct?

I The articles of association of a company limited by shares contain the internal regulations of the company.

II The articles of association form a contract between the shareholders and the company.

A I only

B II only

C Both I and II

D Neither I nor II

9 Alteration of articles

General rule

- The articles can usually be altered by a special resolution (75% majority).
- Copies of the amended articles must be sent to the Registrar within 15 days.

Exceptions

1 Entrenchment

It is possible to entrench some of the articles. This means that a specified procedure (e.g. unanimous consent) may be required to change them.

2 Members increase liability

S25 CA06 prevents a member being bound by any alteration made after he or she becomes a member that requires him or her to increase his or her liability or contribute further to the company.

3 Common law restriction

Any change to the articles must be 'bona fide in interests of the company as a whole': **Allen v Gold Reefs of Africa (1900)**.

- It is for the members to decide whether the change is bona fide in the interests of the company as a whole.
- The court will not interfere unless no reasonable person would consider the change to be bona fide **(Greenhalgh v Arderne Cinemas Ltd (1950), Brown v British Abrasive Wheel Co (1919)** and **Sidebottom v Kershaw, Leese & Co (1920)**.
- If the change is bona fide, it is immaterial that happens to inflict hardship or has retrospective operation.
- The change will be void if actual fraud or oppression takes place.

- An alteration is not invalid merely because it causes a breach of contract – but that does not excuse breach **(Southern Foundries (1926) Ltd and Federated Foundries Ltd v Shirlaw (1940))**.

Greenhalgh v Arderne Cinemas Ltd (1950)

Facts: The issue was the removal from the articles of the members' right of first refusal of any shares which a member might wish to transfer; the majority wished to make the change in order to admit an outsider to membership in the interests of the company.

Held: The benefit to the company as a whole was held to be a benefit which any **individual hypothetical member** of the company could enjoy directly or through the company and not merely a benefit to the majority of members only. The test of good faith did not require proof of actual benefit but merely the honest belief on reasonable grounds that benefit could follow from the alteration.

In several cases the court has held that actual and foreseen detriment to a minority affected by the alteration was not in itself a sufficient ground of objection if the benefit to the company test was satisfied.

Brown v British Abrasive Wheel Co (1919)

Facts: The articles were altered to enable the majority to purchase at 'a fair value the shares of the minority'. The intention was to invoke the clause against some minority members who were refusing to inject further capital into the company. They objected to the alteration.

Held: This was not a bona fide alteration as it would benefit the majority shareholders, rather than the company as a whole.

Sidebottom v Kershaw, Leese & Co (1920)

Facts: The alteration was to expel a member who carried on a business competing with the company.

Held: It was a valid alteration.

Allen v Gold Reefs of West Africa Ltd (1900)

Facts: Z held fully paid up and partly paid up shares in the company. The company's articles provided for a lien for all debts and liabilities of any member upon all partly paid shares held by the member. The company by special resolution altered its articles so that the lien was available on fully paid up shares as well.

Held: The company had power to alter its articles by extending the lien to fully paid shares.

Southern Foundries (1926) Ltd and Federated Foundries Ltd v Shirlaw (1940)

Facts: Alteration of the articles empowered the company to remove the managing director.

Held: The alteration was valid, but the MD could sue for breach of contract.

Test your understanding 11

Explain the meaning and effect of a company's articles of association, paying particular attention to the following issues:

A the operation of the model articles of association

B the effect of the articles on both members and non-members

C the procedure for altering the articles of association.

(Adapted from ACCA June 2004 examination)

10 Statutory books, returns and records

Registers

Register	Contents
Members	Names, addresses, date became/ceased, number of shares, class of share, amount paid up. Any member of the company can inspect the register without charge. A member of the public has the right of inspection but must pay.
Directors and company secretary	Name (present and former), address, date of birth, occupation, nationality, other directorships within the last five years. The register does not include shadow directors (see chapter 10). The register must be open to inspection by a member without charge or by any other person for a fee.
Charges	This register contains details of fixed or floating charges created over the company's property (see chapter 8). The register will have details of the name of chargee, type of charge, brief description of property charged, amount and date created. The company must also keep copies of every instrument creating a charge at its registered office or some other place of which the Registrar has been notified. Any member or creditor may inspect the register free of charge, any other member of the public can inspect for a fee.

Persons with significant control	A person with significant control (PSC) is anyone in the company who: • owns more than 25% of the company's shares • owns more than 25% of the company's voting rights • has the right to appoint or remove a majority of the board of directors • has significant influence or control over the company • has significant influence or control over a trust or firm. The register should have details of name, service address, residential address, country and state of residence, nationality, date of birth, date they became a PSC and the nature of company control.
Other documents	Minutes of general meetings.
Resolutions and meetings	Records must be kept for a minimum period of 10 years.

The registers must normally be kept at the company's registered office (although the register of members and register of directors' interests can be kept where they are made up) and must be available for public inspection by a member free of charge or by any other person for a fee.

Requests for inspection must provide details about the person seeking the information, the purpose of the request and whether the information will be disclosed to others. The company may apply to the court for an order that it need not comply with the request.

The register of directors' addresses should now contain service addresses rather than details of the directors' residential addresses. The service address can be simply 'the company's registered office'.

The company must also keep a separate register of the directors' residential addresses. Both the service and the residential addresses will need to be supplied to the Registrar of Companies.

The residential addresses will be withheld from the public register. However, they will generally remain available to the Registrar and certain specified public bodies and credit reference agencies.

Under the SBEEA 2015 private companies can opt out of maintaining separate private registers and instead keep certain information on the public register at Companies House.

Annual confirmation statement

The annual confirmation statement must be filed with Companies House which states that the company has provided all of the information it was required to provide within the previous 12 months. This statement must be provided within 14 days of expiry of the previous 12 month period. For new companies, the first statement should be provided 12 months from the date of incorporation of the company.

The confirmation statement must include changes to any of the following:

- the address of the company's registered office
- the type of company
- the company's principal business activities
- details of directors and company secretary where applicable
- the statement of capital
- details of the members of the company as at the return date
- details of members who have ceased to become members since the last return was made
- details of the number of shares of each class held by members at the return date.

Accounting records

The company must keep accounting records containing sufficient information to show and explain the company's transactions and its financial position.

At any time it should be possible:

- to disclose with reasonable accuracy the company's financial position at intervals of not more than six months
- for the directors to ensure that any accounts that need to be prepared comply with Companies Act 2006 and International Accounting Standards.

In particular the records **must** show:

- daily entries of all money received and spent
- a record of assets and liabilities
- statement of stocks at end of the financial year to back up the above
- statements of stocktaking
- statements of all goods sold and purchased, showing the goods and the buyers and sellers (except in the retail trade).

Accounting records must be kept for three years in the case of a private company and six years in that of a public one. They should be kept at the company's registered office or at some other place thought fit by the directors.

Failure to keep sufficient accounting records is an offence by the officers in default.

Annual financial statements

Companies are required to produce annual financial statements including:

- balance sheet/statement of financial position and profit and loss account/statement of comprehensive income showing true and fair view
- directors' report stating the amount of any dividend and likely future developments.

The annual financial statements must be approved and signed on behalf of the board of directors and a copy filed with Registrar.

11 Chapter summary

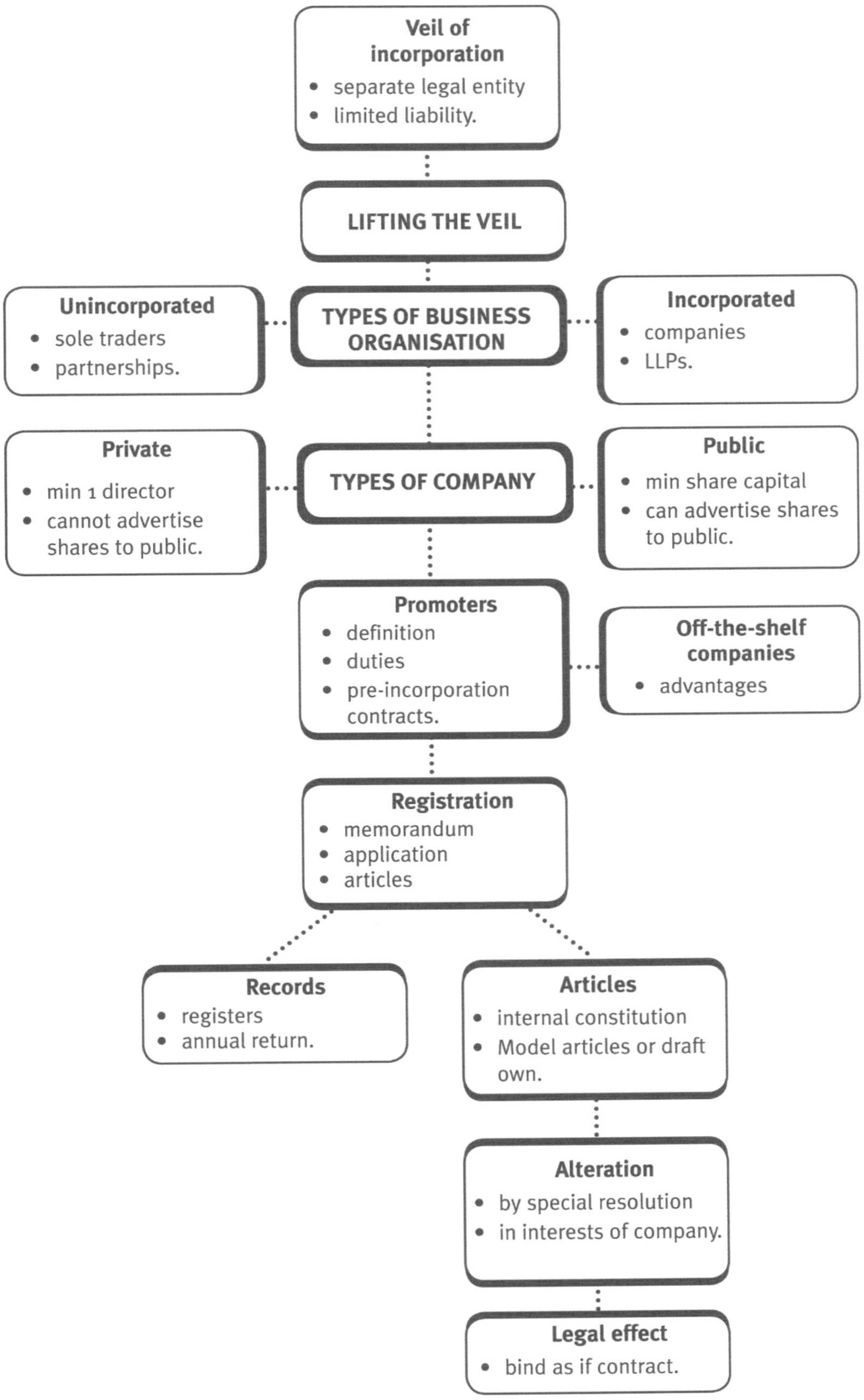

Test your understanding answers

Test your understanding 1

A Whereas English law treats a partnership as simply a group of individuals trading collectively, the effect of incorporation is that a company once formed has its own distinct legal personality, completely separate from its members.

The doctrine of separate or corporate personality is an ancient one, but the case usually cited in relation to separate personality is: **Salomon v Salomon & Co Ltd (1897)**. Salomon had been in the boot and leather business for some time. Together with other members of his family he formed a limited company and sold his previous business to it. Payment was in the form of cash, shares and debentures. When the company was eventually wound up it was argued that Salomon and the company were the same, and since he could not be his own creditor, his debentures should have no effect. Although lower courts had decided against Salomon, the House of Lords held that under the circumstances, in the absence of fraud, his debentures were valid. The company had been properly constituted and consequently it was, in law, a distinct legal person, completely separate from Salomon.

A number of consequences flow from the fact that corporations are treated as having legal personality in their own right.

I Limited liability

No one is responsible for anyone else's debts unless they agree to accept such responsibility. Similarly, at common law, members of a corporation are not responsible for its debts without agreement. However, registered companies, i.e. those formed under the Companies Acts, are not permitted unless the shareholders agree to accept liability for their company's debts. In return for this agreement, the extent of their liability is set at a fixed amount. In the case of a company limited by shares, the level of liability is the amount remaining unpaid on the nominal value of the shares held. In the case of a company limited by guarantee, it is the amount that shareholders have agreed to pay in the event of the company being wound up.

II Perpetual existence

As the corporation exists in its own right, changes in its membership have no effect on its status or existence. Members may die, be declared bankrupt or insane, or transfer their shares, all without any effect on the company. As an abstract legal person the company cannot die, although its existence can be brought to an end through the winding-up procedure.

III Business property is owned by the company

Any business assets are owned by the company itself and not the shareholders. This is normally a major advantage in that the company's assets are not subject to claims based on the ownership rights of its individual members. It can, however, cause unforeseen problems as may be seen in **Macaura v Northern Assurance Co (1925)**. The plaintiff had owned a timber estate and later formed a one-man company and transferred the estate to this company. However, he continued to insure the estate in his own name. When the timber was lost in a fire it was held that Macaura could not claim on the insurance as he had no personal interest in the timber, which belonged to the company.

IV Legal capacity

The company has contractual capacity in its own right and can sue and be sued in its own name. The extent of the company's liability, as opposed to the members, is unlimited and all its assets may be used to pay off debts. The company may also be liable in tort for any injuries sustained as a consequence of the negligence of its agents or employees.

V The rule in Foss v Harbottle (1843)

This states that where a company suffers an injury, it is for the company, acting through the majority of the members, to take the appropriate remedial action. Perhaps of more importance is the corollary of the rule, which is that an individual cannot raise a legal action in response to a wrong suffered by the company.

B **Lifting the veil of incorporation**

There are a number of occasions, both statutory and at common law, when the doctrine of separate personality will not be followed. On these occasions it is said that the veil of incorporation, which separates the company from its members, is 'pierced', 'lifted' or 'drawn aside'. Such situations arise as follows:

I Under statute

If a public company starts to trade without first obtaining a trading certificate, the directors can be made personally liable for any loss or damage suffered by a third party: S767 CA06.

Under the Company Directors Disqualification Act 1986, if a director who is disqualified participates in the management of a company, that director will be jointly or severally liable for the company's debts.

Under the Insolvency Act 1986, members and/or directors held liable for wrongful or fraudulent trading may be made personally liable for losses arising as a result.

II At common law

As in most areas of law that are based on the application of policy decisions, it is difficult to predict when the courts will ignore separate personality. What is certain is that the courts will not permit the corporate form to be used for a clearly fraudulent purpose or to evade a legal duty. Thus in **Gilford Motor Co Ltd v Horne (1933)** an employee had covenanted not to solicit his former employer's customers. After he left their employment he formed a company to solicit those customers and it was held that the company was a sham and the court would not permit it to be used to avoid the contract.

The courts are prepared to ignore separate personality in times of war in order to defeat the activity of shareholders who might be enemy aliens. See Daimler Co Ltd v Continental Tyre and Rubber Co (GB) Ltd (1916).

Where groups of companies have been set up for particular business purposes, the courts will usually not ignore the separate existence of the various companies, unless they are being used for fraud. Although there is authority for treating separate companies as a single group (as in **DHN Food Distributors Ltd v London Borough of Tower Hamlets (1976)**) later authorities have cast extreme doubt on this decision (see **Woolfson v Strathclyde Regional Council (1978)**). More recent cases would appear to suggest that the courts are now more reluctant to ignore separate personality where the company has been properly established **(Adams v Cape Industries plc (1990))**.

Test your understanding 2

1 **B**

The partners of a partnership are fully liable for all of the firm's debts. The fact that the partners in this case are limited companies is irrelevant.

2 **D**

Answer D gives a definition of liability for a limited liability company limited by shares.

3 **A**

A shareholder is a part-owner of the company, but is not a part-owner of the property owned by the company. In law, this property belongs to the company itself, which is a legal person.

Test your understanding 3

1 **A**

A public company must have at least two directors. Statements B, C and D are correct.

2 **D**

A private company cannot invite the public to subscribe for its shares. This is the key difference between a public and a private company.

Test your understanding 4

A the Partnership Act 1890

do not need

...the relationship which subsists between persons carrying on a business in common with a view to profit.

B liability

members

limited

shareholders

...any unpaid portion of the price of their shares.

C more

more

more

do not

D A public limited company must have a minimum allotted share capital of £50,000 and a trading certificate.

Test your understanding 5

1 **A**

The company can always sue the promoter for damages. However, the right to rescission may be lost where, for example, there has been unreasonable delay.

2 **D**

Buying a company off the shelf means that the company has already been incorporated. It saves the time of going through the procedures for incorporation. Other non-urgent changes can then be made, such as changing the company name. A company can be bought off-the-shelf for about £100, which is much cheaper than using a solicitor or accountant to register a new company. However, the registered details (such as the name and directors) may need to be changed. All three statements are therefore correct.

3 **D**

The position at common law is that a company cannot be bound by a contract that was made before it was formed, and after its formation it cannot ratify or formally adopt a pre-incorporation contract. S51 CA06 provides that a person acting for the company should have personal liability on a pre-incorporation contract that he or she enters into.

Test your understanding 6

A Partners are liable for business debts to the extent of their personal wealth, whereas shareholders' liability is limited to the unpaid portion of their shares.

B is

The company cannot make contracts before it comes into existence.

cannot

assigning the contract, making an agreement of novation or acquiring an 'off-the-shelf' company before making the contract.

Test your understanding 7

1 **B**

Regardless of the actual date of registration, the only date that matters is the date on the certificate of incorporation.

2 **A**

Provisional contracts are valid although if not paid within 21 days, the directors become jointly and severally liable with the company.

3 **B**

It is not necessary to submit articles of association and if a company limited by shares does not do so, the model articles will apply.

Test your understanding 8

A joint and several

B
- I An Application
- II Articles of association (unless the model articles are to apply)
- III Memorandum of association
- IV A statement of capital and initial shareholdings
- V A statement of proposed officers containing the names of the first directors and company secretary (if applicable)
- VI A statement of compliance

C Certificate of incorporation

D Adam and Ben are only liable for any unpaid portion of the price of their shares

Test your understanding 9

1 **B**

S54 CA06 prohibits a company, unless given approval by the Secretary of State for the Department for Business and Trade from having a name that would be likely to give the impression that the business is carried on in connection with the government or a local council. Here, the use of the word 'Council' in the business name would not be permitted.

2 **A**

A company cannot take the same name as a company that has been registered already with the same name. Once registered, a company can change its registered office, and must notify the registrar of any such change.

3 **B**

The fact that the name ends with the letters 'Ltd' indicates that it is a private limited company.

Test your understanding 10

C

The articles of association form a contract between the shareholders and the company, in respect of the rights of the ordinary shareholders. The articles set out the internal regulations or constitution of the company, e.g. the articles set out the rights of shareholders and the powers of the directors.

Test your understanding 11

A Model articles are prescribed by the Secretary of State. They apply where a company is formed without registering articles or where the articles registered do not exclude or modify the model articles.

A company:

– may adopt the model articles in full or in part

– is deemed to have adopted the model articles if there is no express or implied provision to exclude them; or

– may draft its own unique articles.

B S33 CA06 states that the provisions of a company's constitution bind the company and its members to the same extent as if there were covenants on the part of the company and of each member to observe those provisions. This section has three effects.

I The documents establish a contract which binds each member to the company. Thus in **Hickman v Kent or Romney Marsh Sheepbreeders' Association (1920)**, the company was able to enforce an article against a member that provided that disputes involving the member and the company should go to arbitration.

II The company is contractually bound to each of its members. On this basis in **Pender v Lushington (1877)** a member was able to sue in respect of the wrongful denial of his right to vote at a company meeting.

III The articles constitute a contract between the members. In **Rayfield v Hands (1958)**, the articles of the company provided that, where shareholders wished to transfer their shares, they should inform the directors of the company, who were obliged to take the shares equally between them at fair value. When the directors refused to purchase the plaintiff's shares, the court held that the directors were bound as members by the articles and therefore had to comply with the procedure set out there. Articles only operate as a contract in respect of membership rights and obligations. Consequently it has been held that, although members can enforce them, non-members, or members suing in some other capacity than that of a member, will not be able to enforce promises established in the company's articles.

In **Eley v Positive Government Security Life Assurance Co (1876)**, the articles of a company stated that the plaintiff was to be appointed as the company's solicitor. It was held that Eley could not use the articles to establish a contract between himself and the company as those articles only created a contract between the company and its members. Although Eley was in fact a member, he was not suing in that capacity but in the capacity of solicitor, which was not a membership right.

C **A company can normally alter its articles by passing a special resolution. However, if certain provisions are entrenched, they can only be altered by following the specified procedure; this may require unanimous consent.**

Any alteration must be made 'bona fide in the interest of the company as a whole', although the exact meaning of this phrase is not altogether clear. It is evident that it involves a subjective element in that those deciding the alteration must actually believe they are acting in the interests of the company. There is additionally, however, an objective element. In **Greenhalgh v Arderne Cinemas Ltd (1950)** it was stated that any alteration had to be in the interests of the 'individual hypothetical member'.

In **Brown v British Abrasive Wheel Co (1919)** an alteration to the articles of the company was proposed to give the majority shareholders the right to buy the shares of the minority. It was held that the alteration was invalid as it would benefit the majority shareholders rather than the company as a whole. However, in **Sidebottom v Kershaw, Leese & Co (1920)**, an alteration to the articles gave the directors the power to require any shareholder, who entered into competition with the company, to transfer their shares to nominees of the directors at a fair price. It was held that under those circumstances the alteration was valid as it would benefit the company as a whole.

Chapter

9

Capital and financing

Chapter learning objectives

Upon completion of this chapter you will be able to:

- understand the different meanings of capital
- illustrate the difference between various classes of shares
- explain the procedure for the variation of class rights
- define companies' borrowing powers
- explain the meaning of debenture
- distinguish loan capital from share capital
- explain the concept of a company charge and distinguish between fixed and floating charges
- describe the need and the procedure for registering company charges
- explain the doctrine of capital maintenance and capital reduction
- examine the effect of issuing shares at either a discount or a premium
- explain the rules governing the distribution of dividends in both private and public companies.

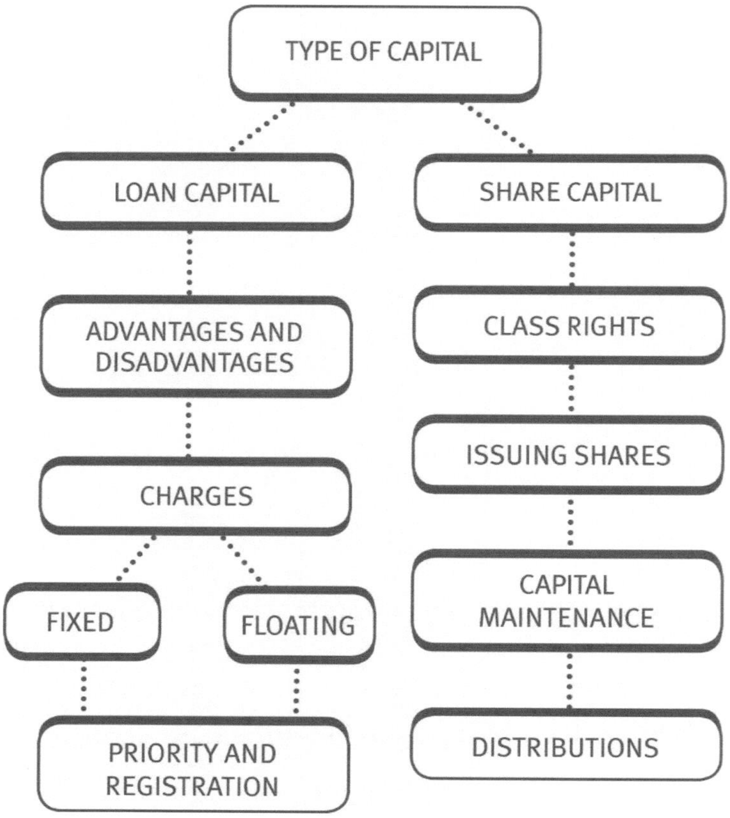

1 Share capital

Definition of a share

A share is 'the interest of a shareholder measured by a sum of money, for the purpose of a liability in the first place, and of interest in the second, but also consisting of a series of mutual covenants entered into by all the shareholders': **Borland's Trustee v Steel Bros & Co Ltd (1901)**.

A shareholder is a member of the company and therefore has voting rights, depending on the class of shares held. They are also entitled to dividends depending on the availability of profits.

In the event of liquidation, depending on the type of share, a shareholder receives payment after all other creditors, but can participate in surplus assets.

2 Types of shares

	Preference shares	Ordinary shares (equity)
Voting rights	None, or restricted by the articles of association.	Full.
Dividend rights	Fixed dividend paid in priority to other dividends, usually cumulative.	Paid after preference dividend. Not fixed.
Surplus on winding up	Prior return of capital, but cannot participate in surplus.	Entitled to share surplus assets after repayment of preference shares.

Test your understanding 1

Freeco is a public limited company. Geoffrey owns 11,000 6% $1 preference shares in the company and his sister, Gertrude, owns 10,000 $1 ordinary shares.

A **Delete as appropriate and complete the sentence.**

Both Geoffrey and Gertrude are/are not members of the company. Geoffrey can/cannot attend general meetings. He can/cannot usually vote in the same way as Gertrude. Gertrude and Geoffrey can/cannot receive a dividend.

On liquidation, the position of both in relation to creditors is ....

(Your answer must not exceed 20 words.)

B **Explain why Geoffrey's investment may be seen as less risky than Gertrude's.**

(Your answer must not exceed 30 words.)

3 Class rights

What are they?

Class rights are the special rights attached to each class of shares, such as dividend rights, distribution of capital on a winding up and voting. (See above concerning the different rights that normally attach to ordinary shares and preference shares.)

How can they be varied?

The procedure for varying class rights depends on whether any procedure is specified in the articles:

Is procedure to vary specified?	Method of variation
Yes	Procedure set out in articles must be followed.
No	Variation needs special resolution or written consent of 75% in nominal value of the class: S630 CA06.

Minority protection

Under S633 CA06, the holders of 15% of the nominal value of that class, who did not consent to the variation, may ask the court to cancel the variation within 21 days of the passing of the resolution.

The court may confirm or cancel the variation. However, it will only cancel the variation if the petitioner proves it is unfairly prejudicial.

The court draws a distinction between:

- a variation that affects the value, enjoyment or power derived from the rights and
- a variation that changes the rights themselves.

The court will only intervene in the latter case.

Cumbrian Newspapers Group Ltd v Cumberland & Westmorland Herald (1986)

Facts: The claimant and the defendant were both publishers of newspapers. They negotiate a transaction whereby D would acquire one of C's papers and C would acquire 10 per cent of D's share capital. D issued the 10 per cent shareholding and as part of the agreement under which the shares were issued amended its articles to give C certain rights including pre-emption rights over other ordinary shares. The purpose of such rights was to enable C as a shareholder to prevent a takeover. Subsequently, a few years later D called a meeting to pass a special resolution to cancel the articles which gave special rights to C. C sought a declaration that the rights were class rights which could not be cancelled without his consent.

Held: The declaration was granted. The special rights granted were rights which could not be varied or cancelled without C's consent.

White v Bristol Aeroplane Co (1953)

Facts: The company made a bonus issue of new ordinary and preference shares to the existing ordinary shareholders who alone were entitled to participate in bonus issues under the articles. The existing preference shareholders objected on the basis that this reduced their proportion of the class of preference shares and was a variation of class rights to which they had not consented.

Held: Bonus issue is not a variation of class rights since the existing preference shareholders had the same number of shares as before.

Greenhalgh v Arderne Cinemas Ltd (1950)

Facts: The company had two classes of ordinary shares, 50p and 10p shares, with every share carrying one vote. A resolution was passed to subdivide each 50p share into five 10p shares, thereby multiplying the votes of that class by five.

Held: The subdivision of shares is not a variation of class rights. The rights of the original 10p shares had not been varied since they still had one vote per share as before.

4 Terminology

Issued share capital	Issued share capital comprises share capital that has actually been issued, released or sold by the company.
Paid up share capital	The amount which shareholders have actually paid on the shares issued.
Called up share capital	The amount of unpaid share capital which has been called for from shareholders but not yet paid.
Uncalled share capital	The amount of unpaid share capital that has not yet been called for from shareholders and therefore also remains unpaid.
Statutory pre-emption rights	New shares offered to existing shareholders in proportion to their shareholdings. Raises new funds. Purpose is not to dilute individual member shareholding. Only applies to ordinary shares which must be paid for in cash. The offer is open for 21 days. Pre-emption rights can be disapplied by provision in the articles of association or by a special resolution being passed by the members.

Bonus issues	Also referred to as scrip issue or capitalisation issue. Are normally issued at no cost to the shareholders in which case do not raise any new funds. Sometimes the company issues partly paid-up bonus shares in which case the shareholders may have to make some contributions in the future. Carried out by some of the company's non-distributable reserves to issue fully paid shares to existing shareholders in proportion to their shareholdings. For example a company may issue two free preference shares for every ordinary share held. Must never be funded from a company's ordinary capital.
Rights issues	New shares offered to existing shareholders in proportion to their shareholdings to raise new funds. Can be used where the statutory pre-emption rights have been disapplied. Offer is open for 21 days during which it cannot be withdrawn. Applies to both ordinary and preference shares. Shares usually offered at discount to current market value (but not at discount to nominal value). Shareholders who do not want to buy the new shares themselves may sell the rights to a third party. A member who does not wish to take up the right can sell his or her right on. Any shares which are not accepted may then be allotted on the same (or less favourable terms) to non-members.

Test your understanding 2

A public company with a stock market listing has just sold a new issue of ten million $1 ordinary shares. All the shares were bought by existing shareholders in the company.

Which one of the following conclusions can be inferred from this statement?

A The company has undertaken a rights issue.

B The company has raised exactly $10 million to finance the expansion of the business.

C As a new issue, the shares could be sold only to personal shareholders and not to institutional shareholders.

D Since there were no new shareholders, the company's share capital was not extended.

5 Issuing shares

Allotment of shares

This is where the shares are allocated to a person under a contract of allotment. Once the shares are allotted and the holder is entered in the register of members, they become a member of the company.

Authority

The directors need authority in order to allot shares. This may be given:

- by the articles, or
- by passing an ordinary resolution.

The authority must state:

- the maximum number of shares to be allotted
- the expiry date for the authority (maximum five years).

The directors of a private company with only one class of shares may allot shares of that class unless it is prohibited by the articles: S550 CA06.

Issue at discount

Every share has a **nominal value** which is fixed at the time of incorporation of the company in the statement of capital and initial shareholding. The nominal value of the share represents the extent of a shareholders potential liability.

The common law rule is that a company cannot issue its shares for a consideration which is at a discount on their nominal value.

Ooregum Gold Mining Co of India v Roper (1892)

Facts: Shares in a company which had a nominal value of £1 were trading at a market price of 12.5p. In an honest attempt to refinance the company, new £1 preference shares were issued and credited with 75p as paid up. The company subsequently went into liquidation.

Held: The holders of the shares were required to pay a further 75p per share.

The common law rule is given statutory effect in S580 CA 2006. In addition S582 CA 2006 states that shares are only treated as paid up to the extent that the company has received money or money's worth.

If this rule is breached the issue is still valid, but the allottee must pay up the discount plus interest. This applied to any subsequent holder of such a share who was aware of the original underpayment: S588 CA 2006.

Under S590 CA 2006 it is an offence to contravene these rules and the company and company and any officers in default are liable to a fine.

Issue at premium

Where a share is allotted at a value greater than its nominal value, the excess over the nominal value is share premium. This is where the market value of the share is greater than the fixed nominal value.

S610 CA 2006 requires any premium to be credited to a share premium account, which may only be used for:

- writing off the expenses of the issue of those shares
- writing off any commission paid on the issue of those shares
- issuing bonus shares.

Paying for shares – private companies

Private companies may issue shares for non-cash consideration. The court will interfere with the valuation only if there is fraud or the consideration is 'illusory, past or patently inadequate'.

Paying for shares – public companies

There are a number of additional rules relating to the issue of shares in public companies contained in CA 2006:

S584	Subscribers to the memorandum must pay cash for their subscription shares.
S585	Payment for shares must not be in the form of work or services.
S586	Shares cannot be allotted until at least one-quarter of their nominal value and the whole of any premium have been paid.
S587	Non-cash consideration must be received within five years.
S593	Non-cash consideration must be independently valued and reported on by a person qualified to be the company's auditor. The independent valuation must be carried out six months prior to allotment.

Test your understanding 3
What can the share premium account be used for?

6 Capital maintenance

Purpose

The capital of a limited company is regarded as a buffer fund for creditors. (Note that the creditors' buffer is an accounting fund, not real money. The actual cash or assets subscribed can be used by the company.)

The rules on maintenance of capital exist in order to prevent a company reducing its capital by returning it to its members, whether directly or indirectly. This means that, **as a general rule**, a limited company cannot reduce its share capital or purchase its own shares. There are, however, an exception to this general rule and these are which is discussed below.

Exception

Reduction of capital

Under S641 CA 2006, a company can reduce its capital at any time, for any reason.

Reduce or cancel liabilities on partly-paid shares, i.e. the company gives up any claim for money owing.

Return capital in excess of the company's needs, i.e. the company reduces its assets by repaying cash to its shareholders.

Cancel the paid-up capital that is no longer represented by the assets, i.e. if the company has a debit balance on reserves it can write this off by reducing capital and thereby does not need to make good past losses.

Procedure for public companies:

Pass a special resolution

Apply to the court to confirm the special resolution.

If reduction involves one of the first two methods above, court must require company to settle a list of creditors entitled to object.

The court must not confirm the reduction until it is satisfied that all creditors have either consented to the reduction or had their debts discharged or secured.

The company must file documents with the Registrar. If the share capital of a public company falls below $50,000, it must re-register as a private company.

Simplified procedure for private companies:

Pass a special resolution supported by a solvency statement.

The solvency statement is a statement by each of the directors that the company will be able to meet its debts within the following year.

A solvency statement made without reasonable grounds is an offence punishable by fine and/or imprisonment.

Copies of the resolution, solvency statement and a statement of capital must be filed with the Registrar within 15 days.

Test your understanding 4

A public company limited by shares may reduce capital by:

A passing an ordinary resolution and obtaining the court's permission

B passing a special resolution and obtaining the court's permission

C passing an ordinary resolution with special notice

D passing a special resolution with special notice

7 Treasury shares

Definition

These are created when a company purchases its own shares from distributable profits. The shares do not have to be cancelled. Up to 10% of the shares can be held 'in treasury' which means they can be re-issued without the usual formalities.

Previously treasury shares could only be created by public companies but since 30 April 2013 they can be created by private companies as well.

General rule

Shares which are purchased by a company must be cancelled and the amount of the company's share capital account reduced by the nominal value of the cancelled shares.

Exception

Under S724 CA 2006, companies can buy, hold and resell their shares.

The shares must be purchased from distributable profits and the company can cancel or sell them at any time.

Under S726 CA 2006, the shares will not give the company any voting rights in respect of those shares. In addition, no dividend or other form of distribution can be made in respect of them.

S728 CA 2006, prescribes that when treasury shares are sold or transferred for the purpose of an employee's share scheme, the company must deliver a return to the Registrar not later than 28 days after the shares are disposed of.

Any consideration received on a sale of treasury shares is to be treated as profits for distribution purposes.

Under S729 CA 2006, in the event the shares are cancelled, there will be a reduction in capital but there is no need for a special resolution of the members or authorisation by the court.

S730 CA 2006 states that where treasury shares are cancelled, the company must deliver a return to the Registrar not later than 28 days after the shares are cancelled. The return must state with respect to shares of each class cancelled:

(a) the number and nominal value of the shares, and

(b) the date on which they were cancelled.

The notice must be accompanied by a statement of capital which must state with respect to the company's share capital immediately following the cancellation:

(a) the total number of shares of the company

(b) the aggregate nominal value of those shares

(c) for each class of shares

  (i) prescribed particulars of the rights attached to those shares

  (ii) the total number of shares of that class, and

  (iii) the aggregate nominal value of shares of that class

(d) the amount paid up and the amount (if any) unpaid on each share (whether on account of the nominal value of the share or by way or premium).

Treasury shares can also be created when a company initially issues shares to the public but keeps a portion in its treasury to be sold at a later date.

8 Distributions

Introduction

A company can only make a distribution (e.g. pay a dividend) out of profits available for that purpose, i.e. distributable profits.

Distributable profits

Distributable profits are the accumulated realised profits (so far as not previously utilised by distribution or capitalisation) less the accumulated realised losses (so far as not previously written off in a reduction of capital): S830 CA06.

Profit and loss

This can be from trading activities and capital transactions.

Accumulated profits

This looks at the cumulative profit/loss, not just the current year in isolation. For example if a company made a trading loss of $1,000 in year 1 and $2,000 in year 2, but made a trading profit of $1,000 in year 3, it must make a profit in excess of $2,000 in year 4 before any dividend can be paid.

Realised profits

A profit or loss is deemed to be realised if it is treated as realised in accordance with generally accepted accounting principles.

Provisions such as depreciation are deemed realised.

If a general revaluation of all the fixed assets has taken place and results in a deficit, that deficit does not need to be treated as realised.

Additional rules for a public company

A public limited company can only declare a dividend if both before and after distribution its net assets are not less than the aggregate of its called up share capital and undistributable reserves.

Undistributable reserves are:

- share premium account
- capital redemption reserve
- unrealised profits (i.e. revaluation reserve)
- reserves that the company is forbidden to distribute.

The latest audited accounts are used to make the calculations.

Model articles

Under the model articles, the directors recommend the payment of a dividend and the company declares it by passing an ordinary resolution. The amount paid cannot exceed the amount recommended by the directors.

However, a shareholder is not entitled to a dividend as of right.

Test your understanding 5

A company had a balance on its profit and loss account reserve at the beginning of its accounting year of losses of $3,000. During the year the company made trading profits of $7,000 and revalued its fixed assets by $5,000.

What are the profits available for distribution?

Consequences of an unlawful dividend

If a dividend is not paid in accordance with the rules on distributions then the company can recover the distribution from:

- shareholders who knew or had reasonable grounds to know the dividend was unlawful
- any director unless he or she can show he or she exercised reasonable care in relying on properly prepared accounts
- the auditors if the dividend was paid in reliance on erroneous accounts.

However, if a director has to make good to the company an unlawful dividend he or she may claim indemnity from the shareholders who when they received the dividend knew it was an unlawful dividend.

9 Loan capital

All companies have the implied power to borrow for the purpose of business.

Loan capital comprises all the longer term borrowing of a company such as:

- permanent overdrafts at the bank
- unsecured loans either from a bank or other party
- loans secured on assets either from a bank or other party.

Companies often issue long-term loans in the form of **debentures**.

A debenture is a document issued by a company containing an acknowledgment of its indebtedness whether charged on the company's assets or not.

There are three main types of debentures:

- a single debenture e.g. a company obtains a secured loan or overdraft facility
- debentures issued as a series and usually registered
- debenture stock subscribed by a large number of lenders.

Advantages of debentures

- The board does not (usually) need the authority of a general meeting to issue debentures.
- As debentures carry no votes they do not dilute or affect the control of the company.
- Interest is chargeable against the profit before tax.
- Debentures may be cheaper to service than shares.
- There are no restrictions on issuing debentures at a discount or on redemption.
- They are freely transferable.

Disadvantages of debentures

- Interest must be paid out of pre-tax profits, irrespective of the profits of the company. If necessary must be paid out of capital.
- Default may precipitate liquidation and/or administration if the debentures are secured.
- High gearing will affect the share price.

Test your understanding 6

Edward and Frederick wish to invest in Fizz, a listed plc. They have the choice of investing by buying shares or by subscribing to an issue of debentures.

A **Fill in the gaps and complete the sentence.**

Most people understand a debenture to mean a

....

Strictly speaking it is a ....

(Your answer must not exceed 10 words.)

B **Fill in the gaps and delete as appropriate.**

Edward and Frederick will have the choice of being

.... shareholders or

.... shareholders. The ....

have the real voting rights while the .... will have a less risky investment.

C **List three differences between debentures and shares.**

10 Fixed versus floating charges

Fixed charge

A fixed charge is a legal or equitable mortgage on a specific asset (e.g. land), which prevents the company dealing with the asset without the consent of the mortgagee.

A fixed charge has three main characteristics:

- It is on an identified asset.
- The asset is intended to be retained permanently in the business.
- The company has no general freedom to deal with (e.g. sell) the asset.

In certain circumstances a fixed charge can be set aside by a liquidator or an administrator if it can be shown that the company sought to put a creditor in a preferential position. This is covered in more detail in Chapter 13 Section 4.

Floating charge

The judge in **Re Yorkshire Woolcombers' Association (1903)** stated that a floating charge has three main characteristics:

- It is on a class of assets, present and future.
- The assets within the class will change from time to time.
- The company has freedom to deal with the charged assets in the ordinary course of its business.

A floating charge cannot be created by an ordinary partnership.

Crystallisation

A floating charge does not attach to any particular asset until crystallisation.

Crystallisation means the company can no longer deal freely with the assets. It occurs in the following cases:

- liquidation
- the company ceases to carry on business
- any event specified (e.g. the company is unable to pay its debts; the company fails to look after its property; the company fails to keep stock levels sufficiently high).

Advantages of a floating charge

A floating charge has the following advantages for the company:

- The company can deal freely with the assets.
- A wider class of assets can be charged.

Disadvantages of a floating charge

A floating charge has a number of disadvantages for the chargee:

- The value of the security is uncertain until it crystallises.
- It has a lower priority than a fixed charge.
- A liquidator can ignore it if it was created within 12 months preceding a winding up. This is to prevent a company from giving preference to one of its unsecured creditors by giving a floating charge over its assets.

Test your understanding 7

JIH Ltd has borrowed money from K Bank plc and has provided security by executing a fixed charge debenture in favour of the bank.

A fixed charge is:

A a charge over specific company property that prevents the company from dealing freely with the property in the ordinary course of business

B a charge over a class of company assets that enables the company to deal freely with the assets in the ordinary course of business

C a charge over specific company property that enables the company to deal freely with the assets in the ordinary course of business

D a charge over company land enabling the company to deal freely with the land in the ordinary course of business

11 Priority and registration of charges

Priority

The priority of a charge depends on the type of charge and whether or not it has been registered:

- Equal charges – first created has priority.
- Fixed charge – has priority over a floating charge.
- An unregistered registerable charge has no priority over a registered charge.
- A chargeholder can prohibit the creation of a later charge with priority, but the prohibition is only effective if a subsequent chargee has notice of the prohibition as well as the charge.

Registration

The company must notify the registrar within 21 days of the creation of the charge.

Registration can be undertaken by:

- the company
- the chargeholder.

Failure to register:

- renders the charge void against the liquidator
- results in a fine on the company and every officer in default
- renders the money secured immediately repayable.

If the change relates to land it must also be registered with the Land Registry.

The company must also include the charge in its own register of charges. However, failure to include the charge in the company's own register does not invalidate the charge.

Test your understanding 8

Which one of the following statements is correct?

A A floating charge has priority over a fixed charge.

B The preferential creditors take priority over fixed charge holders.

C A fixed charge has priority over a floating charge.

D Unsecured creditors take priority over floating charge holders.

12 Loan capital versus share capital

Loan capital versus share capital

	Loan capital	**Share capital**
Definition	A debenture is a document issued by a company containing an acknowledgment of its indebtedness.	A share is the interest of a shareholder in a company measured by a sum of money. It is a bundle of rights and obligations.
Voting rights	A debenture is a creditor of the company and therefore has no voting rights.	A shareholder is a member (owner) of the company and therefore has voting rights, depending on the class of shares held.
Income	A debenture has a contractual right to interest, irrespective of the availability of profits.	Dividends depend on the availability of profits.
Liquidation	A debenture has priority with respect to repayment.	Depending on the type of shares, shareholders receive repayment after creditors, but can participate in surplus assets.
Maintenance of capital	Does not need to be maintained.	Must be maintained.

13 Chapter summary

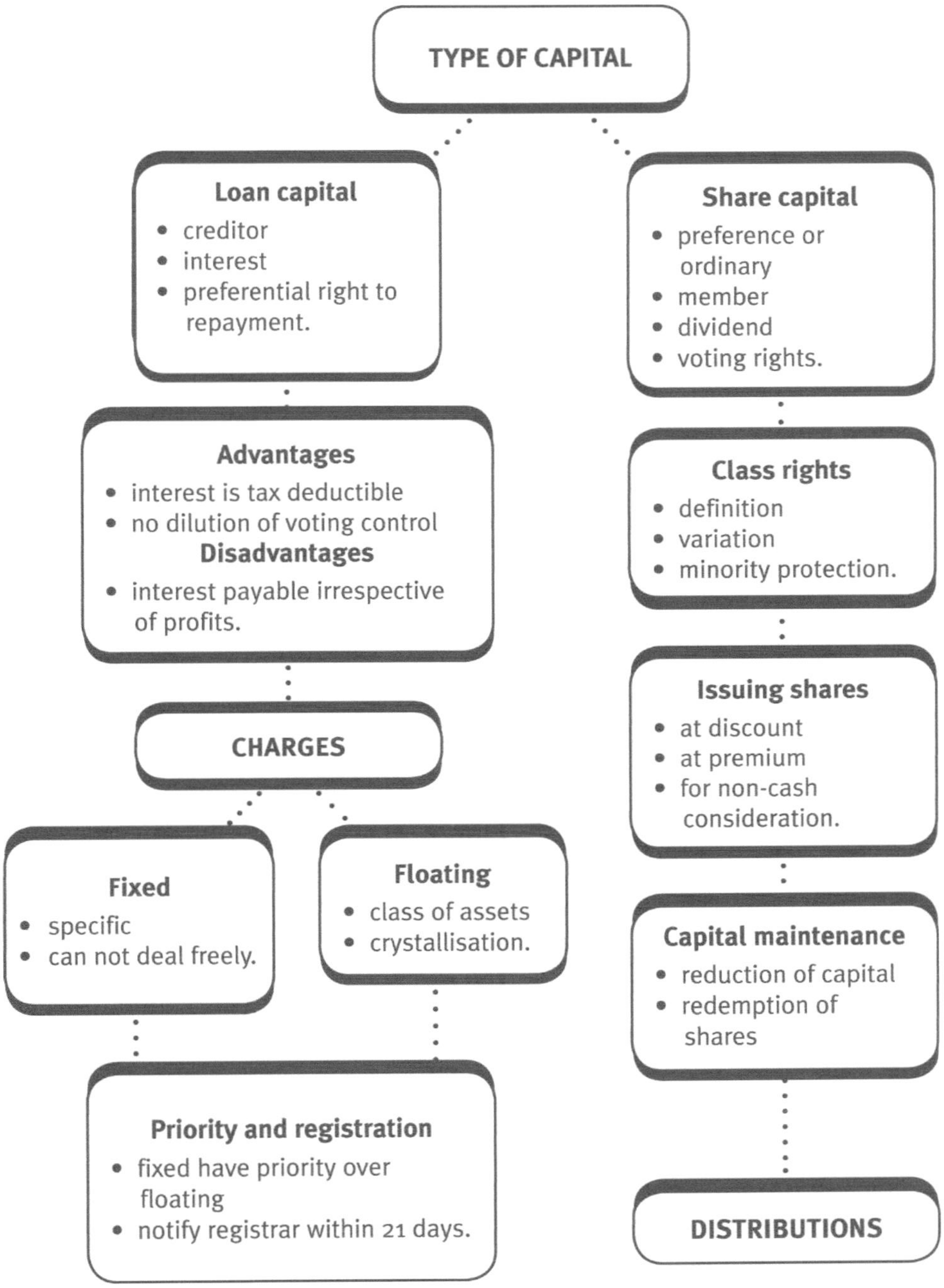

Test your understanding answers

Test your understanding 1

A are

can

cannot

can

...that they cannot receive any payment until all amounts due to creditors have been paid.

B The dividend is fixed. Preference shares have priority when dividends are declared and on winding up. Dividends are cumulative and arrears of dividend will be paid when profits are available.

Test your understanding 2

A A sale of a new issue of shares to the existing shareholders is a rights issue.

Test your understanding 3

The share premium account may only be used for:

- writing off the expenses of the issue of those shares
- writing off any commission paid on the issue of those shares
- issuing bonus shares.

Test your understanding 4

B

Once the special resolution to reduce the share capital has been passed, it must be approved by the court. The procedure involving a special resolution supported by a solvency statement is only available to private companies.

Test your understanding 5

The company can distribute up to $4,000. This represents the $7,000 profit for the year, less the accumulated losses of $3,000. The unrealised profit on the revaluation of fixed assets is excluded.

Test your understanding 6

A loan

...written acknowledgment by a company of an amount owed.

B ordinary

preference

ordinary shareholders

preference shareholders

C (i) Shareholders are members, debenture holders are creditors.

(ii) Shareholders receive a dividend, debenture holders receive interest.

(iii) Shares cannot be issued at a discount, debentures can.

Test your understanding 7

A

A fixed charge is a charge over a specific asset which attaches to the asset immediately upon its creation. This means that the company cannot deal freely with the asset in the ordinary course of business.

Test your understanding 8

C

A fixed charge has priority over a floating charge (over the same asset or assets), even if the floating charge was created at an earlier date.

Chapter

10

Directors

Chapter learning objectives

Upon completion of this chapter you will be able to:

- explain the role of directors in the operation of the company
- discuss the ways in which the directors are appointed, can lose their office or be subject to a disqualification order
- distinguish between the powers of the board of directors, the managing director and individual directors to bind the company
- explain the duties that directors owe to their companies
- demonstrate an understanding of the way in which statute law has attempted to control directors.

PER

One of the PER performance objectives (PO4) is to contribute effective governance in your area. You evaluate, monitor and implement risk management procedures, complying with the spirit and the letter of policies, laws and regulations. Working through this chapter should help you understand how to demonstrate that objective.

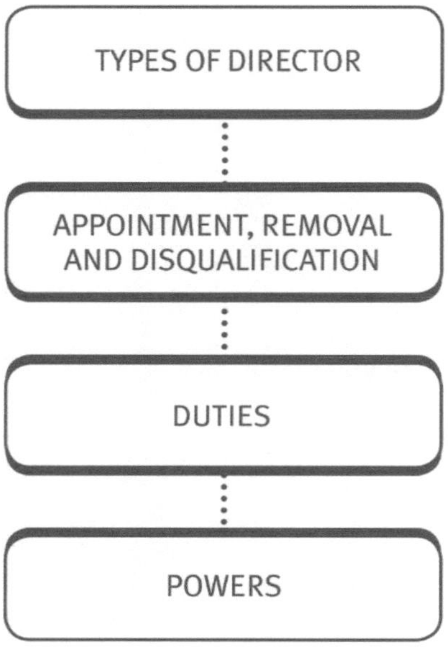

1 Directors

Definition of director

The term 'director' includes 'any person occupying the position of director, by whatever name called': s250 CA06.

The decision as to whether someone is a director is therefore based on their function not their title.

A director must normally be aged at least 16. Under the SBEEA 2015 all directors must be natural persons.

De Jure Director

A person who is formally and legally appointed or elected as director in accordance with the articles of association and gives written consent to hold the office of a director.

De Facto Director

A person who is not a de jure director but performs the acts or duties of a director.

Any person, who is not technically a director, but according to whose directions and instructions other directors and employees are accustomed to act, is legally deemed a de facto director.

A de facto director owes the same duties to the company as a de jure director, i.e. he or she is subject to both statutory duties and prohibitions, and he or she also owes fiduciary duties to the company.

Types of director

Managing director (MD)/Chief executive officer (CEO)	• A director appointed to carry out overall day-to-day management functions. • The model articles allow the board to delegate to the MD/CEO any powers they see fit. • The MD/CEO has a dual role – member of board and also executive officer. • **Freeman & Lockyer (A Firm) v Buckhurst Park Properties (Mangal) Ltd (1964)** – the MD/CEO has the apparent authority to enter into all contracts of a commercial nature.
Shadow director	• 'A person in accordance with whose directions or instructions the directors of a company are accustomed to act': s251 CA06. As discussed earlier this means that it is a person's function rather than their title that defines them as a director. • Used to regulate activity by those who exercise control over a company but try to evade their responsibilities and potential liabilities as a director. • Not a shadow director if advice is given only in a professional capacity e.g. accountants and lawyers.
Executive director	• Likely to be a full-time employee involved in management. • Performs a specific role under a service contract. • May be distinguished by a special title such as 'Sales Director' or Finance Director'.
Non-executive director (NED)	• Part-time. • Brings outside expertise to board. • Not an employee. • Contributes an independent view. • Exerts control over executive directors. • Subject to the same duties, controls and potential liabilities as executive directors.

Chairman of board	• Chairs meetings of board. • Acts as a spokesman for the company. • Has a casting vote.
Alternate director	• Appointed by a director to attend and vote for them at board meetings which they are unable to attend. • Can be another director within the same company or more usually an outsider.

2 Appointment, disqualification and removal

Appointment

First Directors	• Public companies need a minimum of two; private companies need one. • There is no statutory maximum, but the articles may specify a maximum number.
Appointment procedure	• Usually appointed by the existing directors or by ordinary resolution. • Directors of public companies should generally be voted on individually: s160 CA06. • A director's actions are valid notwithstanding that his or her appointment was defective: s161 CA06.
Model articles for public companies	• At the first annual general meeting (AGM) all the directors retire and offer themselves for reelection by ordinary resolution. • At each AGM one-third retire (those most senior). They can be re-elected. • Casual vacancies are filled by the board until the next AGM when the new directors must stand for election.
Publicity	The company must notify Companies House within 14 days of new appointments and any changes in particulars. It must also enter details in the register of directors.

Service contracts	• Cannot exceed two years unless they have been approved by the shareholders by ordinary resolution: s188 CA06. • If s188 CA06 is breached the service contract is deemed to state that the company can terminate the contract at any time by giving reasonable notice. • The service contract must be kept open for inspection at the registered office. • The directors of a quoted company must prepare a director's remuneration report for each financial year of the company. The report will contain for each person who was a director during the year: (a) date of the contract, the unexpired term and the details of any notice periods (b) any provision for compensation payable upon early termination of the contract; and (c) such details of other provisions in the contract as are necessary to enable members of the company to estimate the liability of the company in the event of early termination of the contract.
Compensation for loss of office	• Gratuitous payments must be disclosed to all members and approved by ordinary resolution. If not approved, director holds payment on trust for the company.

Disqualification

Model articles – Directors must vacate their office if they become bankrupt.

Company Directors (Disqualification) Act 1986(CDDA 1986)

The CDDA 1986 was introduced to prevent the misuse of the limited liability status of companies by directors who would set up a new company to carry on essentially the same business as an old company which had ceased trading with unpaid debts.

A disqualified director cannot be concerned in the management of a company directly or indirectly or act as a liquidator, receiver or promoter.

The CDDA 1986 identifies three distinct categories of conduct:

1 General misconduct in connection with companies. This includes:
   - Conviction of a serious offence in connection with the management of a company either in the UK or abroad (maximum fifteen years disqualification).
   - Persistent breaches of CA06, e.g. failure to file returns (maximum five years disqualification).
2 Disqualification for unfitness. This includes:
   - Where an investigation by the Department for Business and Trade finds the director unfit to be concerned in the management of the company.
   - Where a liquidator's report finds the director unfit to be concerned in the management of a company (minimum two years and maximum fifteen years disqualification).
3 Other cases for disqualification. This includes:
   - Participation in fraudulent or wrongful trading (maximum 15 years disqualification).
   - Where an undischarged bankrupt has been acting as a director.
   - Where a person acts on behalf of a disqualified director.
4 Breach of a disqualification order:
   - This is a criminal offence, which could result in a fine and imprisonment.
   - The disqualified director (or any person who acts on his or her instructions) is personally liable for the debts of the company while so acting.

Removal

Under s168 CA06, a company may by ordinary resolution remove a director before expiration of his or her period of office notwithstanding anything in:

- its articles, or
- any agreement between him or her and it.

Thus a director can be removed despite any provision to the contrary in his or her service contract, although he or she can sue for damages if the removal is in breach of his or her contract.

The company must follow this procedure to remove a director:

Special notice (28 days) is required of the resolution by persons wishing to remove a director.

The company must forward a copy of the resolution to the director concerned.

Notice of the meeting goes to the director and all members entitled to attend and vote.

The director in question can require the company to circulate written representations to members.

At the meeting, the director can read out representations if there was no time for prior circulation.

The director must be allowed to attend the meeting and to speak.

An ordinary resolution is needed to remove the director.

The power of the members to remove a director may be limited:

Bushell v Faith (1970)

Facts: A provision in the articles tripled the number of votes of shares held by directors on a resolution to remove them. Statute only required an ordinary resolution and made no provision as to how it could be obtained or defeated.

Held: The weighted voting rights provided in the articles were valid.

Test your understanding 1

Which of the following states the requirements for removal of a director?

A Special resolution with ordinary notice

B Ordinary resolution with special notice

C Ordinary resolution with ordinary notice

D Special resolution with special notice

3 Duties

General duties

Prior to the Companies Act 2006, common law rules, equitable principles and fiduciary duties made up the law on directors' duties. A fiduciary duty is a duty imposed upon certain persons because of the position of trust and confidence that they are in.

These have now been replaced by the specific statutory duties provided in the Companies Act 2006 (s170). However, the old case law still has relevance in interpreting the new legislation and illustrating its application.

Duty to act within powers: s171

A director must act in accordance with the company's constitution and only use his or her powers for the purpose which they were given. They have a fiduciary duty to the company to exercise their powers bona fide in what they honestly consider to be the interests of the company.

If this rule is not adhered to the transaction will be void, unless it is approved by the shareholders.

Hogg v Cramphorn (1967)

Facts: The directors issued further shares and gave financial assistance for their purchase in an attempt to fight off a takeover bid, believing it to be in the best interests of the company.

Held: The directors had acted in what they believed to be the best interests of the company, but were in breach of the duty to act within their powers. Therefore, it was open to the members to ratify their actions, which they did.

Duty to promote the success of the company: s172

A director must act in good faith, in a way which promotes the success of the company and for the benefit of the members as a whole.

The Act introduced the concept of 'enhanced shareholder value' and requires the directors to have regard to:

- the likely consequences of any decision in the long term
- the interests of the company's employees
- the need to foster the company's business relationships with suppliers, customers and others
- the impact of the company's operations on the community and the environment
- the desirability of the company maintaining a reputation for high standards of business conduct and
- the need to act fairly as between members of the company.

Companies may have wider purposes than just the benefit of members such as charitable companies and community interest companies. S172(2) provides that where that is the case, then the duty of the director is to act in a way that would be most likely to achieve that purpose.

S172(3) provides that the general duty is subject to any specific enactment or rule of law requiring directors to consider or act in the interests of creditors of the company. This provision therefore formally recognises that the duty to the shareholders is displaced when the company is insolvent or heading towards insolvency (this is looked at in more detail in **Chapter 13: Fraudulent Behaviour**).

Duty to exercise independent judgment: s173

A director of a company must exercise independent judgment.

This duty is not infringed by a director acting:

- in accordance with an agreement duly entered into by the company that restricts the future exercise of discretion by its directors, or
- in a way authorised by the company's constitution.

Duty to exercise reasonable care, skill and diligence: s174

The standard expected of a director is that of a reasonably diligent person with:

- the general knowledge, skill and experience that could reasonably be expected of a director, and
- the actual knowledge, skill and experience held by the director.

The reasonableness test therefore consists of two elements:

1 An objective test

A director in carrying out his or her functions, must show such care as could reasonably be expected from a competent person in that role. It is not a defence for a director to claim lack of expertise.

2 A subjective test

A director is expected to show the degree of skill which may reasonably be expected from a person of his or her knowledge and experience.

Re City Equitable Fire Insurance Co (1925)

Facts: The company was in liquidation and it was discovered there was a shortage of funds mainly due to the deliberate fraud of the chairman, for which he had been convicted. The liquidator brought an action against the other directors of the company for negligence on the basis that they had left the management of the company entirely in the hands of the chairman.

Held: The liquidator failed and the judge laid down the duties of care and skill to be expected of a director:

(a) A director need not exhibit in the performance of his duties a greater degree of skill than may reasonably be expected from someone of his knowledge and experience.

(b) A director is not bound to give continuous attention to the affairs of the company.

(c) Where duties may properly be left to some other official, a director is justified, in the absence of grounds for suspicion, in trusting that official to perform his duties honestly.

The low level of care shown in **Re City Equitable Fire Insurance Co (1925)** was raised in:

Dorchester Finance Co Ltd v Stebbing (1989)

Facts: The company was a money-lending company and had three directors, Parsons, Hamilton and Stebbing. All three had considerable accountancy and business experience (Parsons and Hamilton were chartered accountants). No board meetings were ever held and Parsons and Hamilton left all the affairs of the company to Stebbing. Parsons and Hamilton did, however, turn up from time to time and signed blank cheques on the company's account which they left Stebbing to deal with. Stebbing loaned the company's money without complying with statutory regulations applying to money lending, such that the loans were unenforceable.

Held: All three were liable in negligence. If a director has a special skill (e.g. as an accountant) he is expected to use it for the benefit of the company.

Duty to avoid conflicts of interest: s175

A director must avoid any situation which places him or her in direct conflict with the interests of the company or the performance of any other duty.

IDC v Cooley (1972)

Facts: Cooley, the managing director of IDC, had been negotiating a contract on behalf of the company, but the third party wished to award the contract to him personally and not to the company. Without disclosing his reason to the company (or its board) he resigned in order to take the contract personally.

Held: He was in breach of fiduciary duty as he had profited personally by use of an opportunity which came to him through his directorship: it made no difference that the company itself would not have obtained the contract. He was therefore accountable to the company for the benefits gained from the contract.

The IDC case illustrates that an individual may still be subject to the duties even after he or she ceases to be a director.

The accountability arises from the mere fact of having made a profit, it is not a question of loss to the company.

Regal (Hastings) Ltd v Gulliver (1942)

Facts: The claimant company owned one cinema and wished to buy two others with the object of selling all three together. They formed a subsidiary to buy the cinemas but could not provide all the capital needed to finance the purchase. The directors bought some of the shares in the subsidiary to enable the purchases to be made and later sold their shares at a profit.

Held: The directors must account to the claimant company for the profit on the grounds that it was only through the knowledge and opportunity they gained as directors of that company that they were able to obtain the shares and consequently to make the profit.

Duty not to accept benefits from third parties: s176

A director must not accept any benefit from a third party which arises by reason of him or her being a director or performing/not performing an act as a director, unless acceptance cannot reasonably be regarded as likely to give rise to a conflict of interest.

Boston Deep Sea Fishing & Ice Co v Ansell (1888)

Facts: Ansell was managing director of the claimant company. He accepted a 'commission' (bribe) from a supplier to order goods from that supplier, on behalf of the company. When the company found out, he was dismissed.

Held: The defendant was in breach of his fiduciary duty as the agent of the company. Therefore the company could recover the commissions paid to him.

Duty to declare interest in proposed transaction or arrangement: s177

A director is required to declare the nature and extent of any interest, either direct or indirect through a connected person, that they have in relation to a proposed transaction or arrangement with the company. Even if the director is not a party to a transaction, the duty may apply if they are aware or ought reasonably to have been aware of the interest.

This declaration can be made in writing, at a board meeting or by a general notice that he or she has an interest in a third party.

Aberdeen Railway v Blakie (1854)

Facts: A company bought some chairs from a firm. At the time of the contract one of the company's directors, unknown to the company, was a partner in the firm.

Held: The company, could avoid the contract, because of this undisclosed interest in the transaction.

Breach of directors' duties

Directors owe their duties to the company as a whole, not to individual members.

Percival v Wright (1902)

Facts: A director of a company bought shares from a member at a price less than that for which the director knew that a third party had expressed interest in buying all the shares in the company. The third party interest came to nothing, but the selling member sued the director for breach of duty to the member in not disclosing the interest expressed by the third party.

Held: The purchasing director was under no obligation to disclose to the selling member the third party interest. A director's duties are owed to the company and not to individual members.

Breach of duty may carry the following consequences:

- The director may be required to make good any loss suffered by the company.
- Contracts entered into between the company and the director may be rendered voidable.
- Any property taken by the director from the company can be recovered from him or her if still in his or her possession.
- Property may be recovered directly from a third party, unless that third party acquired it for value and in good faith.
- An injunction may be an appropriate remedy where the breach has not yet occurred.

S232 CA06 provides that any provision to exempt a director from or indemnify him or her against any liability for breach of duty or negligence is void.

S239 CA06 states that the company can ratify a breach of duty by passing an ordinary resolution.

Test your understanding 2

Jack has acted in breach of his duty to disclose his interest in a contract as a director of JK Ltd.

Which one of the following is correct?

A The breach cannot be ratified by the shareholders.

B The breach may be ratified by a written or ordinary resolution.

C The breach may be ratified by a provision in the company's articles.

D The breach may be ratified by a resolution of the board of directors.

4 Powers

The division of power within a company

The legal theory is that all decisions about the running of the company's business should be taken by the members in general meeting. However, the members usually delegate the power to manage the business to the directors and they exercise all the powers of the company on a day-to-day basis.

Directors are required to exercise their powers in accordance with the company's constitution. This requirement caused problems prior to the Companies Act 2006 as companies normally had very narrow objects, which had the effect of severely restricting the directors' powers. Companies now have unrestricted objects, unless the articles specifically restrict them.

Note that the power to manage the business of the company is given to the board as a whole, not to the individual directors. Where a company's articles delegate the management of the company's business to the board, the members have no right to interfere in decisions made by the board. Directors are not agents of the members and are not subject to their instruction as to how to act.

In **Shaw v John Shaw (1935)** it was held that it was for the board to decide whether or not the company should commence litigation and therefore an ordinary resolution instructing the board to discontinue litigation had no legal effect.

There are some restrictions which mean that power is placed in the hands of the members rather than the directors:

- some actions require a special resolution
- a director can be removed at any time by an ordinary resolution of the members and they may see fit to exercise this right should their views be ignored
- the members can alter the articles by passing a special resolution. This power could therefore be used to restrict the directors' powers.

The control of directors

Although the directors manage the company on a day-to-day basis, a company is ultimately controlled by its members. Most decisions require a majority of over 50% (although some require 75%) therefore shareholders who are in the minority may find that their wishes are ignored.

Members can exercise their votes in their own interests. They are not required to act for the benefit of the company.

Under Model Article 4, the shareholders may by special resolution, direct the directors to take, or refrain from taking, specified action.

Statutory control over directors

Certain matters require the approval of the members in a general meeting in order to be valid.

Directors' service contracts: s188 CA06

Directors' service contracts lasting more than two years must be approved by the members.

Substantial property transactions: s190 CA06

A substantial property transaction occurs where a director acquires from the company (or vice versa) a substantial non-cash asset.

An asset is 'substantial' if its value either exceeds £100,000 or exceeds 10% of the company's asset value and is more than £5,000.

Failure to obtain the members' approval results in the following consequences:

- the transaction is voidable by the company, unless the members give approval within a reasonable period
- the director is liable to account to the company for any gain or indemnify it against any loss.

Loans to directors: s197 CA06

Any loans given to directors, or guarantees provided as security for loans provided to directors, must be approved by members.

Non-contractual payments to directors: s217 CA06

Any non-contractual payments to directors for loss of office must be approved by the members.

Authority of directors

Individual directors cannot bind the company without being given authority to do so. There are three ways in which this authority may be given:

Express	• Where authority is expressly given, all decisions taken are binding.
Implied	• Authority flows from a person's position. • The person appointed as the managing director has the implied authority to bind the company in the same way as the board. • The MD/CEO is assumed to have all powers usually exercised by an MD/CEO.
Apparent/ Ostensible	• Such authority arises where a director is held out by the other board members as having the authority to bind the company. • If a third party acts on such a representation, the company is estopped from denying its truth: **Freeman & Lockyer v Buckhurst Park Properties (1964)** (see Chapter 6).

Transactions beyond the board's powers

S40 CA06 states that the power of the directors to bind the company, or to authorise another to bind the company, will not be limited by anything in the company's constitution, **provided** the other party is acting in good faith.

S40 goes on to state that even where there is **actual knowledge** of the lack of authority this is not enough to count as lack of good faith so, on the face of it, any contract entered into by the board of a company will be binding.

Where, however, the third party to the transaction is also a director of the company or a person associated with a director, the transaction becomes **voidable** at the company's instance: s41 CA06. Moreover, the third party director or associate, and any director who authorised the transaction, is then liable to **compensate** the company for any profit made or to indemnify the company for any loss or damage arising, whether the company chooses to avoid the contract or not.

5 Chapter summary

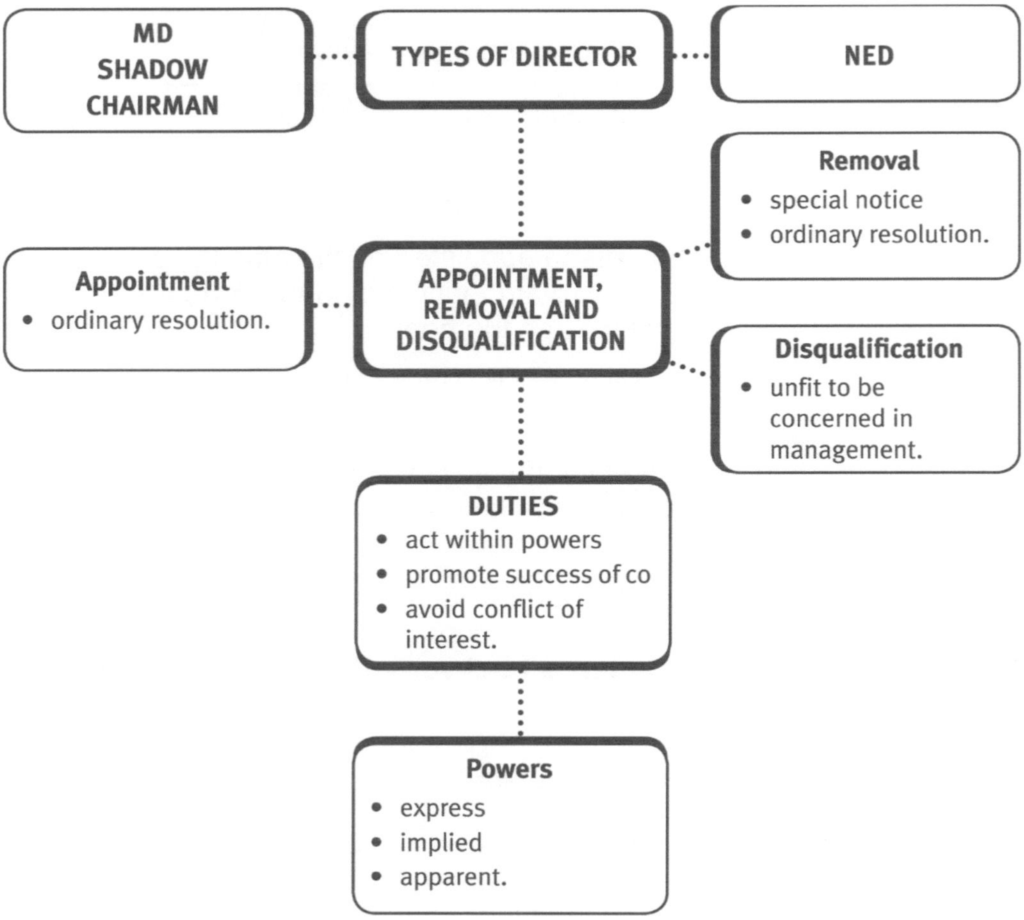

Test your understanding answers

Test your understanding 1

B The removal of a director requires an ordinary resolution with special notice.

Test your understanding 2

B S239 CA06 states that where an interest has not been disclosed, the action can be ratified by passing an ordinary resolution.

Chapter

11

Corporate administration

Chapter learning objectives

Upon completion of this chapter you will be able to:

- discuss the procedure relating to, and the duties and powers of, a company secretary
- discuss the procedure relating to, and the duties and powers of, the company auditors
- distinguish between types of meetings: ordinary general meetings and annual general meetings
- explain the procedure for calling such meetings
- detail the procedure for conducting company meetings
- distinguish between types of resolutions: ordinary, special, and written.

PER

One of the PER performance objectives (PO1) is to always act in the wider public interest. You need to take into account all relevant information and use professional judgement, your personal values and scepticism to evaluate data and make decisions. You should identify right from wrong and escalate anything of concern. You also need to make sure that your skills, knowledge and behaviour are up-to-date and allow you to be effective in your role. Working through this chapter should help you understand how to demonstrate that objective.

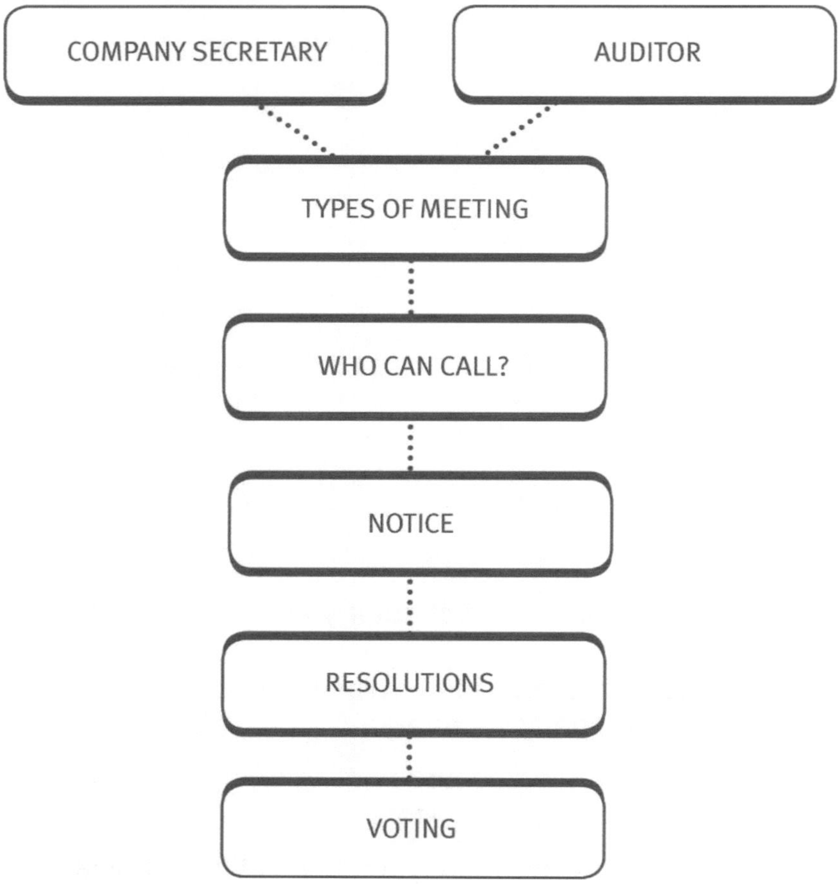

1 Company secretary

Introduction

Every public company must have a qualified company secretary. Private companies may choose to appoint a secretary, but are not obliged to do so.

The secretary is usually appointed and removed by the directors.

Qualifications

The secretary of a **public** company must be **qualified** under one of the following conditions:

- Must have held the office of company secretary in a public limited company (plc) for at least three out of the preceding five years.
- They must be a solicitor, barrister or member of ICAEW, ACCA, CIMA, ICSA, CIPFA.
- They must appear to be capable of discharging the functions by virtue of another position or qualification.

Duties

There are no statutory duties, therefore the duties will be whatever the board decides. The company secretary will typically undertake the following:

- check that documentation is in order
- make returns to the Registrar
- keep registers
- give notice and keep minutes of meetings
- countersign documents to which the company seal is affixed.

Powers

The company secretary has the authority to bind the company in contract. There are two types of authority:

- actual authority – this is the authority delegated by the board
- implied authority regarding contracts of an administrative nature.

Panorama Developments (Guildford) v Fidelis Furnishing Fabrics (1971)

The company secretary ordered services for his own, not the company's, use. It was held that the contract was binding on the company as the contract was of the sort that a company secretary should be able to carry out.

'He is no longer a mere clerk...He is entitled to sign contracts connected with the administrative side of a company's affairs, such as employing staff, and ordering cars, and so forth.'

However, two other cases indicate that there is a limit to the company secretary's authority:

- It does not extend to making commercial as opposed to administrative contracts: **Re Maidstone Building Provisions (1971)**.
- It does not usually carry the authority to borrow money: **Re Cleadon Trust Ltd (1938)**.

Test your understanding 1

In relation to the company secretary, which one of the following statements is correct?

A Both a public and a private company must have a company secretary

B The company secretary is appointed by the members

C In a public company the company secretary must be qualified

D Company secretaries can bind companies in a contract if acting outside their actual or apparent authority

2 The auditor

This section introduces you to various aspects in relation to auditors. These will be revisited when you undertake your Audit and Assurance exam.

Qualifications

The auditor must be either:

- a member of recognised supervisory body (ICAEW, ICAS or ACCA) and eligible under their rules, or
- qualified by a similar overseas body and authorised by the Department for Business and Trade.

The auditor must not be:

- an officer or employee of the company
- the partner of an officer or employee of the company.

Appointment – private companies

The auditors should generally be appointed by the shareholders by ordinary resolution. However, the directors can appoint the company's first auditor and fill casual vacancies.

An auditor will automatically be deemed to be re-appointed at the end of his or her term unless:

- he or she was appointed by the directors
- the company's articles require actual re-appointment
- members with at least 5% of the voting rights have given notice to the company by the end of the company's financial year
- there has been a resolution that the auditor should not be reappointed or
- the directors decide that they do not need auditors for the following year.

A company must inform the Secretary of State if it has failed to appoint an auditor within 28 days of circulating its accounts. The Secretary of State has power to appoint an auditor in those circumstances.

Appointment – public companies

Auditors are generally appointed by the shareholders by ordinary resolution in the general meeting at which the company's accounts are laid. However, the directors can appoint the company's first auditor and fill casual vacancies.

An auditor of a public company holds office until the end of the meeting at which the accounts are laid, unless re-appointed. Where there is a change of auditor, the term of office of the incoming auditor does not begin before the end of the previous auditor's term. This means that a new auditor's term will usually begin immediately after the end of the meeting at which the accounts are laid.

A company must inform the Secretary of State if it fails to appoint an auditor at the general meeting considering the accounts. The Secretary of State has power to appoint an auditor in those circumstances.

Audit exemption

For financial years starting on or after 1 January 2016, to qualify for a total audit exemption a company must meet two out of the following three criteria:

- turnover < £10.2m; and
- net assets < £5.1m; and
- < 50 employees.

However, these exemptions do not apply to public companies, banking or insurance companies or those subject to a statute-based regulatory regime.

Resignation

An auditor can resign at any time by giving written notice to the company: s516 CA06.

The resignation is effective from the date it is delivered to the company's registered office, or from a specified later date. To be effective it must be accompanied by the statement required by s519 (see below).

A company whose auditor resigns is required to inform the registrar: s517 CA06. Failure to do so is an offence.

Under s518 CA06, an auditor who resigns can require the directors to convene a general meeting to consider his or her explanation of the circumstances that led to his or her resignation. The directors have 21 days to send out a notice convening a meeting and it must be held within 28 days of the notice.

Removal

An auditor can be removed by ordinary resolution: s510 CA06. The resolution must be passed at a general meeting; a written resolution cannot be used to remove an auditor.

Special notice of the resolution is needed (i.e. 28 days). The company must send a copy of the resolution to the auditor and he or she has the right to make a statement of his or her case. The company then has to circulate his or her statement to the shareholders. However, if time does not allow for circulation, the statement can be read out at the meeting.

Notice of the resolution removing the auditor must be sent to the Registrar within 14 days.

Statement by departing auditor

Under s519 CA06, a departing auditor is required to make a statement and to deposit it with the company:

- For quoted companies, this statement must explain the circumstances surrounding his or her departure.
- For other public companies and all private companies, it should explain the circumstances surrounding his or her departure, unless the auditor thinks that there is no need for them to be brought to the attention of the shareholders or creditors. In that case, the statement should state that there are no such circumstances.

Unless there are no circumstances to be brought to the attention of shareholders and creditors, the company is obliged to circulate the statement to everyone to whom it needs to send the annual accounts. It must do this within 14 days of receiving it.

If the company does not want to circulate the statement, it can apply to the court for an order that it need not circulate the statement.

Duties

The auditor has a statutory duty to report to the members on whether the accounts:

- give a true and fair view and
- have been properly prepared in accordance with the Companies Act and the relevant financial reporting framework.

The auditor must investigate and form an opinion as to whether:

- proper books of accounting records have been kept
- proper returns adequate for their audit have been received from branches not visited by them
- the accounts are in agreement with the books of account and returns
- the information given in the directors' report is consistent with the accounts.

If the auditor is dissatisfied with the findings of his or her investigation he or she must qualify the audit report.

The report (whether qualified or unqualified) must state the name of the audit firm, or if an individual has been appointed as auditor, his or her name. Where the auditor is a firm, the senior statutory auditor must sign the report in his or her own name on behalf of the firm.

Under s507 CA06 it is a criminal offence to knowingly or recklessly cause an audit report to include anything that is misleading, false or deceptive, or to omit a required statement of a problem with the accounts or audit. The offence carries an unlimited fine.

Companies Act liability for auditor's report and audited accounts

S507 of the Companies Act 2006 (CA06) makes it an offence for an auditor to recklessly cause an auditor's report to contain any matter that is misleading or false to a material extent. The offence is punishable by a fine.

s532 CA06 makes any provision exempting auditors from or indemnifying them against liability for negligence void in relation to providing audited accounts.

s534 CA06 provides that a company may enter into a liability limitation agreement with an auditor, limiting his or her liability for negligence (among other things) in the course of auditing accounts.

Powers

The auditor has the right to:

- receive notice of, attend and speak at general meetings
- access the books at all times
- require such information and explanations from the company's officers and employees as the auditor thinks fit for the performance of his or her duties (it is a criminal offence to fail to provide the information requested, unless it was not reasonably practicable to do so).

Test your understanding 2
If a company's auditor is to be removed before his or her term of office expires, what type of resolution is required and what period of notice must be given?

3 Meetings

Annual general meeting (AGM)

Timing	Public companies must hold an AGM within the six months following their financial year end: s336.
Failure to hold	The company and every officer in default can be fined if an AGM is not held. Any member can apply to the Department for Business and Trade to convene the meeting.
Private companies	Private companies are not required to hold an AGM.
Notice	**21 days' notice** is required unless every member entitled to attend and vote agrees to a shorter period. The notice must state that the meeting is an AGM.

Business	Usual business includes: • consider accounts • appoint auditors • elect directors • declare dividends.
Resolutions	• Members holding at least 5% of the voting rights (or at least 100 members holding on average £100 paid-up capital) have the right to propose a resolution for the AGM agenda and to require the company to circulate details of the resolution to all members. • If the members' request is received before the financial year end, the members are not required to cover the costs of circulation. Otherwise, the members requesting the resolution must deposit a sum to cover the company's costs.

General meetings (GM)

Timing	Held **whenever required**. Must be held by a plc if a serious loss of capital has occurred, i.e. net assets have fallen to less than half of the called up share capital.
Notice	At least 14 days.
Business	The person who requisitions the meeting sets the agenda.

Class meetings

Purpose	Meeting of a class of shareholders, usually to consider a variation of their class rights.
Procedure	Notice, etc. as for general meetings.
Quorum	Two persons holding or representing by proxy at least one-third in nominal value of the issued shares of the class in question.

4 Calling a meeting

Who can call a meeting?

Directors	The articles usually delegate the power to the directors.
Members	Members may require the directors to call a GM if they hold at least 5% of the paid up voting capital. The directors must call a meeting within 21 days of receiving a requisition. The meeting must take place within 28 days of the notice convening the meeting. If the directors do not call a meeting, the members who requested the meeting (or any members holding over 50% of the total voting rights) may themselves call a meeting to take place within three months of the initial request and recover their expenses from the company.
Resigning auditor	A resigning auditor may require the directors to convene a meeting so he or she can explain the reasons for his or her resignation.
Court	A court can call a meeting on the application of a director or member where it would otherwise be impracticable e.g. to break a deadlock.

Notice

Who must receive notice?	Every member and every director: s310.
Failure to give notice	Accidental failure to give notice to one or more persons does not invalidate the meeting: s313.
Contents of notice	Date, time and place of the meeting. The general nature of the business to be transacted. The text of any special resolutions.
Length of notice period	**AGM – 21 days** Less if every member entitled to attend and vote agrees. **GM – 14 days** Less if members holding at least 95% of shares agree. (Where company is private, can be reduced to 90%).
Special notice	Requires 28 days' notice. Required for the removal of a director or auditor.

5 Resolutions

Resolutions are the way in which companies take decisions. They are voted on by the members in person or by proxy. There are three types of resolution:

Type	% required to pass	To Registrar?	Purpose of resolution
Special	≥75%	Yes – within 15 days	• Alter name. • Wind up company. • Alter articles. • Reduce share capital.
Ordinary	≥50%	Only if required by statute	Used whenever the law or the articles do not require a special resolution.
Written (private companies only)	Same majority as required in GM	Yes if a 75% majority is required	The purpose can be anything apart from resolutions requiring special notice. Members cannot revoke their agreement. The date of the resolution is the date when the necessary majority has been reached. The resolution must be passed within 28 days from its circulation.

Test your understanding 3

Fill in the gaps:

1 An annual general meeting requires .... days' notice.

2 Members may require the directors to call a GM if they hold at least .....% of the paid up voting capital.

3 Special notice requires .... days' notice.

4 A special resolution must be filed with the Registrar within ..... days.

6 Procedure at meetings

A **quorum** is the minimum number of members that needs to be present at a meeting in order to validate business. It is generally two persons; members or proxies: s318 CA06.

Voting is by a **show of hands** initially, unless a poll is demanded. A show of hands means one member one vote, irrespective of the number of shares held.

A **poll** may be demanded by members holding at least 10% of the total voting rights (or by not fewer than 5 members having the right to vote on the resolution). A poll means one vote per share. The result of a poll replaces the result of the previous show of hands. Quoted companies must publish the results of polls on their website: s341 CA06.

Members have a statutory right under s 324 CA06 to appoint one or more persons as their '**proxy**'. A proxy can attend meetings, vote and speak on behalf of the member for whom he or she is acting.

7 Chapter summary

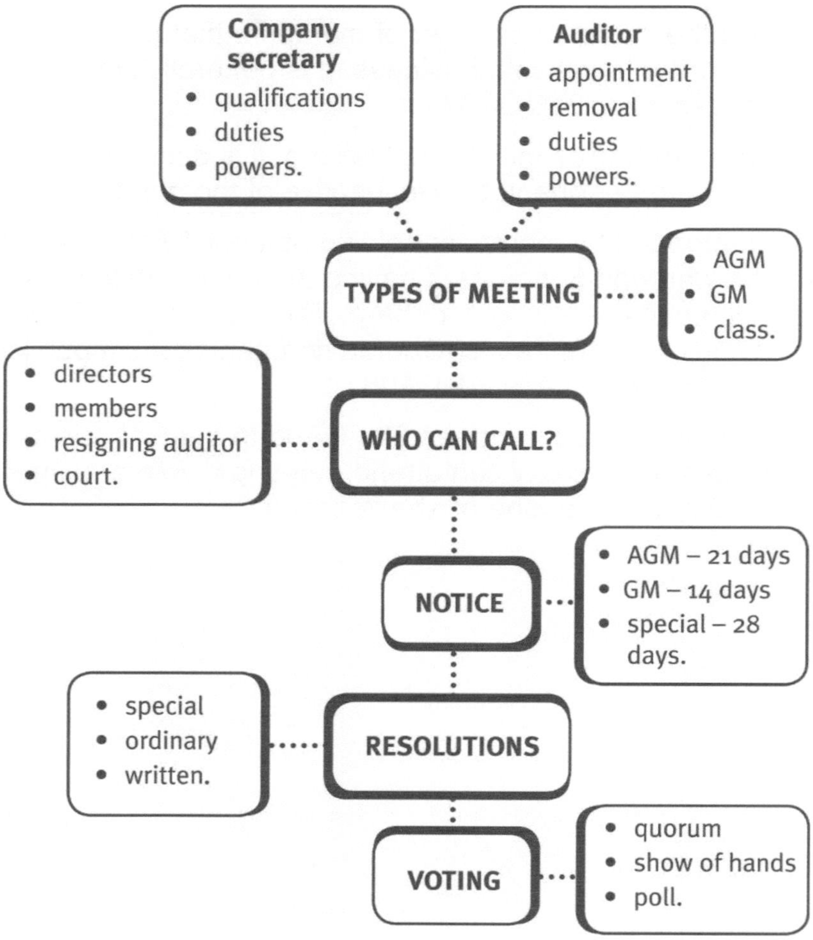

Test your understanding answers

Test your understanding 1

C Only a public company is required to have a company secretary. The secretary is appointed by the directors and must be qualified. To bind a company, the secretary must be acting within his or her actual and/or apparent authority.

Test your understanding 2

Removal of an auditor before his or her term of office expires requires an ordinary resolution of which 28 days' special notice has been given.

Test your understanding 3

1 An annual general meeting requires **21** days' notice.

2 Members may require the directors to call a GM if they hold at least **5%** of the paid up voting capital.

3 Special notice requires **28** days' notice.

4 A special resolution must be filed with the Registrar within **15** days.

Chapter

12

Insolvency

Chapter learning objectives

Upon completion of this chapter you will be able to:

- explain the meaning of and the procedure involved in voluntary liquidation
- explain the meaning of and the procedure involved in compulsory liquidation
- explain administration as an alternative to liquidation.

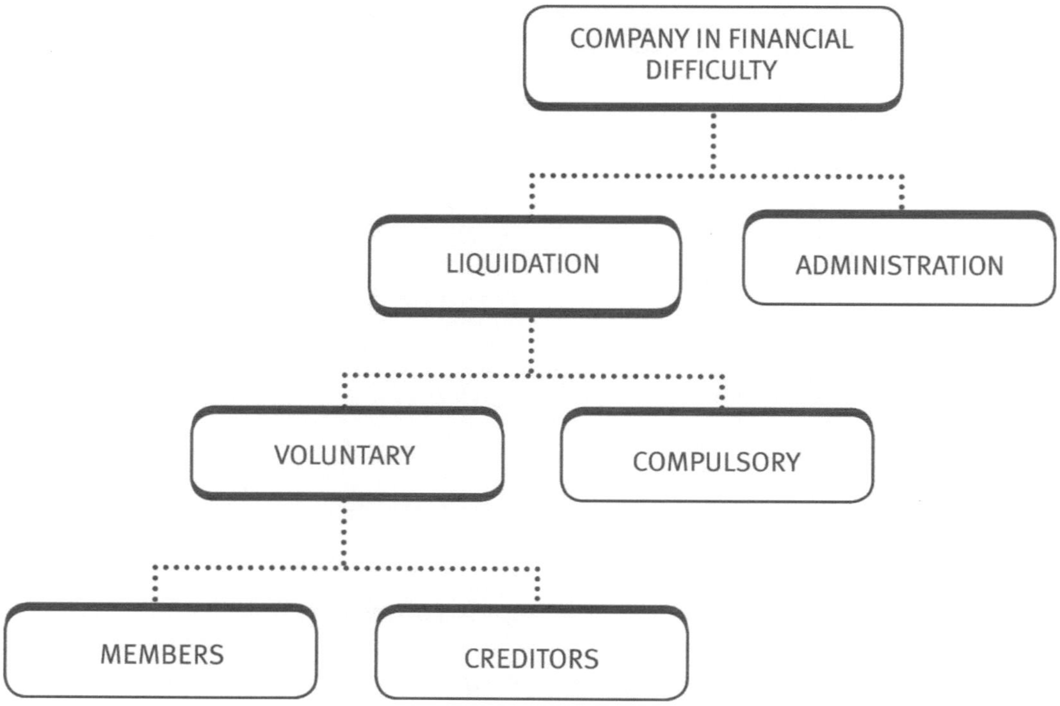

1 Introduction

If a company finds itself in financial difficulty, the two main options available to it are:

- Administration. This aims to rescue the company so that it may continue trading as a going concern.
- Liquidation. This winds up the company, thus bringing its life to an end.

2 Voluntary liquidation: s84 Insolvency Act (IA 1986)

A voluntary liquidation occurs where the members pass a resolution to go into liquidation. The type of resolution needed depends on the circumstances:

- Where the period fixed for the duration of the company expires or an event occurs upon which the articles provide that a company should be wound up, an **ordinary resolution** must be passed.
- A **special resolution** must be passed if the company is being wound up for any other reason.

There are two types of voluntary liquidation:

- A members' voluntary liquidation is used where the company is solvent.
- A creditors' voluntary liquidation is used where the company is insolvent.

Members' voluntary winding up

THE DIRECTORS MAKE A **DECLARATION OF SOLVENCY** UNDER S 89 IA 1986 STATING THAT THEY ARE OF THE OPINION THAT THE COMPANY WILL BE ABLE TO PAY ITS DEBTS WITHIN 12 MONTHS. IT IS A CRIMINAL OFFENCE TO MAKE A FALSE DECLARATION.

⋮

WINDING UP COMMENCES FROM THE PASSING OF THE APPROPRIATE RESOLUTION (S86 IA 1986)

⋮

THE MEMBERS **APPOINT A NAMED INSOLVENCY PRACTITIONER AS LIQUIDATOR** (S91 IA 1986).

⋮

THE LIQUIDATOR IS RESPONSIBLE FOR REALISING THE ASSETS AND DISTRIBUTING THE PROCEEDS.

⋮

THE LIQUIDATOR PRESENTS THEIR REPORT TO A **FINAL MEETING** OF THE MEMBERS (S93 IA 1986).

⋮

THE LIQUIDATOR **INFORMS THE REGISTRAR** OF THE FINAL MEETING AND SUBMITS A COPY OF THEIR REPORT (S94(3) IA 1986).

⋮

THE REGISTRAR REGISTERS THE REPORT AND THE COMPANY IS **DISSOLVED** 3 MONTHS LATER.

Creditors' voluntary winding up

WINDING UP COMMENCES FROM THE PASSING OF THE APPROPRIATE RESOLUTION (S86 IA 1986).

THE MEMBERS APPOINT A LIQUIDATOR. THE DIRECTORS MUST THEN DELIVER A NOTICE TO THE CREDITORS SEEKING THEIR DECISION ON THE LIQUIDATOR. THE DIRECTORS MUST ALSO SEND TO THE CREDITORS A **STATEMENT OF AFFAIRS** WITHIN 7 WORKING DAYS.

THE CREDITORS CAN APPROVE THE LIQUIDATOR EITHER BY VIRTUAL MEETING OR BY THE 'DEEMED CONSENT PROCESS'. UNDER THIS PROCESS, APPROVAL IS DEEMED UNLESS 10% OF THE CREDITORS OF THE COMPANY RAISE OBJECTIONS TO THE PROPOSED LIQUIDATOR. THE MEMBERS AND CREDITORS MAY APPOINT UP TO FIVE PERSONS TO SERVE ON A **LIQUIDATION COMMITTEE**

THE LIQUIDATOR SUBMITS THEIR FINAL REPORT TO THE MEMBERS AND CREDITORS

THE LIQUIDATOR SUBMITS A COPY OF THEIR REPORT TO THE REGISTRAR

THE REGISTRAR REGISTERS THE REPORT AND THE COMPANY IS **DISSOLVED** 3 MONTHS LATER

Converting a members' voluntary liquidation into a creditors' voluntary liquidation

If the liquidator discovers that the company's debts will not be paid in full within the time specified in the declaration of solvency, he or she must convert the members' voluntary liquidation into a creditors' voluntary liquidation. This is executed by following the process for a creditors' voluntary liquidation.

Test your understanding 1
Compare and contrast the characteristics of a members' voluntary winding up and a creditors' voluntary winding up.

3 Compulsory liquidation

Grounds for winding up: s122 IA 1986

A compulsory winding up commences when a petition for a winding up order is presented to and approved by the court. The possible grounds for the petition are set out in s122 IA 1986:

- The company has passed a special resolution to be wound up by the court.
- A public company has not been issued with a trading certificate within a year of incorporation.
- The company has not commenced business within a year of being incorporated or has suspended its business for over a year.
- The company is unable to pay its debts. A company is deemed to be unable to pay its debts where a creditor who is owed at least £750 has served a written demand for payment and the company has failed to pay the sum due within three weeks.
- A dissatisfied member may petition the court for the company to be wound up on the just and equitable ground. However, the court will not make an order under this ground if some other more reasonable remedy is available.

Petitioners

The following persons may petition the court for a compulsory liquidation:

- the company itself.
- the Official Receiver, who is a civil servant in The Insolvency Service and is an officer of the Court.
- the Department for Business and Trade.
- a contributory. This is any person who is liable to contribute to the assets of the company when it is being wound up. (The contributory must prove that the company is solvent).
- a creditor who is owed at least £750.

Effect of winding up

The winding-up petition has the following effects:

- The liquidation is deemed to have started when the petition was first presented.
- All actions for the recovery of debt against the company are stopped.
- Any floating charges crystallise.
- Any legal proceedings against the company are halted, and none may start unless leave is granted from the court.
- The company ceases to carry on business except where it is necessary to complete the winding up, e.g. to complete work-in-progress.
- The powers of the directors cease, although the directors remain in office.
- The employees are automatically made redundant, but the liquidator can re-employ them to help him or her complete the winding up.

Subsequent procedures

ON THE MAKING OF THE WINDING-UP ORDER, THE OFFICIAL RECEIVER BECOMES LIQUIDATOR

↓

WITHIN THREE MONTHS, THE OFFICIAL RECEIVER WILL SUMMON MEETINGS OF THE CONTRIBUTORIES IN ORDER TO APPOINT A LICENSED INSOLVENCY PRACTITIONER TO TAKE OVER THE JOB OF LIQUIDATOR

↓

CREDITOR APPROVAL OF THE LIQUIDATOR IS SOUGHT VIA THE 'DEEMED CONSENT' PROCESS. IF 10% OR MORE OBJECT AN ALTERNATIVE DECISION MAKING PROCEDURE SUCH AS VIRTUAL MEETING SHOULD BE USED

↓

THE LIQUIDATOR IS RESPONSIBLE FOR REALISING THE ASSETS AND DISTRIBUTING THE PROCEEDS

↓

THE LIQUIDATOR RETURNS TO THE COURT AND THE COURT PASSES AN ORDER DISSOLVING THE COMPANY

↓

THE LIQUIDATOR FILES THE ORDER AND THEIR FINAL REPORT WITH THE REGISTRAR

↓

THE REGISTRAR REGISTERS THE REPORT AND THE COMPANY IS DISSOLVED AS FROM THE DATE OF THE ORDER

Test your understanding 2

Fill in the gaps in the following sentences:

The possible grounds for a compulsory liquidation petition are set out in....................:

A The company has passed a.............................resolution to be wound up by the court.

B A.......................... company has not been issued with a trading certificate within .... of incorporation.

C A creditor who is owed at least.......................has served a written demand for payment and the company has failed to pay the sum due within ....

D It is .... to wind up the company.

Application of assets

The liquidator must repay debts in the following order:

- fixed charge-holders.
- expenses of liquidation.
- preferential creditors
  - wages or salaries due in the four months preceding the commencement of winding up (maximum £800 per employee)
  - all accrued holiday pay.

  All preferential creditors rank equally amongst themselves.
- secondary preferential creditors – HMRC in respect of VAT, PAYE Income Tax and employees National Insurance Contributions.
- floating charge-holders.
- unsecured creditors – rank equally amongst themselves. The Enterprise Act 2002 introduced into the Insolvency Act 1986 a ring-fencing mechanism where part of assets which are subject to a floating charge are available to unsecured creditors. The amount ring-fenced is 50% of the first £10,000, plus 20% of the rest up to a maximum ring-fenced fund of £800,000.
- post-liquidation interest.
- members – declared but unpaid dividends.
- members – return of capital (in accordance with class rights).
- any surplus to be distributed to members.

Test your understanding 3

Sharepak Ltd is being wound-up. Rank the following persons in the order in which they will be paid by the liquidator:

Preference shareholders.

Mrs Patel – an employee who is owed holiday pay of £1,000.

Barlloyd Bank – which has a charge over all the company's current assets.

Midwest Bank – which has a charge on the company's headquarters.

Ordinary shareholders.

4 Administration

Purpose

Administration involves the appointment of an insolvency practitioner, known as an administrator, to manage the affairs, business and property of a company. It was first introduced by Schedule 16 IA 1986, but has subsequently been amended by the Enterprise Act 2002.

Administration is often used as an alternative to putting a company into liquidation, e.g. to:

- rescue a company in financial difficulty with the aim of allowing it to continue as a going concern
- achieve a better result for the creditors than would be likely if the company were to be wound up
- realise property to pay one or more secured or preferential creditors.

The administrator can only use the third option where:

- he or she thinks it is not reasonably practicable to rescue the company as a going concern, and
- he or she thinks that he or she cannot achieve a better result for the creditors as a whole than would be likely if the company were to be wound up, and
- he or she does not unnecessarily harm the interests of the creditors of the company as a whole.

Who can appoint an administrator?

An administrator can be appointed by any of the following persons:

- the court in response to a petition by, e.g. a creditor, the directors or the company itself
- the holder of a qualifying floating charge over the company's assets
- the company or its directors provided that winding up has not already begun.

The court will only agree to appoint an administrator if it is satisfied that:

- the company is or is likely to become unable to pay its debts, and
- the administration order is likely to achieve its objectives.

Consequences of administration

The appointment of an administrator has the following effects:

- the rights of creditors to enforce any security over the company's assets are suspended
- there can be no enforcement of charges, retention of title clauses or hire-purchase agreements against the company
- any outstanding petition for winding up is dismissed
- no resolution may be passed to wind up the company
- the directors still continue in office, but their powers are suspended.

Carrying out the administration

The administrator has a number of tasks:

- He or she is the company's agent, but must act in the best interests of all the company's creditors. He or she can do anything necessary for the management of the company.
- He or she has wide powers to manage the business and property of the company, including the power to bring and defend legal proceedings, sell assets and borrow money. With regards to selling assets this includes property which is subject to both fixed and floating charges, which may be disposed of without the consent of the charge holder, although they retain first call against any money realised by the sale of the asset. In respect of assets subject to fixed charges, this will require the court's permission.
- He or she has the power to remove and replace directors and employees. If an employee's contract is not adopted by the administrator within 14 days, that employee is made redundant.
- He or she can pay out monies to secured or preferential creditors without the need to seek approval of the court. He or she can also pay out monies to unsecured creditors but this must be with the approval of the court.

The administrator also has a number of legal duties. As soon as is reasonably practicable after appointment:

- He or she must send notice of appointment to the company and publish notice of appointment.
- He or she must obtain a list of company creditors and send notice of appointment to each.
- Within 7 days of appointment, he or she must send notice of appointment to the Registrar.

- He or she will arrange for a statement of affairs of the company to be drawn up.
- He or she must ensure that every business document of the company bears his or her identity as administrator and a statement that the company affairs and property are being managed by him or her.
- Based on the statement of affairs, he or she must draw up a statement of his or her proposals within eight weeks of his or her appointment.
- The proposals must be approved by the creditors of the company. This approval can be given by:
  - Deemed consent process
  - Virtual meeting
  - Some other reasonable method.
- The creditors have the right to form a creditors meeting of between 3 to 5 creditors. If formed the administrator must hold a meeting of the creditors within 6 weeks of its establishment.
- If the creditors do not approve the proposals, the court may dismiss the administrator or make such provisions as it sees fit.
- If the creditors approve the proposals, the administrator can carry them out.

Ending the administration

The administration will end when it is completed or when the administrator is discharged by the court:

- The administration must normally be completed within 12 months of the date on which it commenced. However, this term can be extended with the consent of the court or the secured creditors.
- The administrator may apply to the court for discharge at any time. He or she must make an application when the purpose of the order has been achieved. He or she must also notify the Registrar and all of the creditors.

5 Chapter summary

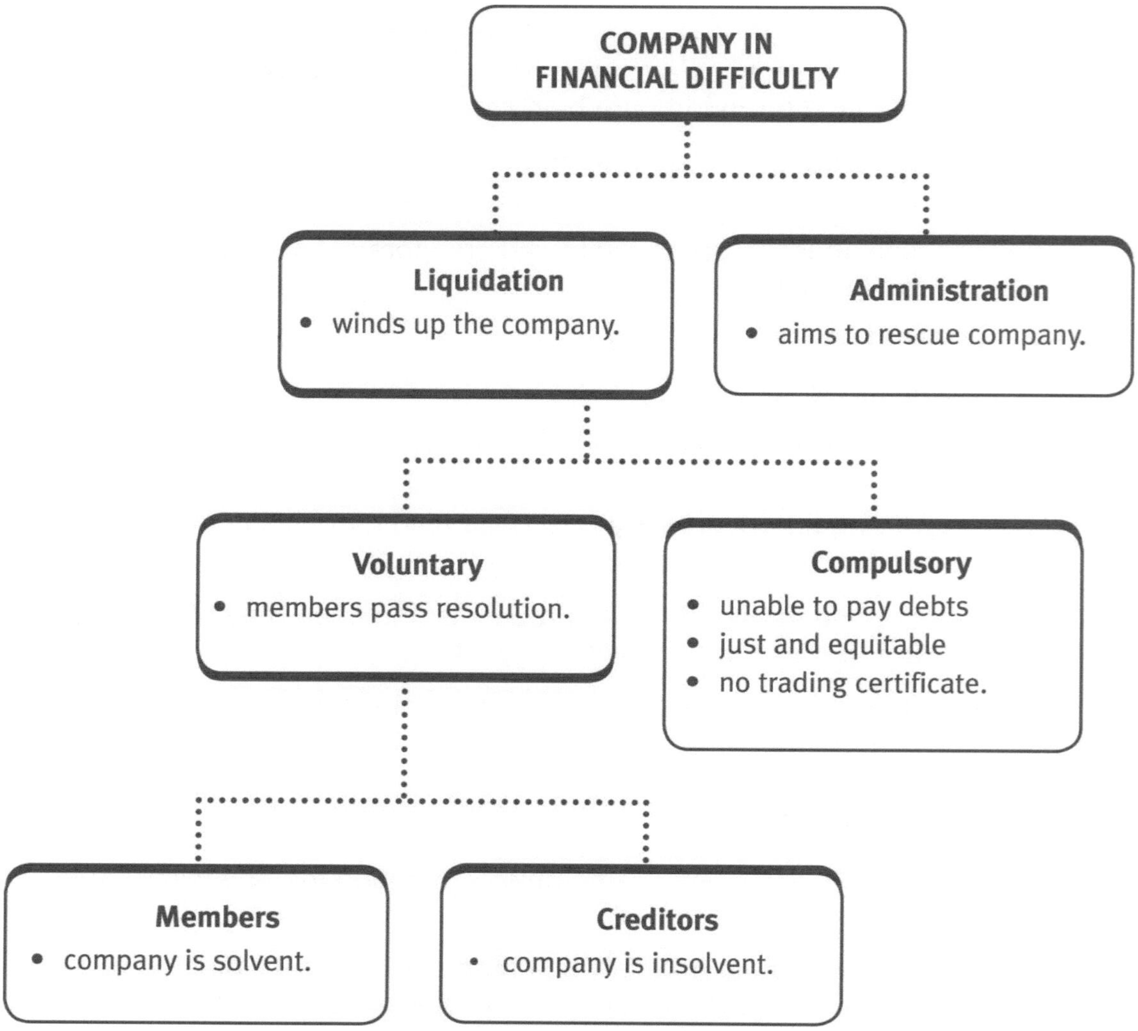

Test your understanding answers

Test your understanding 1

A voluntary winding up takes place when the company resolves by special resolution to be wound up for any cause whatsoever: S84 Insolvency Act 1986.

In both cases of voluntary winding up the passing of the resolution, which must be advertised within 14 days in the Gazette, has the following consequences:

I The winding up commences from the time of the passing of the resolution.

II The company ceases to carry on business, except in so far as is necessary for its beneficial winding up.

III All transfers of shares, except those made with the concurrence of the liquidator, are void.

In the case of a members' voluntary winding up, the directors make a declaration of solvency stating that after full inquiry into the company's affairs they are of the opinion that the company will be able to pay its debts within 12 months of the commencement of the winding up. In a creditors' voluntary winding up, such a declaration is not possible owing to the circumstances leading to the winding up. In a members' voluntary winding up, the liquidator is appointed by the members and is accountable to them. In a creditors' voluntary winding up, the members appoint a liquidator which is followed by the directors delivering notice to the creditors seeking their decision on the liquidator. The creditors can approve the liquidator either by virtual meeting or the 'deemed consent' process. Under this process approval is deemed unless 10% of the creditors of the company raise objections to the proposed liquidator. The members and creditors may appoint up to five persons to serve on a liquidation committee. Here the liquidator is primarily accountable to the creditors.

Test your understanding 2

The possible grounds for a compulsory liquidation petition are set out in s122 IA 1986:

A The company has passed a special resolution to be wound up by the court.

B A public company has not been issued with a trading certificate within a year of incorporation.

C A creditor who is owed at least £750 has served a written demand for payment and the company has failed to pay the sum due within three weeks.

D It is just and equitable to wind up the company.

Test your understanding 3

The liquidator will repay in the following order:

Midwest Bank – the charge on the company's headquarters is a fixed charge.

Mrs Patel – employees who are owed holiday pay are classed as preferential creditors.

Barlloyd Bank – the charge over all the company's current assets is a floating charge.

Preference shareholders.

Ordinary shareholders – the ordinary shareholders will share in any surplus assets.

Chapter

13

Corporate and Fraudulent behaviour

Chapter learning objectives

Upon completion of this chapter you will be able to:

- recognise the nature and legal control over insider dealing
- recognise the nature and legal control over market abuse
- recognise the nature and legal control over money laundering
- recognise the nature and legal control over bribery
- discuss potential criminal activity in the operation, management and winding up of companies
- distinguish between fraudulent and wrongful trading.

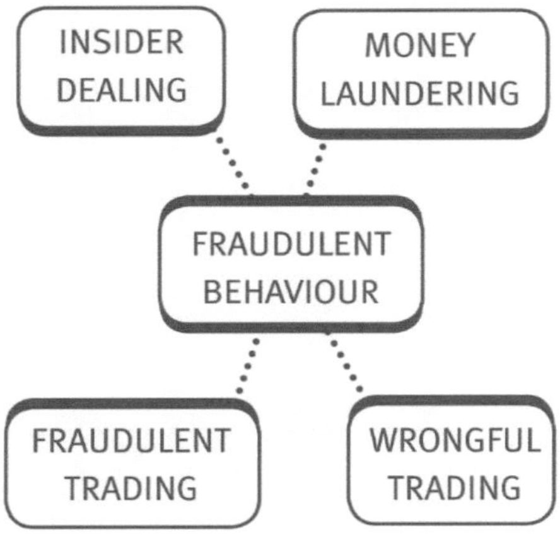

1 Insider dealing

The value of a share reflects the profitability and future prospects of a company. This type of information is usually only available to a prospective purchaser after it has been made available publicly. However, if a prospective purchaser could gain access to such information before it was made public, he or she could anticipate which way the price was likely to move and thereby make a profit. This is known as 'insider dealing'. Insider dealing has been made a criminal offence as it is perceived to undermine the integrity of the stock market.

Legislation

Insider dealing is a crime under part V of the Criminal Justice Act 1993.

The offences

The Criminal Justice Act 1993 sets out the three distinct offences in s52.

An individual will be guilty of insider dealing if they have **information** as an **insider** and:

- they **deal** in price-affected securities on the basis of that information
- they **encourage another person** to deal in price-affected securities in relation to that information
- they **disclose the information** to anyone other than in the proper performance of their employment, office or profession.

Dealing

Dealing is defined in s55 as acquiring or disposing of securities, whether as a principal or agent, or agreeing to acquire securities.

Inside information

S56 defines inside information as information which:

- relates to particular securities or to a particular issuer of securities
- is specific or precise
- has not been made public
- if made public would be likely to have a significant effect on the price.

Insider

S57 states that a person has information as an insider only if they know that it is inside information and they have it from an inside source.

A person has information from an inside source if:

- he or she has it through being a director, employee or shareholder of issuer of securities
- he or she has it through having access to the information by virtue of his or her employment, office or profession
- the direct or indirect source of the information is a person within either of these categories.

Defences

When dealing in securities, or encouraging another to do so, a person will not be guilty of insider dealing where the individual is able to show that he or she did not, at the time, expect the dealing to result in a profit or in the avoidance of a loss in relation to the inside information which he or she knew.

It is also a defence where the insider believed on reasonable grounds that the information had been disclosed widely enough to ensure that none of those taking part in the dealing would be prejudiced by now having the information.

Where the defendant is able to show that he or she would have dealt with the securities in the same way or encouraged another to deal with the securities in the same way, even if he or she had not possessed the inside information, he or she will have a defence.

Consequences

On summary conviction an individual found guilty of insider dealing is liable to a fine not exceeding the statutory maximum and/or a maximum of six months imprisonment.

On indictment the penalty is an unlimited fine and/or a maximum of ten years imprisonment (for offences committed before 1 November 2021 the maximum term is seven years).

If the individual concerned is a director, he or she is in breach of his or her fiduciary duty and may be liable to account to the company for a profit made.

Test your understanding 1	
1	**Which statute contains the legislation on insider dealing?**
2	**What are the three sub-categories of the offence of insider dealing?**
3	**What are the three general defences to a charge of insider dealing?**

2 Market Abuse

Legislation

The Financial Services and Markets Act 2000 introduces the concept of market abuse.

Under s118 (1) market abuse is defined as:

- behaviour in relation to any qualifying investment
- likely to be regarded by regular users of the market as falling below the standard reasonably expected of a person in that position; and
- that falls within at least one of three categories:
  1. Based on information not generally available to users of the market which, if available to a regular user, would be likely to be regarded by him or her as relevant in regard to the terms on which to deal in those investments.
  2. Is likely to give a regular user a false or misleading impression as to the market value of such investments.
  3. Is regarded by a regular user as likely to distort the market in such investments.

Qualifying investments are those which are traded on the UK's 'prescribed markets', as well as those traded on other European regulated markets.

The Financial Services Authority have also drawn up a Code of Market Conduct to detail the ways in which market abuse can occur.

There are seven types of behaviour which can amount to market abuse.

Insider dealing

As discussed above in section 1, insider dealing is when an insider deals, or tries to deal, on the basis of inside information.

Improper disclosure

This is where an insider improperly discloses inside information to another person and is also classified as insider dealing.

e.g **Illustration 1**

An employee finds out that his or her company is about to become the target of a takeover bid. Before the information is made public, he or she buys shares in his or her company because he or she knows a takeover bid may be imminent. He or she then discloses the information to a friend.

This behaviour creates an unfair market place because the person who sold the shares to the employee might not have done so if he or she had known of the potential takeover. The employee's friend also has this information and could profit unfairly from it.

Misuse of information

This is any behaviour based on information that is not generally available but would affect an investor's decision about the terms on which to deal. This is also a type of insider dealing.

e.g **Illustration 2**

An employee learns that his or her company may lose a significant contract with its main customer. The employee then sells his or her shares, based on his or her assessment that it is reasonably certain.

This behaviour creates an unfair market place as the person buying the shares from the employee might not have done so had he or she been aware of the information about the potential loss of contract.

Manipulating transactions

This is trading, or placing orders to trade, that gives a false or misleading impression of the supply of, or demand for, one or more investments, raising the price of the investments to an abnormal or artificial level.

e.g **Illustration 3**

A person buys a large number of a particular share near the end of the day, aiming to drive the stock price higher to improve the performance of their investment. The market price is pushed to an artificial level and investors get a false impression of the price of those shares and the value of any portfolio or fund that holds the stock. This could lead to people making the wrong investment decision.

Manipulating devices

This is trading, or placing orders to trade, which employs fictitious devices or any other form of deception or contrivance.

e.g

Illustration 4

A person buys shares and then spreads misleading information with a view to increasing the price. This could give investors a false impression of the price of a share and lead them to make the wrong investment decision.

Dissemination

This is the giving out of information that conveys a false or misleading impression about an investment or the issuer of an investment where the person doing this knows the information to be false or misleading.

e.g

Illustration 5

A person uses an internet bulletin board or chat room to post information about the takeover of a company. The person knows the information to be false or misleading. This could artificially raise or reduce the price of a share and lead to people making the wrong investment decisions.

Distortion and misleading behaviour

This is behaviour that gives a false or misleading impression of either the supply of, or demand for an investment, or behaviour which otherwise distorts the market in an investment.

e.g

Illustration 6

There is movement of an empty cargo ship that is used to transport a particular commodity. This could create a false impression of changes in the supply of, or demand for, that commodity or the related futures contract. It could also artificially change the price of that commodity or the futures contract, and lead to people making the wrong investment decisions.

Consequences

Market abuse is defined in the Code can result in an unlimited fine and a public reprimand by the Financial Services Authority under civil law.

3 Money laundering

Money laundering is a serious matter for accountants as they have certain responsibilities, which if not met can carry harsh consequences. This topic also comes up in the Advanced Audit and Assurance exam.

Definition

Money laundering is the process by which the proceeds of crime are converted into assets which appear to have a legal rather than an illegal source. The aim of disguising the source of the property is to allow the holder to enjoy it free from suspicion as to its source.

Legislation

Money laundering is primarily regulated by the Proceeds of Crime Act 2002.

The legislation imposes some important obligations upon professionals, such as accountants, auditors and legal advisers. These obligations require such professionals to report money laundering to the authorities and to have systems in place to train staff and keep records.

The three phases

Money laundering usually comprises three distinct phases:

- Placement – the initial disposal of the proceeds of criminal activity into an apparently legitimate business activity or property.
- Layering – the transfer of money from business to business, or place to place, in order to conceal its initial source.
- Integration – the culmination of the previous procedures through which the money takes on the appearance of coming from a legitimate source.

The offences

The Proceeds of Crime Act 2002 created three categories of criminal offence: laundering, failure to report, and tipping off.

Laundering

It is an offence to conceal, disguise, convert, transfer, or remove criminal property from England, Wales, Scotland or Northern Ireland: s327 Proceeds of Crime Act 2002.

Concealing or disguising criminal property includes concealing or disguising its nature, source, location, disposition, movement or ownership, or any rights connected with it.

'Criminal property' is defined as property which the alleged offender knows (or suspects) constitutes or represents benefit from any criminal conduct.

'Criminal conduct' is defined as conduct that:

- constitutes an offence in any part of the UK
- would constitute an offence in any part of the UK if it occurred there.

Failure to report

Under s330 individuals carrying on a 'relevant business' may be guilty of an offence of failing to disclose knowledge or suspicion of money laundering where they know or suspect, or have reasonable grounds for knowing or suspecting, that another person is engaged in laundering the proceeds of crime.

This offence only relates to individuals, such as accountants, who are acting in the course of business in the regulated sector.

Any individual who is covered by s330 is required to make disclosure to a nominated money laundering reporting officer within their organisation, or directly to the National Crime Agency, as soon as is practicable.

Tipping off

Section 333A states that it is an offence to make a disclosure likely to prejudice a money laundering investigation. It therefore covers the situation where an accountant informs a client that a report has been submitted to the National Crime Agency.

Penalties

The maximum penalty for the s327 offence of money laundering is 14 years' imprisonment.

Failure to report is punishable on conviction by a maximum of five years' imprisonment and/or a fine. Tipping off is punishable on conviction by a maximum of two years' imprisonment and/or a fine.

Money Laundering Regulations 2017

Secondary regulation is provided by the Money Laundering Regulations 2017.

The Money Laundering Regulations 2017 implemented the EU's Fourth Money Laundering Directive.

The Regulations require firms to put preventative measures in place. They require firms to ensure that they know their customers by conducting customer identification and verification and undertake ongoing monitoring where applicable, to keep records of identity and to train their staff on the requirements of the Regulations.

At a minimum, an anti-money laundering program should incorporate:

- Money laundering and terrorist financing risk assessment.
- Implementation of systems, policies, controls and procedures that effectively manage the risk that the firm is exposed to in relation to money laundering activities and ensure compliance with the legislation.

- Compliance with customer due diligence, enhanced due diligence and simplified due diligence requirements.
- Enhanced record keeping and data protection systems, policies and procedures.

The Regulations cover most financial firms such as banks, building societies, money transmitters, bureaux de change, cheque cashers and savings and investments firms. In addition the Regulations cover legal professionals, accountants, tax advisers, auditors, insolvency practitioners, estate agents, casinos, high value dealers when dealing in goods worth over 15,000 Euro and trust or company service providers.

There are various regulators and professional bodies who have been given supervisory authority. For example, the Financial Services Authority supervises all financial firms covered by the Regulations and the Office of Fair Trading supervises all consumer credit firms and estate agents.

Money laundering and terrorist financing risk assessment

A written risk assessment must be carried out to identify and assess the risk of money laundering. The risk assessment must take into account information provided by the supervisory authority on risk factors in the sector. The following risk factors must also be taken into account:

- The firm's customers
- The countries or geographic where the firm operates
- The firm's products or services
- The firm's transactions, and
- The firm's delivery channels.

The risk assessment should be used to:

- Develop policies, procedures and controls to mitigate the risk of money laundering.
- Apply a risk based approach to detecting and preventing money laundering.

The firm must establish and maintain written policies, controls and procedures to effectively manage and mitigate the money laundering and terrorist financing risks identified in the risk assessment. These must be proportionate to the size and nature of the business, approved by senior management, regularly reviewed and updated and communicated internally within the firm.

Officer responsible for compliance

Firms must appoint a Money Laundering Compliance Principal (MLCP) and this person must be on the board of directors or a member of senior management. Sole practitioners with no employees are exempt from this requirement.

Firms must also appoint a nominated officer, Money Laundering Reporting Officer (MLRO), to receive internal suspicious activity reports and assess whether a suspicious activity report should be made to the appropriate regulatory body. The MLRO and MLCP may be the same person if the MLRO is sufficiently senior.

Employees

Firms must assess the skills, knowledge, conduct and integrity of employees involved in identification, preventing or detecting money laundering.

Staff training must be provided on an ongoing basis in how to recognise and handle transactions and activities which may be related to money laundering.

Customer due diligence

Accountants are required to establish that new clients are who they claim to be by obtaining satisfactory evidence of identity from the client. This is often referred to as 'customer due diligence' or 'know your customer' procedures.

Customer due diligence is an essential part of the anti-money laundering requirements. It ensures that accountants:

- know who their clients are, and
- do not unknowingly accept clients which are too high risk.

Customer due diligence must be performed as soon as is reasonably practicable after contact is first made between the two parties.

Enhanced due diligence

For higher risk clients, enhanced due diligence must be carried out. Enhanced due diligence procedures include examining the background and purpose of the transaction and increased monitoring of the business relationship.

Simplified due diligence

For clients presenting a lower risk of money laundering, simplified due diligence may be carried out.

Office for Professional Body Anti-Money Laundering Supervision

The Office for Professional Body Anti-Money Laundering Supervision (OPBAS) was established by the Government in 2018 under the OPBAS Regulations 2018. The Regulations give OPBAS duties and powers to ensure that the 22 accountancy and legal professional body anti-money laundering supervisors meet the standards required by the Money Laundering Regulations 2017 and they have powers to investigate those that do not.

Test your understanding 2	
1	**Which Act contains the legislation on money laundering?**
2	**To which organisation must you report suspicions of money laundering?**
3	**Which of the three money laundering offences only applies to individuals, such as accountants, who are in business in the regulated sector?**
4	**What is meant by the term 'money laundering'?**

4 Bribery

Definition

Bribery is an act implying money or gift given that alters the behaviour of the recipient. It is the offering, giving, receiving, or soliciting of any item of value to influence the actions of an official or other person in charge of a public or legal duty.

Legislation

The Bribery Act 2010 came into force on 1 July 2011.

The Act creates four offences:

- bribing a person to induce or reward them to perform a relevant function improperly (S1)
- requesting, accepting or receiving a bribe as a reward for performing a relevant function improperly (S2)
- using a bribe to influence a foreign official to gain a business advantage (S6)
- a new form of corporate liability for failing to prevent bribery on behalf of a commercial organisation (S7).

Commercial organisation has a wide meaning and includes partnerships, limited liability partnerships and companies which carry on business.

Defence

Under S9 for a commercial organisation it is a defence to have in place 'adequate procedures' to prevent bribery. This may include implementing anti-bribery procedures. It is important that firms consider what adequate procedures are most appropriate for their firm given the risks they face and the way they run their business. The procedures should be proportionate to the risk posed.

For some firms there will be no need to put bribery prevention procedures in place as there is no risk of bribery on their behalf. Other firms may need to put in place measures in key areas, such as gifts and hospitality, as this is the area where they have identified a risk.

Penalties

The penalty for individuals is a maximum sentence of 10 years.

For commercial organisations there may be an unlimited fine.

Deferred prosecution agreement

Deferred prosecution agreements (DPA) became available to prosecutors in the UK in February 2014 under the Crime and Courts Act 2013.

A DPA allows commercial organisations to settle allegations of criminal economic activity without being prosecuted and without any formal admission of guilt.

An agreement is made between the prosecutor and the commercial organisation, under which the prosecutor will bring criminal charges but then immediately suspend the process, on the basis that the organisation has agreed to a number of conditions determined by the prosecutor such as paying a financial penalty or co-operating with the future prosecution of individuals. If the organisation does not honour the conditions, the prosecution may resume.

Test your understanding 3

A manager at a manufacturing company who has overall responsibility for the procurement of a service which is currently subject to re-tender is approached by the current supplier and offered (at the expense of the company) a day trip to London, including lunch in Harrods and a trip on the London Eye. The company says the offer is "to cement and say thank you for our longstanding business relationship".

Advise the company as to whether there are any implication of accepting the proposed hospitality.

5 Potential criminal activity in the operation, management and winding up of companies

Introduction

There are a number of criminal offences that could be undertaken by individuals concerned in the operation, management or winding up of a company. Many of these points have been covered in earlier chapters and so are only dealt with in outline here.

Failure to file accounts or annual returns

Failure to deliver accounts or annual returns on time is a criminal offence. All the directors of a company in default could be prosecuted. If convicted, a director could end up with a criminal record and a fine of up to £5,000 for each offence.

Providing misleading information to an auditor

Under s499 CA 2006, an auditor is entitled to require from the company's officers and employees such information and explanation as he or she thinks necessary for the performance of his or her duties as auditor. It is a criminal offence for an officer of the company to:

- provide misleading, false or deceptive information or explanations, or
- fail to provide information or explanations required by the auditor.

An individual can defend such a charge if he or she can prove that it was not reasonably practicable to provide the information or explanations required.

Companies Act 2006

Under s82 CA 2006 it is a criminal offence to use a business name that requires prior approval, if that approval has not been obtained.

It is also a criminal offence to fail to disclose the business details that the Act requires. These details include stating the company's corporate name and address for the service of documents.

Company Directors Disqualification Act 1986 (CDDA 1986)

Under s13 CDDA 1986, any person who acts in contravention of a disqualification order (or while an undischarged bankrupt) is guilty of an offence. The maximum penalty is:

- two years' imprisonment and/or a fine on conviction on indictment
- up to six months' imprisonment and/or a fine not exceeding the statutory maximum on a summary conviction.

S15 CDDA 1986, provides that anyone who is involved in the management of a company while disqualified, or who acts on the instructions of someone who is disqualified, shall be personally liable for the company's debts incurred during the time they acted.

Phoenix companies

S216 and s217 Insolvency Act 1986 (IA 1986) are aimed at so-called 'phoenix companies'. They apply where a person was a director or shadow director of a company at any time in the period of 12 months ending with the day before the company went into liquidation.

The provisions apply for the five years following liquidation. They prevent the person being a director of a company with a similar name, or a name which suggests an association with the previous company, without leave of the court.

It is a criminal offence to contravene the provisions, punishable by imprisonment and/or a fine. In addition, the director will be personally liable for any debts of the new company which are incurred when he or she was involved in its management.

The Fraud Act 2006

The Fraud Act 2006 radically changed the law of criminal fraud.

Before the Fraud Act came into force, the statutory fraud offences under the Theft Act 1978 were based on deception. They included:

- Obtaining property by deception.
- Obtaining a money transfer by deception.
- Obtaining a pecuniary advantage by deception.
- Obtaining services by deception.

The Fraud Act swept all of the old statutory deception offences away. Instead a new offence of fraud has been defined as follows:

- The defendant must have been dishonest, and have intended to make a gain or to cause a loss to another; and
- The defendant must carry out one of these acts:
  - s2: fraud by making a false or misleading representation, this being where any person makes "any representation as to fact or law ... express or implied" which they know to be untrue or misleading.
  - s3: fraud by failing to disclose information whereby a person fails to disclose any information to a third party when they are under a legal duty to disclose such information.
  - s4: fraud by abuse of position where a person occupies a position where they are expected to safeguard the financial interests of another person, and abuses that position; this includes cases where the abuse consisted of an omission rather than an overt act.

The current offence of fraud is intended to be wide and also flexible. There is no reliance on the concept of "deception". It does not matter whether the false information actually deceives anyone, it is the misleading intention which counts.

Failure to prevent fraud

The Economic Crime and Corporate Transparency Act 2023 sets out the corporate offence on failure to prevent fraud.

The offence can make an organisation criminally liable where an employee, agent, subsidiary or other 'associated person' commits a fraud which benefits the organisation or its customers and the organisation did not have reasonable fraud prevention procedures in place. It sits alongside existing fraud legislation for example the Fraud Act offences, which would make an individual liable for prosecution under that legislation and the organisation would face prosecution under the Economic Crime and Corporate Transparency Act.

The offence applies to large incorporated organisations and partnerships both inside and outside the UK, which meet two of the following criteria:

- More than 250 employees
- More than £36 million annual turnover
- More than £18 million total balance sheet assets

The Crown Prosecution Service or the Serious Fraud Office can bring a prosecution. If convicted, an organisation can receive an unlimited fine.

Failure to prevent tax evasion

The Criminal Finances Act 2017 sets out the corporate offence on failure to prevent the criminal facilitation of criminal tax evasion.

The offence can make a 'relevant body' criminally liable if it fails to prevent the facilitation of UK or non-UK tax evasion by an employee or 'associated person'. The offence applies to both UK and non-UK companies as well as partnerships, as if they were corporations.

An 'associated person' can be an individual, corporate entity or an employee of a corporate associated person, carrying out services on behalf of the 'relevant body'.

A 'relevant body' is defined in the act as a company or a partnership.

The offence is of strict liability and no knowledge or intention is required. There is no requirement for the tax evader to have been prosecuted for evasion, or for the facilitator to have been prosecuted for facilitation.

The legislation focuses on the procedures that should be in place to prevent the criminal facilitation of tax evasion by an employee or associated person.

There are three stages to the offence:

- **Stage one:** The criminal evasion of tax.
- **Stage two:** The criminal facilitation of this offence by an associated person.
- **Stage three:** The relevant body failed to prevent the associated person from committing that facilitation.

There is a statutory defence where at the time of the offence the relevant body had reasonable prevention procedures in place to prevent tax evasion facilitation offences or where it is unreasonable to expect such procedures. The reasonable prevention procedures are judged by six guiding principles:

1 Risk assessment
2 Proportionality of risk-based prevention procedures
3 Top level commitment
4 Due diligence
5 Communication
6 Monitoring and review

The penalty is an unlimited fine for the relevant body and potential reputational damage.

6 Transactions at an undervalue and preference

A liquidator may apply to the court to set aside company transactions at an undervalue (s238 Insolvency Act 1986) or where the company gives a preference (s239 Insolvency Act 1986).

Undervalue

A company enters into a transaction at an undervalue if the company makes a gift or otherwise enters into a transaction on terms that the company receives not consideration or insufficient consideration.

The transaction would not be set aside if it was entered into in good faith on the reasonable belief that it would benefit the company.

Preferences

A company gives a preference if it does anything to put a creditor in a better position in the event of the company's insolvent liquidation than they would otherwise be.

The court will not make an order unless the company was influenced by a desire to prefer the creditor. Therefore, a payment or charge created in favour of a creditor who is threatening legal proceedings might be a defence. However, if the preference was given to a connected person it is presumed that the company was influenced by its desire to give a preference.

7 Fraudulent and wrongful trading

Fraudulent trading

Fraudulent trading occurs where the company's business is carried on with intent to defraud creditors or for any fraudulent purpose.

Fraudulent trading can give rise to:

- civil liability under s213 Insolvency Act 1986 if the company is in the course of being wound up
- criminal liability under s993 CA06 whether or not the company is in the course of being wound up.

It is necessary to establish **dishonest intent**. In **Re William C Leith Bros (1932)** it was said that if the directors carry on the business and cause the company to incur further debts at a time when they know that there is no reasonable prospect of those debts being paid this is a proper inference of dishonesty. The court also added that if the directors honestly believed the debts would eventually be paid there would be no intent to defraud.

R v Grantham (1984)

Facts: The directors ordered a consignment of potatoes on a month's credit at a time when they knew that payment would not be forthcoming at the end of the month when it was due.

Held: The directors were convicted of fraudulent trading.

The second point required to establish liability is that the person concerned shall be **knowingly a party** to the fraudulent trading.

In **Re Maidstone Buildings (1971)** it was established that a person is not 'party' merely by reason of knowledge. They must take some active step, such as the ordering of goods.

Fraudulent trading can give rise to the following consequences:

- The court can order the individual to contribute to the company's assets.
- If a director, they may be disqualified for 15 years under CDDA86.
- If found guilty of the criminal offence, the individual can be fined and/or imprisoned for up to 10 years.

Wrongful trading

Wrongful trading occurs where on a winding-up it appears to the court that the company has gone into insolvent liquidation and, before the start of winding up, the director knew or ought to have known that there was **no reasonable prospect that the company would avoid going into insolvent liquidation**: S214 Insolvency Act 1986.

The provision of 'wrongful trading' contained in S214 IA86 is designed to remove one of the difficult obstacles to the establishment of being party to fraudulent trading – namely proving dishonesty. **It applies only to directors and shadow directors.**

The director is expected to reach those conclusions and take such steps as a reasonably diligent person would take.

The legislation also expects such a director to:

- have the general knowledge, skill and experience which may reasonably be expected of a person carrying out the same functions as were carried out by that director (i.e. this is an objective test)
- use the general knowledge, skill and experience he or she himself has (i.e. this is a subjective test).

When considering the director's functions, the court will have regard not only to those functions he or she carried out but also to those entrusted to him or her. This means that the director could be made liable for those actions he or she should have carried out but failed to.

Re Produce Marketing Consortium Ltd (No 2) (1989)

Facts: The company, after trading successfully for nine years, built up an overdraft, had a continuing trading loss and had an excess of liabilities over assets. In February 1987 the directors recognised that liquidation was inevitable but carried on trading until October 1987, arguing that this period of trading minimised the loss to creditors by allowing an orderly disposal, for value, of the company's goods.

Held: The court required them to contribute £75,000 to the assets of the company (equating to the net debts incurred during the wrongful trading period) on the grounds that:

- they would have known that liquidation was inevitable in July 1986 had the company produced timely internal accounts and this therefore marked the beginning of the period from which they should have been minimising losses to creditors
- while trading on to dispose of assets might sometimes be justifiable, the directors had done no more than dispose of assets and so had failed to take every step to minimise losses.

Wrongful trading can give rise to the following consequences:

- a liquidator may apply to the court for an order that the director should make such contribution to the company's assets as the court thinks fit, thereby increasing the assets available for distribution to the creditors
- they may be disqualified for 15 years under CDDA86.

Test your understanding 4

Explain the main differences between a director fraudulently trading and wrongfully trading.

(Your answer must not exceed 40 words.)

8 Chapter summary

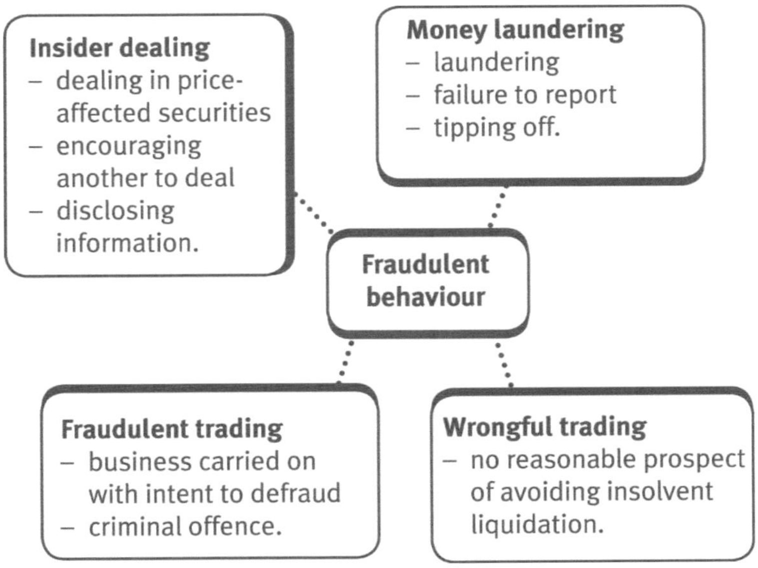

Test your understanding answers

Test your understanding 1

1 Criminal Justice Act 1993.

2 Dealing in securities.

Encouraging another person to deal.

Disclosing information.

3 Did not expect the dealing to result in a profit. Believed the information had been disclosed. Would have done what he or she did even without the information.

Test your understanding 2

1 The Proceeds of Crime Act 2002.

2 National Crime Agency.

3 Failure to report.

4 Money laundering is the process by which the proceeds of crime are converted into assets which appear to have a legal rather than an illegal source. The aim of disguising the source of the property is to allow the holder to enjoy it free from suspicion as to its source.

Test your understanding 3

This could be interpreted as an attempt to influence the manager actions in the current tendering and therefore be considered bribery under the Bribery Act 2010. The offer of hospitality should be refused.

Test your understanding 4

Fraudulent trading is trading with intent to defraud creditors and is a criminal offence. Wrongful trading occurs when it was known or ought to have been known that insolvency was unavoidable, and is not a criminal offence.

Chapter

14

Question and Answers

1 Essential elements of legal systems

Question 1

Which of the following is not true of judicial precedent?

A Precedents must be based on points of law

B Precedents must be based on points of fact

C Precedents must have been made by a superior court

D Precedents can be overruled by a superior court. The Supreme Court can overrule itself

Question 2

Which of the following is a general principle of civil law?

A The law is certain

B Judges create law

C Statutes are drafted in great detail

D There is no custom

Question 3

B

Statute law is:

A Law made in Parliament

B Law made by judges

C Law found in the Quran

D Law established by a country's constitution

Question 4

In Sharia law, the sayings of the Prophet are known as:

A Quran

B Figh

C Ahadith

D Madhab

2 International Commercial Arbitration

Question 5

If the parties do not agree to a specified number of arbitrators in their arbitration agreement, there shall be:

A 2

B 3

C 4

D 5

Question 6

An arbitral award may be set aside:

A because it conflicts with public policy

B because the party requesting the setting aside did not have proper notice of the arbitration proceedings taking place

C because the dispute fell outside of the scope of the arbitration agreement

D all of the above

Question 7

A request for an additional award not made in the official arbitral decision must be made within:

A 10 days

B 20 days

C 30 days

D 60 days

3 International business transactions: formation of the contract

Question 8

Faisal has received a letter from Gertrude. She is interested in buying some FLD457 parts.

Hee has received a letter from Ingrid. She states she would like to buy some ET396 parts at the catalogue price to be delivered to Ingrid by Hee. Hee receives a fax from Ingrid cancelling her interest in his parts before he has contacted her to accept.

Assume that the UNCCISG applies when answering the following questions.

1 **Gertrude's letter to Faisal is classified as:**

A an offer

B an invitation to treat

C an acceptance

D a rejection

2 **Ingrid's letter to Hee is classified as:**

A an offer

B an invitation to treat

C an acceptance

D a revocation

3 **Ingrid's fax to Hee is classified as:**

A a counter-offer

B a withdrawal

C a revocation

D an acceptance

4 International business transactions: obligations

Question 9

Alastair and Balvinder had a contract in which Alastair was to deliver fresh flowers to Balvinder. The contract specifies that the goods must be delivered on a particular day when they are required for a specific contract. When the flowers arrived, they were extremely wilted and past their best and Balvinder wishes to seek a remedy from Alastair.

Balvinder's best remedy is:

A to declare the contract avoided

B to request that Alastair repair the goods

C to reduce the price

D there is no appropriate remedy

Question 10

Seller has delivered the goods required under the contract to Buyer. Buyer has inspected the goods and given notice to the Seller that the goods do not conform to the contract and that the value of the goods has been reduced by 40%. Buyer needs to sell the goods immediately to his client, who has indicated that she will accept the goods regardless of the deficiency in the quality.

Buyer could seek which of the following remedies?

A Avoidance

B Repair of the goods by the seller in a set period of time

C Damages

D Reduction in the price of the contract

Question 11

Kabogo and Lisette have a contract for Lisette to buy goods from Kabogo. Lisette is to collect the goods from Kabogo's place of business. The contract states that Lisette will not be handed the goods until the price has been paid.

When must the price be paid?

A When Kabogo tells Lisette that the goods are ready

B When Lisette arrives at Kabogo's premises

C When Lisette has inspected the goods for quality

D When Lisette has removed the goods from Kabogo's premises

Question 12

Yolande and Zani have a contract for Yolande to make 20 machines for Zani. The contract refers to the need for Zani to provide a specification for the machines, but it is now past the date when Yolande indicated that she would be producing the machines and she needs the relevant specification.

Which of the following steps may Yolande take before she can make the machines?

A Request details of the specification from Zani

B Produce the specification herself

C Either of the above

D Neither of the above

Question 13

Nils and Olly have a contractual relationship. Nils is manufacturing a boiler to be delivered and installed in Olly's factory. Nils was late in delivering the boiler and as a result, Olly lost normal profits for a week and the opportunity to do a rush contract for a new customer which arose after the contract with Nills had been agreed.

In claiming damages, Olly will be able to include:

I the lost normal profits

II the lost profit on the contract for the new customer.

Which of the statements are correct?

A I only

B II only

C Both I and II

D Neither I or II

5 International business transactions: risk and payment

Question 14

Noelle and Oscar have a contract for Noelle to deliver goods from La Rochelle by sea to London, where Oscar will collect the goods. Assuming the goods are clearly appropriated to the contract and that the contract makes no further reference to risk, risk passes to Oscar:

A when the goods leave Noelle's premises

B when the goods pass the ship's rail in La Rochelle

C when the goods are collected by Oscar in London

D when the goods arrive at Oscar's premises

Question 15

Trevor and Uhuru are in contract negotiations for Uhuru to buy a portion of a consignment of cans of peaches from Trevor. Trevor purchased the goods in Sudenten, where he inspected them and they were in good condition. The goods are being shipped on Trevor's own boat, and he has received no notification of any problems with the journey. Trevor has agreed to deliver Uhuru's portion of the cargo to a different carrier when he arrives in Nordesten, whereupon the goods will be delivered to Uhuru in Weston.

Risk passes to Uhuru:

A In Sudenten

B On Trevor's boat in transit

C In Nordensten

D In Weston

Question 16

Abdul and Bruce agreed a contract for Bruce to buy 20 tonnes of coal by collection from the premises of a third party on 30 May. Abdul is storing 100 tonnes of coal at the third party premises. The coal is stored in a heap. Abdul contacts Bruce on 1 June and tells him that he may pick up the coal from the third party premises any time during the following two weeks. Bruce sends his lorries on 4 June. The coal is loaded on the lorries that afternoon, but Bruce does not take the coal away until 5 June.

Risk passes to Bruce on:

A 30 May

B 1 June

C 4 June

D 5 June

Question 17

Gio, from Colombia, has drawn up an international bill of exchange in favour of Helen, from Chile, through an Argentine bank. The bill of exchange states that it is for three thousand pesos.

Helen will receive:

A 3,000 Colombian pesos

B 3,000 Chilean pesos

C 3,000 Argentine pesos

6 International business forms – agency

Question 18

Which of the following is incorrect in relation to a contract made by an agent acting within his or her authority?

A The principal can sue on the contract

B The third party can sue on the contract

C The agent can be sued on the contract

D The principal can be sued on the contract

Question 19

Simon lives in Devon and one day he sees an Aston Martin parked on the beach. No one is in sight but the tide is coming in rapidly. Simon calls his neighbour and arranges for him to come and tow the Aston Martin up the beach to safety. The neighbour is happy to oblige but wants payment for what he has done. When the owner, Mike, returns, he refuses to pay because he says the action was not necessary.

Which of the following best describes the legal position?

A An agency of necessity has arisen because Simon is unable to contact Mike.

B An agency of necessity has arisen because there is an emergency situation and a pressing need for action.

C No agency of necessity has arisen because the Aston Martin is not a perishable good and Simon's action was not reasonable.

D No agency of necessity has arisen because there is no existing pre-contractual relationship between Simon and Mike.

Question 20

Preparing for her 50th birthday party, Jean went into Wine Warehouse and ordered three cases of wine, saying she was buying them in her capacity as agent for Dame Helen, a well known celebrity who lived in the same village and was planning a summer ball in the grounds of her country house. Wine Warehouse supplied the wine and then invoiced Dame Helen.

Is there an agency by holding out or estoppel?

A Yes

B No

Can Wine Warehouse demand payment from Dame Helen?

C Yes

D No

Question 21

Andrea worked for Lady Gertrude and part of her job was to buy plants, ornaments and furniture for the gardens of her country manor house. When her daughter, Harriett, was about to finish studying at university, she told Andrea that Harriett would be taking on these responsibilities.

A few weeks later, Andrea ordered some very expensive roses and marble statues from Lady Gertrude's main supplier and collected the goods the next day for her own garden. The invoice was delivered to Lady Gertrude.

Task 1 **(2 marks)**

With regards to an agency relationship which of the following statements is correct?

- **The contract is made between the principal and the agent**
- **The contract is made between the principal and the third party**
- **The contract is made between the agent and the third party**
- **A binding contract cannot be created**

Task 2 **(2 marks)**

In the above situation, which ONE of the following best describes the agency relationship between Andrea and Lady Gertrude?

- **There is an agency relationship by ratification**
- **There is an agency relationship by express agreement**
- **There is an agency relationship by implied agreement**
- **There is an agency relationship by necessity**

Task 3 **(2 marks)**

Identify which of the following statements are true or false.

	True	**False**
Andrea has the express authority to purchase roses and statues		
Lady Gertrude would be liable to settle the invoice for the roses and statues		

(Total: 6 marks)

7 Partnerships

Question 22

Are the following statements true or false?

An ordinary partnership is a separate legal entity from its partners.

A True

B False

The Partnership Act 1890 governs the rights and duties of partners in an ordinary partnership, in the absence of an express provision to the contrary.

C True

D False

Question 23

Which of the following is NOT recognised as a separate legal entity?

A A limited liability partnership

B A private limited company

C A public limited company

D A general partnership

Question 24

Sharon and Tracy formed a partnership 5 years ago. Two years ago the partnership employed Frank as its manager. Sharon and Tracy subsequently left much of the day-to-day work to Frank who has let it be known generally that he has become a partner, although he has not. In January of this year Frank entered into a large contract with a longstanding customer, Dorian, who had dealt with the partnership for some three years.

Dorian believed Frank's claim that he was a partner in the business.

This contract has gone badly wrong leaving the partnership owing $30,000 to Dorian and unfortunately the business assets will only cover the first $15,000 of the total debt.

Task 1 **(2 marks)**

Which of the following TWO are not features of a general partnership?

- **The partners have unlimited liability**
- **The partners have joint and several liability**
- **There must be a partnership agreement**
- **The partnership must be registered at Companies House**

Task 2 **(2 marks)**

Identify whether the following statements are true or false.

	True	False
A partnership is liable for contracts made by a partner if he is acting within his or her express authority only		
Dorian cannot make a claim against the partnership as she entered into the contract with Frank		

Task 3 **(2 marks)**

Who is liable for the $15,000 shortfall of the debt?

- Sharon and Tracy only
- Frank only
- Sharon, Tracy and Frank
- None of the above

(Total: 6 marks)

8 Corporations and legal personality

Question 25

A public limited company cannot commence business or borrow money until the nominal value of the company's allotted share capital is not less than:

A £12,500

B £25,000

C £40,000

D £50,000

Question 26

Within what period of time after the year end must a company file its accounts with the Registrar?

A Three months for a public company and six months for a private company.

B Nine months for a public company and seven months for a private company.

C Six months for a public company and nine months for a private company.

D Ten months for a public company and twelve months for a private company.

Question 27

The articles of association of a company forms a contract between:

A The shareholders and the company in all respects.

B The shareholders and the directors in all respects.

C The company and the directors in respect of directors' rights only.

D The company and the shareholders in respect of shareholder rights only.

Question 28

Sarah, a promoter, is in the process of incorporating Super Ltd, and has ordered goods to be used by the company. She has signed the order form 'Sarah, for and on behalf of Super Ltd'. Who is liable if the goods are not paid for?

A Super Ltd

B Sarah

C Sarah and Super Ltd jointly

D Neither Sarah nor Super Ltd as there is no contract

Question 29

Pam was formerly employed by Dallas Ltd. Her employment contract had a covenant to the effect that she should not compete with Dallas Ltd. The covenant is reasonable and not in restraint of trade. Pam has formed a company, Pam (Services) Ltd, which has started to trade in competition with Dallas Ltd.

Will Dallas Ltd be able to get an injunction to prevent Pam (Services) Ltd from trading?

A No, because Pam (Services) Ltd has a separate legal entity.

B Yes, because the company has been formed as a device to hide Pam's carrying on of that trade.

C No, because a company is not liable for the actions of its shareholders.

D Yes, because Pam (Services) Ltd is engaging in fraudulent trading.

Question 30

Ruby sets up a new company, Super Solutions Ltd, to continue her existing business. She enters into a contract on the 15th June 20X7 on the company's behalf with Ingrid Ltd for the purchase of stock with payment to be made 30 days later.

The certificate of incorporation was issued on the 1st July 20X7, it was received by Ruby on the 8th July 20X7 and the company started trading on the 15th July 20X7.

When the payment date arrives, the newly registered company has no cash available because it has also committed large funds to taking a lease of its new premises.

Task 1 **(2 marks)**

Identify whether the following statements are true or false.

	True	False
Super Solutions Ltd became a legal entity capable of entering into contracts in its own name on the 8th July 20X7		
Ruby is the promoter of Super Solutions Ltd		

Task 2 **(2 marks)**

Identify whether the following statements are true or false.

	True	False
The company is not bound under the contract, but is able to ratify or formally adopt it by ordinary resolution afterwards		
Ruby is personally liable for the contract under common law		

Task 3 **(2 marks)**

Identify whether the following statements are true or false.

	True	False
Ruby could have avoided liability under the contract by delaying completion of the contract until Super Solutions Ltd was registered		
Ruby can avoid liability under the contract by insisting the original contract is discharged, and replaced with a new contract in the name of Super Solutions Ltd		

(Total: 6 marks)

9 Capital and financing

Question 31

How is authority to allot shares required to be given to the directors of a public limited company?

I **By ordinary resolution.**

II **By special resolution.**

III **By the articles of association.**

A I or III only

B II or III only

C III only

D II only

Question 32

A bonus issue is the issue of additional shares, typically fully paid up, to existing shareholders in proportion to their holdings.

A True

B False

By making a rights issue, a company requires existing shareholders to subscribe for additional shares in proportion to their holdings.

C True

D False

Question 33

As a general rule, is a company able to allot shares:

At a premium?

A Yes

B No

At a discount?

C Yes

D No

Question 34

Every charge entered into by a company has to be registered. Within how many days must registration take place?

A 7 days

B 14 days

C 21 days

D 28 days

Question 35

A characteristic of a floating charge is that:

It is a charge over a class of assets present and future:

A Yes

B No

It is a charge over a class of assets, which, in the ordinary course of the business of the company, will change:

C Yes

D No

Question 36

At the start of 20X6 Crums Ltd was faced with the need to raise a large amount of capital, which it was decided to raise through the mechanism of issuing a number of secured loans. In order to raise the capital Crums Ltd entered into the following transactions:

(i) it borrowed £50,000 from Don secured by a floating charge. The loan was given and the charge created on 1 February. The charge was registered on 15 February

(ii) it borrowed £50,000 from Else, also secured by a floating charge. This charge was created on the morning of 1 April and it was registered on 15 April

(iii) it borrowed £100,000 from Flash Bank plc. This loan was secured by a fixed charge. It was created in the afternoon of 1 April and was registered on 20 April

(iv) it borrowed £100,000 from High Bank plc. This loan was secured by a fixed charge. It was created on 5 April and was registered on 15 April.

Task 1 **(2 marks)**

Which of the following statements are correct?

- A charge must be registered at Companies House within 14 days of creation
- A charge must be registered at Companies House within 21 days of creation
- A charge must be registered at Companies House within 28 days of creation
- A charge must be registered at Companies House within 30 days of creation

Task 2 **(4 marks)**

Identify the order of the debts in order of priority.

	1st	**2nd**	**3rd**	**4th**
Don – floating charge of £50,000				
Else – floating charge of £50,000				
Flash Bank plc – fixed charge of £100,000				
High Bank plc – fixed charge of £100,000				

10 Directors

Question 37

Which of the following is NOT one of the matters to which directors must have regard when discharging their duty to promote the success of their company?

A The impact of the company's operations on the community and the environment.

B The interests of the creditors of the company.

C The need to act fairly as between the members of the company.

D The desirability of maintaining a reputation of high standards of business conduct.

Question 38

To dismiss a director under s168 Companies Act 2006 requires:

A An ordinary resolution with 14 days' notice

B A special resolution with 14 days' notice

C An ordinary resolution with 28 days' notice to the company

D A special resolution with 28 days' notice to the company

Question 39

A disqualification order against a director of a company on the ground that his or her conduct makes him or her unfit to be concerned in the management of a company may last for:

A A minimum of 2 years and a maximum of 5 years

B A minimum of 2 years and a maximum of 15 years

C A minimum of 5 years with no maximum

D A maximum of 15 years with no minimum

Question 40

Which ONE of the following statements about the duties of directors is correct?

A The directors have a duty to ensure that no individual shareholder suffers a financial loss as a result of purchasing the company's shares.

B Directors owe their duties to the members and the company.

C Directors owe their duties to the company as a whole.

D Directors have a duty to distribute a dividend to ordinary shareholders each year.

Question 41

If a director breaches his or her duty, which of the following never applies?

A The director may have to account for a secret profit if he or she has made one.

B If the director holds more than 50% of the shares he or she can ratify his or her own breach of duty at an annual general meeting.

C The director can be automatically absolved from breach of duty by the articles of association.

D The director may be liable in tort.

Question 42

Len is a director of Mod plc, but he also owns a majority interest in Nim Ltd.

Last year Mod plc entered into a contract to buy new machinery from Nim Ltd. Len attended the board meeting that approved the contract and voted in favour of it, without revealing any link with Nim Ltd.

At the same meeting the board of Mod plc decided not to pursue the development of a new product that had been offered to them by its inventor. Len, however, liked the new product and arranged for it to be produced by Nim Ltd. It has proved to be a great success and Nim Ltd has made a great deal of money from its production.

Task 1 **(2 marks)**

What of the following TWO statutory duties has Len most likely to have breached as a director of Mod plc?

- **S.172 – Duty to promote the success of the company**
- **S.173 – Duty to exercise independent judgement**
- **S.175 – Duty to avoid conflicts of interest**
- **S.177 – Duty to declare an interest in a proposed transaction or arrangement**

Task 2 **(2 marks)**

Identify whether the following statements are true or false.

	True	False
Len should have declared the full extent of his relationship with Nim Ltd		
Len should have waited at least twelve months before taking on the production of the inventor's product		

Task 3 **(2 marks)**

What remedy is Mod plc most likely to seek in relation to Len's breaches?

- **Damages for loss suffered**
- **An account of any profits made by Len on both contracts**
- **Rescission of contract between Mod plc and Nim Ltd**
- **Compulsory winding up of Nim Ltd**

(Total: 6 marks)

(Adapted from ACCA June 2000 examination)

11 Corporate administration

Question 43

Under which circumstances must the directors of a plc convene a general meeting?

A If the company makes a trading loss.

B If the company's net assets fall to half or less of its issued share capital.

C If the company secretary resigns.

D If the company's net assets fall to half or less of its called-up share capital.

Question 44

What is the quorum for a general meeting of a public limited company?

A Two persons being members or proxies for members

B Five persons being members or proxies for members

C Two persons being members

D Five persons being members

Question 45

Which of the following resolutions cannot be made by a public company?

A Special resolutions

B Written resolutions

C Ordinary resolutions

D Ordinary resolutions with special notice

Question 46

What is the minimum period of notice for an AGM?

A 7 days

B 14 days

C 21 days

D 28 days

12 Insolvency

Question 47

Which ONE of the following statements is incorrect?

A A members' voluntary liquidation is used where the company is solvent.

B A members' voluntary liquidation is usually commenced by the passing of a special resolution.

C A creditors' voluntary liquidation is where the company is insolvent.

D A creditors' voluntary liquidation is commenced by creditors.

Question 48

In a liquidation, how many months after the liquidator files his or her final report with the Registrar will a company be dissolved?

A One month

B Three months

C Six months

D Twelve months

Question 49

Which of the following is not an unsecured debt when a company goes into liquidation?

A Arrears of holiday pay due to employees.

B Money owed to trade creditors.

C Money owed to gas and electricity suppliers.

D Money owed to an engineer for repairs carried out on company machinery.

Question 50

Which of the following is NOT a ground for compulsory winding up under the Insolvency Act 1986?

A A public company has not been issued with a trading certificate within a year of incorporation.

B The company has not paid a dividend during the last two years.

C It is just and equitable to wind up the company.

D The company has passed a special resolution to be wound up by the court.

13 Fraudulent behaviour

Question 51

Insider dealing is the offence of dealing in:

A Shares

B Securities

C Cash

D Property

Question 52

Which of the following Act covers market abuse?

A Criminal Justice Act 1993

B Proceeds of Crime Act 2002

C Financial Services and Markets Act 2000

D Company Director Disqualification Act 1986

Question 53

Which of the following is a money laundering offence?

A Alerting client

B Flagging up

C Tipping off

D Failure to detect

Question 54

Which of the following is a corporate bribery offence?

A Bribing an individual

B Receiving a bribe

C Bribing a public foreign official

D Failure to prevent bribery

Question 55

Nelly and Tim are directors of Bouncy Castles Ltd. Tim is not involved in the running of the business as he is too busy with other business ventures. Three months ago Nelly was told by the company's accountant that the company is facing mounting debts and that its assets and projected income is not sufficient to pay them. In spite of knowing this Nelly orders another 10 bouncy castles. Three months later, the company goes into compulsory liquidation.

Task 1 **(2 marks)**

Which TWO of the following statements are correct?

- **Fraudulent trading can only be a civil action**
- **Fraudulent trading can be a civil action and a criminal action**
- **Wrongful trading can only be a civil action**
- **Wrongful trading can be a civil action and a criminal action**

Task 2 **(2 marks)**

Which TWO of the following statements are correct?

- **Fraudulent trading applies only to directors and shadow directors**
- **Fraudulent trading must include dishonest intent**
- **Nelly is liable for fraudulent trading**
- **Tim is liable for fraudulent trading**

Task 3 **(2 marks)**

Which TWO of the following statements are correct?

- **Tim is not liable for wrongful trading**
- **Tim is liable for wrongful trading**
- **Wrongful trading applies only to directors and shadow directors**
- **Wrongful trading must include dishonest intent**

(Total: 6 marks)

Test your understanding answers

Question 1

B

Precedents must be based on points of law, not fact.

Question 2

A

The law is certain. B & C are features of common law systems. D is not true.

Question 3

A

Question 4

C

Question 5

B

3 – one shall be selected by each party and the two so chosen will select the third.

Question 6

D

Question 7

C

Question 8

1	B
2	A
3	C

Question 9

A

Balvinder should declare the contract avoided. It is not possible for Alastair to 'repair' dead flowers, and as fresh flowers are required for a contract and Balvinder now has no fresh flowers, the breach is a fundamental breach of contract, so he may declare the contract avoided and seek an alternative supply.

Question 10

D

Buyer may reduce the price of the contract and potentially claim damages, as taking advantage of a remedy other than damages does not preclude him from claiming damages as well if necessary. As the breach is not fundamental, and the goods may still be sold to the client, he may not declare the contract avoided. Due to the tight time-frame associated with the contract, requesting Seller repairs the goods is not appropriate.

Question 11

C

The price must be paid before the goods are handed over to Lisette, but she is entitled to inspect the goods for quality before she pays the price.

Question 12

C

As the agreed date for the specification to be available is past, Yolande may either make her own specification or continue to ask Zani for the specification. If she makes the specification herself, she must give details of the specification to Zani and allow a reasonable time period for Zani to come up with an alternative specification. If Zani does not, then Yolande's specification will be binding.

Question 13

A

She may not claim the loss on the contract for the new customer as that could not have been foreseen by the parties.

Question 14

B

When the goods are given to the shipper in La Rochelle, the named port of export and the goods pass the ship's rail.

Question 15

C

Risk passes to Uhuru when the goods are delivered to the carrier in Nordensten, as this is where the goods will be appropriated to the new contract. As Uhuru is only buying a portion of the consignment, the goods will not be clearly marked to the contract until they are passed to the first carrier under the contract.

Question 16

C

Usually risk passes when the buyer is made aware that the goods are available for him or her to collect at the third party premises (which in this case was 1 June). However, risk does not pass until the goods are clearly marked to the contract, and as Bruce is buying unidentified goods from a specific stock, risk does not pass until Bruce loads the goods onto his own lorry, whereby they are identified to the contract.

Question 17

B

3,000 Chilean pesos

Question 18

C

Question 19

D

Although Simon acted in good faith and possibly reasonably, the law is unlikely to say that an agency of necessity has arisen, because it is not inclined to allow a person to be bound by the act of a complete stranger.

Question 20

B

It is the conduct of the principal that might give rise to an agency by estoppel, not the conduct of the 'agent'.

D

The contract can only be enforced against Jean personally.

Question 21

Task 1

- The contract is made between the principal and the third party

Task 2

- There is an agency relationship by express agreement

Task 3

	True	**False**
Andrea has the express authority to purchase roses and statues		X
Lady Gertrude would be liable to settle the invoice for the roses and statues	X	

Question 22

B

This is true of a limited liability partnership but not an ordinary partnership.

C

Question 23

D

A, B and C all have a separate legal personality.

Question 24

Task 1

- There must be a partnership agreement
- The partnership must be registered at Companies House

Task 2

	True	False
A partnership is liable for contracts made by a partner if he or she is acting within his or her express authority only		X
Dorian cannot make a claim against the partnership as she entered into the contract with Frank		X

Task 3

- Sharon, Tracy and Frank

Question 25

D

Question 26

C

Question 27

D

The Eley case illustrates that the statutory rules only apply to rights as a shareholder.

Question 28

B

A company cannot be liable on a pre-incorporation contract as the company does not exist at the time the contract is made.

Question 29

B

This is very similar to the facts of Gilford Motor Co Ltd v Horne.

Question 30

Task 1

	True	False
Super Solutions Ltd became a legal entity capable of entering into contracts in its own name on the 8th July 20X7		X
Ruby is the promoter of Super Solutions Ltd	X	

Task 2

	True	False
The company is not bound under the contract, but is able to ratify or formally adopt it by ordinary resolution afterwards		X
Ruby is personally liable for the contract under common law	X	

Task 3

	True	False
Ruby could have avoided liability under the contract by delaying completion of the contract until Super Solutions Ltd was registered	X	
Ruby can avoid liability under the contract by insisting the original contract is discharged, and replaced with a new contract in the name of Super Solutions Ltd		X

Question 31

A

Question 32

A

D

There is no obligation on the members to take additional shares.

Question 33

A

A sum equal to the premium on each share must be transferred to a share premium account.

D

Shares cannot be issued at a discount on nominal value.

Question 34

C

Question 35

A

A floating charge is typically over a class of assets of a company, present and future, with which the company may continue to deal prior to crystallisation of the charge.

C

A floating charge typically covers assets that change in the ordinary course of business and only fixes to those assets at the time of crystallisation.

Question 36

Task 1

- A charge must be registered at Companies House within 21 days of creation

Task 2

	1st	2nd	3rd	4th
Don – floating charge of £50,000			X	
Else – floating charge of £50,000				X
Flash Bank plc – fixed charge of £100,000	X			
High Bank plc – fixed charge of £100,000		X		

Question 37

B

This is not one of the six matters listed.

Question 38

C

Question 39

B

Question 40

C

Question 41

C

The articles cannot exempt directors from liability.

Question 42

Task 1

- S.175 – Duty to avoid conflicts of interest
- S.177 – Duty to declare an interest in a proposed transaction or arrangement

Task 2

	True	False
Len should have declared the full extent of his relationship with Nim Ltd	X	
Len should have waited at least twelve months before taking on the production of the inventor's product		X

Task 3

- An account of any profits made by Len on both contracts

Question 43

D

Question 44

A

Question 45

B

Question 46

C

For an AGM 21 days notice is required, for a GM 14 days notice is required.

Question 47

D

A creditors' voluntary liquidation is usually commenced by the passing of a special resolution.

Question 48

B

Question 49

A

This would rank as a preferential creditor.

Question 50

B

Question 51

B

Question 52

C

Question 53

C

Question 54

D

Question 55

Task 1

- Fraudulent trading can be a civil action and a criminal action
- Wrongful trading can only be a civil action

Task 2

- Fraudulent trading must include dishonest intent
- Nelly is liable for fraudulent trading

Task 3

- Tim is liable for wrongful trading
- Wrongful trading applies only to directors and shadow directors